The Teachings of the Odd-Eyed One

SUNY series in Hindu Studies

Wendy Doniger, editor

The Teachings of the Odd-Eyed One

A Study and Translation of the Virūpākṣapañcāśikā, with the Commentary of Vidyācakravartin

David Peter Lawrence

State University of New York Press

Cover photo of image in Virūpākṣa Temple at Pashupatinath complex, Nepal, provided by Dina Bangdel.

Published by State University of New York Press, Albany

Printed in the United States of America

For information, contact State University of New York Press, Albany, NY
www.sunypress.edu

Production by Ryan Morris
Marketing by Fran Keneston

This book was printed on acid-free, 50% recycled paper.

Library of Congress Cataloging-in-Publication Data

Lawrence, David Peter, 1959–
The teachings of the odd-eyed one : a study and translation of the Virūpākṣapañcāśikā, with the commentary of Vidyācakravartin / David Peter Lawrence.
p. cm. — (SUNY series in Hindu studies)
Includes bibliographical references and index.
ISBN: 978-0-7914-7553-9 (hardcover : alk. paper)
ISBN: 978-0-7914-7554-6 (pbk. : alk. paper)
1. Virūpākṣanāthapāda. Virūpākṣapañcāśikā. 2. Kashmir Śaivism—Doctrines. I. Virūpākṣanāthapāda. Virūpākṣapañcāśikā. English. II. Vidyācakravartin. Virūpākṣapañcāśikāvivṛti. English. III. Title.

BL1281.1547.V5835 2008
294.5'95—dc22

2007048681

10 9 8 7 6 5 4 3 2 1

For the memory of my mother
Nina Marie Lawrence, 1926–2006

Contents

Illustrations

Preface

The *Virūpākṣapañcāśikā*, "*Fifty Verses of Virūpākṣa*" (actually fifty-three in the present form) was reportedly one of the three favorite texts on spiritual discipline (*yoga śāstra*) of the great twentieth-century tantrism scholar and holy man, Gopinath Kaviraj—the others being Vyāsa's *Yogasūtrabhāṣya* and the *Vijñānabhairava*.[1] Historically and philosophically, the text as well as the *Vivṛti*, "Commentary," on it of Vidyācakravartin, are important as late works from the Pratyabhijñā philosophical tradition of what is now called monistic Kashmiri Śaivism.

As explained in the Introduction, while the *Virūpākṣapañcāśikā* is probably from Kashmir, the *Vivṛti* is most likely from South India. The commentary is of the sort designed to help Sanskrit readers understand both the language and the basic ideas of the original, without much elaboration or controversy. I believe that it also offers much assistance to English readers in understanding the verses' meanings, organization, religious and intellectual contexts, and practical applications.

The *Virūpākṣapañcāśikā* and *Vivṛti* do not engage in the complex and technical investigations of philosophical topics that typify the original Pratyabhijñā works of Utpaladeva and Abhinavagupta. Rather they use Pratyabhijñā theories to structure a series of tantric contemplations. Moreover, the focus of the present texts is not on epistemology and metaphysics, the predominant concerns of the Pratyabhijñā school—but on distinctive features of that tradition's *religious and philosophical psychology*. These present the monistic Śaiva approach to the transformation of egoity and the experience of embodiment.

In the final chapter of the Introduction, I offer some proposals about how the Pratyabhijñā psychology may be engaged dialogically with Western religious and psychoanalytic understandings of narcissism. These proposals follow and build upon the approach to comparative philosophy explored in my previous book, *Rediscovering God with Transcendental Argument.* I must emphasize that, particularly in the engagement with psychoanalysis, my goal is not to describe Śaivism as an alternative approach for trafficking with realia to which that discipline would have privileged access. Rather, I wish to suggest, however briefly, that the Śaiva texts may point toward a religious understanding of narcissism beyond the explanatory scope of the psychoanalytic method. It should go without saying that those who are interested only in the philological and historical representation of the texts may choose to skip that chapter.

Granting the intrinsic interest of the *Virūpākṣapañcāśikā* and *Vivṛti,* I originally chose to publish this translation and study because I thought it would be fairly simple and not very time-consuming. However, the project has proven significantly more complex than anticipated. It has been challenging to finish this work while struggling with some other practical difficulties in the last few years.

This work would not have been possible without much assistance and support from others, while of course the errors that remain are my own responsibility. First, I wish to thank the editor of the SUNY Series in Hindu Studies, Wendy Doniger, for her interest in and encouragement for this project along with much invaluable advice.

My first draft of the translation was completed in Hong Kong by about 2001. Since then, I have traveled to India several times to work on this and other projects, and have benefited immensely from discussing the texts and my translation with my wise mentors there. With Hemendra Nath Chakravarty, I reexamined and discussed the text and commentary line by line. Navjivan Rastogi reviewed my entire translation and provided me with very helpful and detailed comments and suggestions on it, in writing, in our meetings, and on the phone. Srinarayan Mishra likewise assisted with a number of difficult textual and philosophical issues.

I have also received valuable advice in conversations and correspondence with many others, including Lawrence Cohen, David Dubois, Mark Dyczkowski, John Holt, Bernard McGinn, William B. Parsons, T. S. Rukmani, Alexis Sanderson, Gayatri Spivak, and Sthaneshwar Timalsina. Likewise, I am grateful to the anonymous reviewers of the manuscript for their illuminating comments and suggestions.

It was helpful for me to have presented various parts of the Introduction at conferences and seminars: Knowledge Systems in Early and Medieval

India, University of California at Berkeley, February 2002; Conference of the Society for Tantric Studies, Flagstaff, Arizona, October 2002; Language, Consciousness and Culture: East-West Perspectives, Calcutta, January 2004; Kashmir Project Seminar, University of Chicago, April 2004; and the Society for Asian and Comparative Philosophy Meeting at the Annual Meeting of the American Academy of Religion, San Antonio, November 2004.

I also benefited from discussing a number of my ideas with students in my classes: Power and the Body in Hindu and Buddhist Tantrism, which I taught at Concordia University in spring 2003, and the University of Manitoba in fall 2003; Mysticism, which I taught at the University of North Dakota in spring 2006; and Religion and Philosophy in India, which I also taught at the University of North Dakota in spring 2006.

Dina Bangdel is to be thanked for providing the picture for the cover.

Most of all I am grateful to my family for their love and support. This book would never have been possible without the encouragement and inspiration of my wife, Caroline Cheng; our sons, Jeremy and Edwin; and my parents, Nina and Glenn Lawrence. My mother passed away in March 2006 and this book is dedicated to her memory.

Abbreviations

IPK	*Īśvarapratyabhijñākārikā* by Utpaladeva
IPKV	*Īśvarapratyabhijñākārikāvṛtti* by Utpaladeva
IPV	*Īśvarapratyabhijñāvimarśinī* by Abhinavagupta, commentary on IPK
IPVV	*Īśvarapratyabhijñāvivṛtivimarśinī* by Abhinavagupta, commentary on Utpaladeva's *Īśvarapratyabhijñāvivṛti*
MMP	*Mahārthamañjarīparimala* by Maheśvarānanda on his own *Mahārthamañjarī*
SS	*Śiva Sūtra* revealed to Vasugupta
TA	*Tantrāloka* by Abhinavagupta
TAV	*Tantrālokaviveka* by Jayaratha, commentary on TA
VAP	*Virūpākṣapañcāśikā* by Virūpākṣa
VAPV	*Virūpākṣapañcāśikāvivṛti* by Vidyācakravartin, commentary on VAP
YS	*Yoga Sūtra* by Patañjali

Part I

Introduction

Chapter 1

The Texts in their Religious and Intellectual Contexts

This book is an introduction to and translation of a circa twelfth century C.E. contemplative manual, the *Virūpākṣapañcāśikā* (VAP) with the commentary *Vivṛti* (VAPV) of Vidyācakravartin. The VAP purports to give the teachings of an incarnation of Śiva, under the name Virūpākṣa. Virūpākṣa, from *virūpa* and *akṣa,* meaning "the Odd-Eyed One," is a common name for Śiva. It refers to the notion that Śiva's eyes are odd in either number or form, as he possesses in his forehead a third eye that is also awry, perpendicular to the other two.[1]

Whether or not either is actually from Kashmir, the VAP and VAPV may be situated within the Trika stream of tantric, monistic "Kashmiri Śaivism." They are important historically as late works from the tradition of Trika philosophical theology called Pratyabhijñā, which was created by Utpaladeva (c. 900–950 C.E.) and further advanced by Abhinavagupta (c. 950–1025 C.E.). Substantively, the VAP and VAPV are valuable for their elucidation of the distinctive Pratyabhijñā psychological approach to empowering and divinizing the human ego and body.

The present chapter will provide basic information about the religious and intellectual contexts of the texts. The second chapter will discuss the narrative framing the VAP as a dialogue between Virūpākṣa and the Vedic deity Indra, and how this narrative continues the South Asian legacy of myths of the instruction of Indra. The third will exposit the basic teachings of the VAP and VAPV, and the fourth will make suggestions about how the texts may be engaged dialogically by means of comparative or intercultural philosophy. The short fifth chapter will address issues pertaining to the translation.

Names and Dates

There is no evidence presently available to support the identification of Virūpākṣa with any known historical individual. I have wondered whether the narrative of the encounter of Indra with Virūpākṣa might, beyond its religious and philosophical significance, allude to the relationship of a royal patron with a monistic Śaiva scholar-practitioner. However, this is only a conjecture.

Textual references suggest that the VAP is from the eleventh or twelfth century C.E. The terminus a quo is indicated by the heavy use the text makes of the tenth to eleventh century writings of Abhinavagupta. The terminus ad quem is provided by the text's quotation in the twelfth century, South Indian *Mahārthamañjarīparimala* of Maheśvarānanda.[2] The existence of a number of old Śāradā manuscripts of the text suggests that it may have come from the region of Kashmir.

There are more clues about the commentator, but they are again inconclusive. In the closing verses of the VAPV he proclaims, "This light commentary was composed by the glorious (Śrī) Vidyācakravartin, and placed on the touchstone named the intelligence of Govindacandra." Vidyācakravartin thus makes a contextual reference in naming someone who was perhaps his patron or guru. However, the identity of Govindacandra is another mystery. There was a twelfth century king of Kanauj with that name, who was the patron of Lakṣmīdhāra, author of the *Kṛtyakalpataru*. However, I am not aware of any evidence that Vidyācakravartin is referring to that Govindacandra.

There is some evidence suggesting, rather, that Vidyācakravartin was from South India. The only known manuscripts of his commentary have been found in that region, in scripts of South Indian languages. T. Ganapati Sastri for his 1910 edition used a manuscript in Malayalam script, from the Trivandrum Palace Library.[3] Alexis Sanderson has also informed me of the existence of three manuscripts in Telugu script, in Maharaja Serfoji's Sarasvati Mahal Library in Thanjavur.[4]

The author of the VAPV is sometimes identified with a fourteenth century Vidyācakravartin thought to have belonged to the court of King Ballāla III of the Hoysala dynasty. Authorship of a number of works has been ascribed to that Vidyācakravartin, including the short monistic Śaiva text *Daśaślokī*, a *mahākāvya* titled *Rukminīkalyāṇa*, and commentaries on the poetics texts, Rucaka's *Alaṁkārasarvasva* and Mammaṭa's *Kāvyaprakāśa*.[5] It is well established that monistic Śaiva, Śaiva Siddhānta, and other Kashmiri cultural traditions were transmitted to the region of South India during this period, and the aforementioned works are replete with references to Kashmiri religion as well as poetics. However, I do not believe that it has yet been firmly demonstrated that one person was the author of all those texts as well as the VAPV. As an illustration of the complexity of the topic, it may be observed that S. S. Janaki has argued that the ostensible fourteenth century author was the last of a series of three Vidyācakravartins sponsored by the Hoysala dynasty![6]

Sanderson has also thrown into some doubt the common assumption about the commentator's name. The concluding verses of the VAPV refer to the commentator as Śrī-Vidyācakravartin, which I have provisionally translated as "glorious Vidyācakravartin," but designate the patron or guru as Govindacandra. As Sanderson observes, if Śrī were the common honorific title, "glorious," and if Vidyācakravartin were the author of the final verses, it would have been markedly disrespectful for him to omit the honorific for Govindacandra. Sanderson suggests, therefore, that the commentator's proper name might actually have been Śrīvidyācakravartin.[7]

This argument is reasonable. However, I do not believe that it excludes the possible identity of the author of the VAPV with one or more authors from the court of Ballāla III or other Hoysala kings. I have found that the author of the *Saṁjivanī* commentary on the *Alaṁkārasarvasva,* in what are presumably his own benedictory verses, refers to himself as Śrī-Vidyācakravartin and names Rucaka without the Śrī. Also of interest are Janaki's observations regarding that ostensible Vidyācakravartin that "an air of self-consciousness and pride is seen in our author"[8] and that he refers to himself in "exaggerated terms of praise."[9] One might be tempted to speculate whether his "pride" exemplifies the Pratyabhijñā philosophical psychology of perfected egoity that is taught in the VAP and VAPV. Again, however, this is ungrounded.

For the present study, I will continue provisionally to identify the commentator as Vidyācakravartin. I believe that there is a strong possibility that he was patronized by the Hoysala dynasty and that he wrote one or more of the other texts mentioned, but we cannot be certain.

Monistic Kashmiri Śaivism and the Tantric Quest for Power

What is commonly called Kashmir or Kashmiri Śaivism is actually a group of tantric and monistic Śaiva traditions that flourished in Kashmir from the latter centuries of the first millennium C.E. through the early centuries of the second. While these traditions have extended their influence throughout South Asia, they have survived only in a greatly attenuated form in Kashmir itself. Recently, however, there have been efforts to revive them in India and globally. I prefer the designation monistic Śaivism or monistic Kashmiri Śaivism to distinguish these traditions from dualistic Śaivasiddhānta traditions that also flourished in medieval Kashmir.[10]

The classification of the monistic Śaiva traditions as "tantric" requires explanation. Asian and Western scholars have come to recognize that contemporary usages of the terms "tantra," "tantrism," and "tantric" do not agree in extension with those of any premodern South Asian traditions.[11] Nevertheless, there is a growing consensus among scholars toward using the terms to classify together religious movements on the basis of historical and thematic relations, regardless of their self-definitions.[12] Among the movements in the religious and philosophical dynamism of medieval Kashmir now classified as tantric are the interweaving Śaiva and Śākta lineages known as the Kaula, Krama, Spanda, and Trika; the Vaiṣṇava Pāñcarātra and Buddhist Vajrayāna.

What makes these traditions tantric? Probably the most generic and distinctive feature of these and other traditions that contemporary scholars call tantra is the pursuit of *power*. Hindu traditions understand this power as in essence Śakti, the Goddess herself. Tantric practitioners variously endeavor to identify with the Goddess, to be ecstatically possessed by her, or to become her possessor (*śaktiman*) in identifying with her consort (e.g., one of the forms of Śiva or Viṣṇu).[13]

A number of other features of Hindu tantrism are widely accepted by scholars, which may be understood as doctrinal and practical expressions of this quest for Śakti.[14] These include cosmogonic myths of the sexual union of Śakti with a male deity, along with practices that recapitulate that union in contemplation or actual intercourse; circular diagrams of cosmogenesis and cosmocracy (*maṇḍala*); empowered speech formulas (*mantra*); theosophical schemes tracing homologies between the transcendent and immanent modalities of emanating Śakti; the divinization of the experience of embodiment; and the synthesis of embodied enjoyment (*bhoga*) with spiritual practice (*yoga*) and liberation (*mokṣa*).[15]

Much of the variety within tantrism derives from the particular modalities of Śakti that are pursued. Tantric powers range from the relatively limited yogic "proficiencies" (*siddhis*)[16] of local "shamans," through the sovereignty of kings (traditionally great sponsors of Hindu and Buddhist tantric traditions), to the omnipotence of the person who has become liberated by completely identifying with the deity.[17]

In his classic studies, Alexis Sanderson has illuminated the ways in which the tantric pursuit of powers transgresses orthodox, upper-caste

Hindu norms that delimit human agency for the sake of symbolic-ritual purity (*śuddhi*).[18] Many of the tantric rites were originally performed in cremation grounds, which are traditionally viewed in South Asia as extremely impure. Prescriptions for the sexual ritual commonly advocate adultery and caste-mixing, and apparently sometimes even incest.[19] David White has recently argued that tantra originated in ancient Siddha practices that endeavored to gain benefits from *yoginīs* through the transgressive offering and ingestion of sexual fluids.[20] In some traditions, there is the ingestion of urine, excrement, phlegm, and even, allegedly, human flesh.[21]

Historical Transformations of Kashmiri Tantrism: The Philosophical Rationalization of Monistic Śaiva Traditions

Sanderson, White, Mark Dyczkowski, Ronald Inden, and others have documented crucial historical trends in the early Kashmiri tantric traditions. One of these is the traditions' continual appropriation and subordination, which Sanderson calls "overcoding," of the symbolism and ritual of each other as well as of more established traditions.[22] Of course, the hierarchizing aspects of culture have been a central concern throughout the contemporary humanities and social sciences, and analogous processes have been observed in other South Asian religions.[23] Tantric traditions are remarkable for the baroque complexity and convolutedness of this hierarchization.[24]

Another important development was the tantric traditions' efforts to "domesticize" or "Sanskritize" (though their scriptures were already in Sanskrit) by assimilating to more established upper-caste Hindu orthopraxy.[25] Some of the more radical practices, such as those involving cremation grounds and sexual rituals, were toned down and internalized, and the emphasis became more gnoseological. An aspect of this trend that has been emphasized by White is the "dissimulation" by practitioners of their transgressive engagements under the guise of upper-caste, householder propriety.[26] Likewise, increasingly popular soteriologies aiming at identity with the omnipotent deity may be viewed as in a sense "sublimations" of pursuits of more concrete magical and political powers.

My own research has focused on another highly consequential expression of this process of domesticization, the enrichment and "philosophical rationalization" of monistic Śaivism through Sanskritic traditions of academic discourse and philosophical dialogue. Often candidly inspired with a sense of religious mission, monistic Śaiva writers began to consolidate their complex spiritual inheritance in increasingly systematic manuals (*śāstras*) of doctrines and practices. An important expression of this development in the ninth century was the production by Vasugupta and his disciple Kallaṭa of the core texts of the "Spanda system," the *Śiva Sūtra* and the *Spanda Kārikā*.[27] The commentaries on these works continued the project of systematization and justification.

It was a tradition of monistic Śaivism called Trika ("Triadism," referring to its emphasis on various triads of modalities of Śakti and cosmic levels) that produced the first work of full-scale philosophical apologetics against rival schools of Hinduism and Buddhism. This was the *Śivadṛṣṭi*, "*Cognition of Śiva*," by Somānanda (c. 900–950 C.E.). Somānanda's pupil Utpaladeva (c. 900–950 C.E.) continued his teacher's initiative with much greater sophistication in composing the foundational texts and commentaries of the *Īśvarapratyabhijñā* or simply *Pratyabhijñā* system, which became the authoritative system of monistic Śaiva philosophical theology.[28]

The polymathic Abhinavagupta (c. 950–1020 C.E.), a disciple of a disciple of Utpaladeva, wrote long commentaries further elaborating Utpaladeva's philosophical arguments.[29] Despite the paramount philosophical importance of those commentaries, Abhinavagupta's greatest significance in the history of tantrism was his effort in his monumental *Tantrāloka*, "*Illumination of the Tantras*,"[30] and numerous other works, to systematize and provide a critical philosophical structure to *nonphilosophical* Trika theology. Abhinava utilized categories from the Pratyabhijñā philosophy to interpret and organize the diverse aspects of Trika symbolism, doctrine, and practice. And bringing to a sort of culmination the hermeneutics of overcoding, he synthesized under the rubric of this philosophically rationalized Trika an enormous range of symbolism and practice from Kaula, Krama, Spanda, and other Śaiva and Śākta traditions.[31]

Abhinavagupta is also renowned for his works on Sanskrit poetics, in which he interprets aesthetic experience as homologous to and practically approaching the monistic Śaiva soteriological realization. With Utpaladeva and Abhinavagupta, Hindu tantra reached its peak of intellectual sophistication. As further elaborated in the writings of their followers, their ideas had a tremendous influence on tantric as well as bhakti traditions throughout South Asia. The influence of Pratyabhijñā philosophy and soteriology is evident in most later Sanskritic traditions of Hindu tantrism.

Granting the practical antecedency of philology and descriptive history, with what theoretical methods should we endeavor further to understand the Pratyabhijñā philosophy as well as later philosophically rationalized Śaiva and Śākta tantric traditions? The dominant theoretical approaches of the contemporary humanities and social sciences are inclined to explain culture in terms of the advancement, maintenance, and enjoyment of social, political, and economic power. I certainly would not deny the great influence of such motivations throughout world history, but would only question how far we should presuppose that influence to extend.

In South Asian studies it is becoming increasingly common to explain processes such as philosophical rationalization, overcoding, and domestication exclusively in such terms. Thus, according to White, what he calls "the 'high Hindu' Tantric mysticism of the later Tantric exegetes" originated as "an effort to win a certain support base of high-caste householders in Kashmir and, later, in Tamil Nadu."[32] Accordingly, in their philosophical and soteriological aspects:

> Exegetical or scholasticist Tantric works . . . constitute a secondary development, a hermeneutical transformation of an earlier body of practice into a mystical metaphysics, which often systematically distorts the meaning of the original practice itself.[33]

White alleges that:

> Abhinavagupta's "packaging" of Tantra as a path to ecstatic, exalted god-consciousness was pitched at a leisured Kashmiri populace whose "bobo" profile was arguably homologous to the demographics of the twentieth- and twenty-first-century New Age seekers who treat "Tantric sex" as a consumer product.[34]

Some of the most brilliant, erudite, and inspired writers in world history, along with centuries of their followers, are assimilated to the commodified banality of contemporary bourgeois bohemian culture.

While White's and other studies founded on a similar paradigm provide a wealth of valuable knowledge, such claims are exaggerated and prejudicial. In tantra as elsewhere, sometimes it is a straightforward matter to distinguish hermeneutic distortion from creative insight, but often not. The same is the case in ascribing implicit motivations. We may be blinded, ironically, to an insidious hegemonic Orientalism or "ethos-centrism" in our critical reductions of other cultures to the counters of a globalized system obsessed with profit and consumption, political world order, marketing, and media spin. While the achievement and enjoyment of practical advantages have long been acknowledged among the possible benefits of the tantric realization of Power (Śakti), why should we assume that soteriology and philosophy are epiphenomena?

Before pursuing reductionistic theories and social critiques, or endeavoring to debunk tantric *śāstras* by a postulation of pristine and authentic sexual transgression, we should extend the hermeneutic and dialogical charity of attempting seriously to engage with the stated religious and philosophical concerns of Sanskrit writers.[35] For us, as for those writers, attempting to critically understand the monistic Śaiva quest for Śakti leads to complex and fascinating epistemological, metaphysical, psychological, and ethical considerations.

Doctrines and Practices of Empowerment in Monistic Kashmiri Śaivism

As may be gathered from the appellation "monistic Śaivism," a basic doctrinal position of this stream of tantric traditions is that the only reality is the God Śiva. Śiva is thus the true Self of all beings. These traditions overcode the fundamental tantric principle of power, Śakti, within Śiva's metaphysical essence. Śiva is the *śaktiman,* the "possessor" of Śakti, encompassing her within his androgynous nature as his integral power and consort. According to the central monistic Śaiva myth, Śiva divides himself from Śakti and then in sexual union emanates and controls the universe through her.

Liberation, the realization of one's true Self as Śiva, is accomplished through a great variety of ritual and contemplative practices. The basic pattern of praxis, which Sanderson has suggested also reflects the appropriation of Śāktism by Śaivism, is the *approach to Śiva through Śakti.* As the *Vijñāna Bhairava* states, Śakti is Śiva's "door" or "face" (*mukha*).[36] The adept strives to attain identity with Śiva through the recapitulation of the myth, to become the *śaktiman,* the possessor and enjoyer of Śakti. Thus, in the Kaula sexual ritual a man realizes himself as the possessor of Śakti immanent within his partner.[37] In the monistic Śaiva appropriation of Kālī Krama tantrism, one contemplates oneself as the possessor of *śakticakras,* circles of Śaktis. The *Spanda* tradition pursues the possession of *śakticakras* understood as *Spanda,* "Creative Vibration."

Within the historical elaboration of monistic Śaiva theology, and especially in the grand syntheses of Abhinavagupta, an astonishing number of what might be called secondary codes were propounded for the same basic mythic and ritual pattern—in the terms of philosophical theories, pantheons of higher and lower deities, hierarchies of emanating mantras and cosmic principles, *maṇḍala* iconography, and various other symbols, metaphors, and analogies. In the remainder of this chapter, I will review certain of these expressions of monistic Śaiva doctrine and practice that will be helpful in understanding the background to the teachings of the VAP and VAPV.

Pratyabhijñā Philosophy and the Perfection of Egoity

Utpaladeva and Abhinavagupta, belying the Western dichotomy of faith (or mysticism) and reason, conceive the Pratyabhijñā system simultaneously as a philosophical apologetics and an internalized tantric ritual. They structure its discourse according to the most widely accepted Sanskritic standards for publicly assessable philosophical argument, which had been systematized as a set of sixteen categories by the Nyāya school of philosophy. Their proclaimed goal is through this discourse to lead students to the soteriological *recognition* (*pratyabhijñā*) "I am Śiva."[38]

Utpaladeva describes the primary modus operandi of the Pratyabhijñā in accordance with the basic monistic Śaiva mythico-ritual pattern described earlier, as the "revealing of Śakti" (*śaktyāviṣkaraṇa*). In this case, as Abhinavagupta explains, the process is rationalized as a Nyāya syllogism, known as the "inference for the sake of others" (*parārthānumāna*). The inferential subject is oneself, "I," and the predicate is "Śiva." Śakti is now the inferential reason, which is supposed to identify a quality in the subject known to be invariably concomitant with the predicate. Thus, the Pratyabhijñā demonstrates that I am Śiva because I have his quality, that is, Śakti, the capacity of emanating and controlling the universe.

The Pratyabhijñā thinkers also identify the insight gained by the revealing of Śakti with the experience comprehended in a monistic Śaiva cosmological principle called "Pure Wisdom" (*śuddhavidyā*).[39] According to them, Pure Wisdom is the awareness of oneself as the emanator of the universe, expressed "I am this."[40] Abhinava further elaborates that this insight animates what he calls "good reasoning" (*sattarka*) which, counteracting ordinary deluded and dualistic thinking, leads to a "purification of conceptual constructions" (*vikalpasaṁskāra*).[41]

The central moment of the Pratyabhijñā system is the explanation of Śiva's emanation and control of the universe through Śakti as an act self-recognition (*pratyabhijñā, ahampratyavamarśa*).[42] As will be discussed further, Utpaladeva and Abhinavagupta further identify Śiva's self-recognition/Śakti with the principle of Supreme Speech (*parāvāk*), which they derive from the linguistic philosopher Bhartṛhari. Another key category with which they identify it is omnipotent agency (*kartṛtā*).

According to Utpaladeva and Abhinavagupta, Śiva emanates through differentiating his self-recognition (or Speech or agency) into discrete acts of recognitive-linguistic apprehension[43] that idealistically constitute all objects of experience.[44] Śiva recognizes himself even through limited objective judgments such as "This is blue" and "This is yellow." Various epistemological, metaphysical, and linguistic theories, by demonstrating the necessity and foundational status of the recognition "I am Śiva," attempt to lead the student to experience and possess the recognition that "I am Śiva."[45]

In the area of philosophical psychology, the Pratyabhijñā thinkers describe the empowered Śiva-identity recognized by the practitioner as a higher sense of I (*aham*) or, more abstractly, I-hood (*ahambhāva*), which also came to be called "perfect I-hood" (*pūrṇāhaṁtā*). Michel Hulin and Mark Dyczkowski have demonstrated the historical innovativeness of this theory and its great influence on later tantric traditions. Dyczkowski describes it as a conception of "absolute" or "super" "egoity" (not to be confused with the Freudian superego).[46] He explains:

> This concept of Self as pure, absolute ego-consciousness is quite unique in the history of Indian thought. It is found only in monistic Kashmiri Śaiva schools and those traditions (like the Śākta *Śrīvidyā*) that have been directly influenced by them.[47]

A sense of egoity precursory to the Pratybhijñā theory is, in my view, found in earlier tantric and even some Upaniṣadic realizations of empowerment.[48] Nevertheless, Dyczkowski's contention is valid with regard to the Pratyabhijñā philosophical psychological understanding of egoity. Contrary to earlier Hindu and Buddhist thought, the Pratyabhijñā system and Pratyabhijñā-inspired tantrism do not advocate the surrender of ordinary egoistic identity, referred to by such terms as "I-concept" (*ahaṁkāra*), "pride" or "self-conception" (*abhimāna*), "I-am-ness" (*asmitā*), and "I-hood" (*ahaṁtā*). For this mode of thinking, the human ego is an immanent expression of God's identity *that must be universalized and transfigured into its essential nature as perfect I-hood.*[49]

Abhinavagupta further elaborates that integral to the perfect egoity of God is a state of satiety he variously describes as "rest in the self" (*svātmaviśrānti*), "self-enjoyment" (*svātmopabhoga*), and "self-relishing" (*svātmacamatkāra, svaviṣayāsvāda*). Through practices ranging from the Kaula sexual ritual through aesthetic appreciation and philosophical and theosophical contemplations, ordinary selfish pleasures are transfigured into that divine satiety. The richness and profundity of the Pratyabhijñā interpretation of the divinization and empowerment of egoity account for much of the influence of the system on later tantric doctrine and practice.

Semantics and Syntax of the Perfect I

As mentioned, the Pratyabhijñā thinkers identify the Śakti and self-recognition of the Self/Śiva with the principle, Supreme Speech, derived from the Grammarian Bhartṛhari. They accordingly follow Bhartṛhari in explaining emanation as occurring through a bifurcation of Supreme Speech into ordinary expressive speech (*vācaka*) and the objective referents of that speech (*vācya*). The origination of this polarity from a common superlinguistic source makes the entire universe of experience inherently linguistic, and provides the ground for the reconnection of words and objects in conventional linguistic reference.[50] The complete reversal of the cosmic fragmentation occurs in the soteriological recognition.

Utpaladeva and Abhinavagupta expound many philosophical as well as "theosophical" ramifications of this theory throughout their writings. Important to the VAP and VAPV is Abhinava's contemplation of the nature of perfect egoity as encompassing all speech and referents, in terms of an occult etymology of the word *aham*, "I," itself. This also justifies the choice of *aham* as a favorite monistic Śaiva mantra. To mention the relevant aspects of this complex scheme, according to it, *aham* encompasses all Sanskrit phonemes from the first in the traditional enumeration, *a*, through the last, *ha*, and the graphemic *bindu*, *ṁ*—along with the corresponding cosmic cycle of emission and reabsorption.

An overlapping scheme describes emanation and return in terms of two triads of cosmic courses (*adhvan*)—phonemes (*varṇa*), mantras and words (*pada*) on the side of expressive speech (*vācaka*), and cosmic segments (*kalā*), cosmic principles (*tattva*) and cosmic realms (*bhuvana*) as the referents of that speech (*vācya*).[51] On the basis of the conception of semantically foundational Supreme Speech as the essence of scriptural traditions (*āgama*),[52] Abhinavagupta also justifies the overcoding of the authoritative oral and written texts of competing schools of Hinduism, Buddhism, and Jainism. According to him, the scriptures of other traditions provide their followers with progressively more "perfect" or "complete" (*pūrṇa*) realizations of the monistic Śaiva perfect I-hood.[53]

Such semantic speculations are only the beginning of the monistic Śaiva linguistic theory. Correlative to their identification of Śakti and self-recognition as Speech, Utpaladeva and Abhinavagupta further interpret monistic Śaiva empowered identity with a philosophical theory of *syntax* that I have previously described as a "mythico-ritual syntax of omnipotence."[54] The relevant considerations pertain to how verbs expressing action (*kriyā*) relate to declined nouns referring to the concomitants of action (*kārakas*).[55]

Edwin Gerow and I have separately argued that there is a tendency in many traditions of Hindu and Buddhist philosophy to denigrate the role of the agent in the syntactic nexus.[56] Among Hindu schools, this tendency appears to be strongest in Advaita Vedānta, while Buddhists from Nāgārjuna to Dharmakīrti entirely negate the role of the agent in the syntax of dependent origination. In Gerow's view, this tendency culminated in the late Hindu grammarian Nāgeśa's treatment of passive intransitive syntax as most paradigmatic. This denigration of agency seems to reflect not only the agent's bondage to karma in rebirth for Hindus and Buddhists—as emphasized by Gerow[57]—but also its subordination to the order of objective ritual behavior—pertaining to sacrifice, caste, life cycle, and so on—in orthodox Brahmanic norms.

Utpaladeva and Abhinavagupta develop a grammar of omnipotence by taking up and radicalizing earlier understandings of the positive albeit delimited role of the agent, particularly from the Vyākaraṇa and Nyāya traditions. Through his self-recognition, Śiva forms the intention (*icchā*) for action, and is the instigator (*prayojaka*) and encompassing locus (*vyāpārāśraya*) of all processes in the universe along with all their accessories. Whereas God/the Self is "self-determined" or "independent" (*svatantra*) in relation to the operations of all the other factors of action, the latter are "determined by another" (*paratantra*), namely, the agent.[58]

The Pratyabhijñā syntax of agency not only interprets the monistic Śaiva myth, but it is also ritually axiomatic. Utpaladeva describes the Pratyabhijñā philosophy as leading to salvation through the contemplation of one's status as the agent of the universe. Abhinavagupta likewise explains that the aspirant's goal in more concrete ritual action is identification with Śiva as the agent impelling all things indicated by nouns declined as nonagents—the ritual paraphernalia manipulated by the adept epitomizing all other cosmic entities.[59]

There is more to the Pratyabhijñā grammar of empowered identity than the theory of noun-verb relations that I exposited in my first studies.

The VAP and VAPV also advert to Abhinavagupta's further elaboration of this grammar in terms of the semantics and syntax of *grammatical persons.* As expressed in conjugations, personal pronouns, and sometimes declensions, the grammatical persons are the familiar triad of He/She/It/They (called in Sanskrit the "first person" and in English the "third person"), You (Sanskrit "middle person," English "second person") and I/We (Sanskrit "final person," English "first person"). Abhinava's views about grammatical persons are remarkable for ways in which they anticipate theories of later thinkers such as Charles Peirce and Emile Benveniste, although his overarching intellectual and religious agenda is quite different.

Like contemporary thinkers, Abhinava acknowledges that the three persons in ordinary discourse are defined by their mutual distinctions and are arbitrary in their reference. However, he also ranks the persons hierarchically. He affirms the privilege of I/We as indicating the enunciator of discourse, over the addressee You and the noninterlocutory He/She/It, with an observation—anticipating Benveniste—about their degrees of extension. That is, what is called in English the second person You can include the third person He/She/It/They. The first person, as We, can also include You and He, She or They. The wider extension of the first person points to its still much greater, ultimate significance.

According to Abhinava, the ranking of the three persons reflects the basic triadic structure of emanation according to Trika: Śiva, Śakti, Human (*nara*). That is, I as the enunciator of discourse corresponds to the omnipotent Self as Śiva, as the whole universe is ultimately My Supreme Speech. The addressee, You, is identified with Śakti according to the model of Śiva's dialogues with Śakti in tantric scriptures. The noninterlocutory He/She/It represents the unenlightened human reduced to the condition of inert objects. Abhinava prescribes a contemplation of return in which all forms of He/She/It are *personalized* as absorbed into You as Śakti. And You as Śakti are realized to be *My* integral power and consort.[60]

Universalization of the Body and Reflected Identity

Another approach to empowered identity in monistic Śaivism that is especially important to the VAP and VAPV is the transformation of the sense of embodiment. Tantric traditions resonate with contemporary cultural theories in conceiving *embodiment* as integral to human identity. They do not, however, celebrate the status quo experience of the human body. For them, rather, the ordinary experience of the body is an extremely limited and inadequate realization of much greater possibilities. Developing precedents in the Vedas, Upaniṣads, Bhagavad Gītā, and earlier tantrism, the monistic Śaivas interpret the Self's/Śiva's entire cosmic emanation through Śakti as the true *body*.[61] The *Śiva Sūtra* thus proclaims that all that is observable (*dṛśya*), that is, the universe, is one's body.[62]

The limited human body is a microcosm that replicates the macrocosmic body emanated by Śiva through Śakti. Gavin Flood explains how the fleshly body manifests the transcendent-cum-immanent Ultimate Reality:

> The human body, which is a consequence of the contraction of consciousness, is thought to contain the higher universe beyond it and also the absolute consciousness of Śiva with which it is ultimately identical and of which it is a projected form. The human body is, therefore, homologous with the cosmical hierarchy, which we might call the 'manifest cosmic body,' and contains within its transcendent source, which we might call the 'essential cosmic body.'[63]

By such reasoning the human body becomes one of the primary foci for monistic Śaiva transformative practices:

> The body is regarded as the vehicle of transformation, being of central importance in Śaiva yoga and in the Trika liturgies, during which awareness of identity with supreme Śiva is thought to expand and to fill the body. Such an expansion of awareness is, for the Śaiva monist, an expansion of awareness through the cosmos and a recognition that both universe and absolute are identical with the body.[64]

The monistic Śaivas thus employ various tantric techniques for what may be described equally as the "universalization" of the human body and the "corporification" of the universe. Such techniques in effect "overcode" the routine cultural techniques—of action, rest, washing, life cycle, and so on—that Marcel Mauss described as constituting the bodily "habitus" of ordinary men and women.[65] This transformation is evinced in the purification of the elements (*bhūtaśuddhi*) and the projection of divinizing mantric syllables (*nyāsa*) on the body and ritual implements, which are performed as preliminaries to worship. Through these practices, the adept resolves the gross elements of his or her physical body into their subtle essences. The adept symbolically burns away the limitations of the physical body, and through the contemplative infusion of divine nectar manifests his or her divinized body.[66]

A variety of tantric practices are conceived to awaken Śakti as Kuṇḍalinī, often symbolized in the form of a serpent, dormant in the energy center (*cakra*) at the base of the spine. As she ascends through higher energy centers she divinizes the subtle physiology of the human body.[67] In the sexual ritual, the male and female partners physically become Śiva and Śakti, and realize their primordial unity in their very genitalia and sexual fluids.[68] I also mention that the transformation of embodiment in tantric traditions is often understood greatly to improve the health or strength of the practitioner's human body, or even to make it immortal.[69]

Another important monistic Kashmiri Śaiva code for the myth and ritual of Śakti possession, closely related to those of egoity and embodiment, makes use of the metaphor or analogy of reflection (*pratibimba*). Although this code is not directly addressed by the VAP and VAPV, I believe that a review of it will help us to understand those texts.

The analogy of reflection actually has a long and complex history in South Asian religious and philosophical traditions for explaining the relation of the Ultimate Reality, God, or the higher Self to the multiplicity of limited subjects and objects that constitute the universe. Moreover, as Phyllis Granoff has shown, reflection is often said to constitute the *body* of the Ultimate Reality or of the enlightened being. As manifest in *iconography or imaginary forms* the reflection (*pratibimba, pratimā*) provides Hindu, Buddhist, and Jain traditions an accessible mode of approach to the Ultimate.[70]

It was Abhinavagupta who fully established the use of the model of reflection to articulate the basic mythic and recapitulatory ritual structures of monistic Śaivism.[71] The pattern is similar to that observed by Granoff regarding images or reflections as the body and immanent mode of access to the divine. For Abhinavagupta, however, just as the whole universe is the Śakti-body of the Self as Śiva, it is also one's *own* reflection.

Abhinava thus interprets various modes of practice as leading to identification with Śiva through the realization *that the entire emanated universe is one's reflection.* Techniques that he describes in this manner include the Pratyabhijñā philosophy itself, theosophical meditations in the *Tantrāloka, Tantrasāra,* and *Parātrīśikāvivaraṇa* on emanating mantric phonemes and cosmic principles,[72] and even the Kaula congregation (*yoginīmelaka*) and aesthetic experience.

Abhinava's explanations of the myth and practice of empowered identity in terms of reflection were further diffused along with the rest of his theology to other intellectual traditions of Hindu tantrism. The authors of the VAP and VAPV would certainly have been aware of these interpretations, even though they do not mention them. It will be useful to keep these teachings on reflection in mind as we recount, in chapter 2, an Upaniṣadic teaching on reflected identity, and endeavor in chapter 4 to engage the Odd-Eyed One's instructions on divine egoity with Western conceptions of "narcissism."

Chapter 2

The Instruction of Indra

The Narrative Context

The *Virūpākṣapañcāśikā* is framed as a dialogue between an incarnation of Virūpākṣa/Śiva and the deity Indra. Indra was the most prominent high God of early Vedic religion, celebrated as the God of the rains, and for his victories over Vṛtra, "the Restrainer," and other demons. Vidyācakravartin provides an interesting narrative framework for the conversation between the deities: Once, in sport, Śiva assumed a body in this world. Wandering about, he came upon Indra. Indra, presuming himself (*abhimanyamānam*) to be the Supreme Lord, was exhibiting a fight between rutting elephants. Virūpākṣa displayed before Indra a fight between two great mountains. Indra was humiliated and asked Virūpākṣa to explain the seed of his yogic proficiency (*siddhi*). Virūpākṣa then propounded the text in order to enlighten Indra.[1]

The Subordination of the Vedic High God

This narrative instantiates an old and widespread mythic pattern. The status of Indra in the early Vedic literature had declined greatly over the centuries. Beginning in late Vedic and early Buddhist texts, and continuing in the Hindu epics and Purāṇas are numerous accounts of the God's humiliation, subordination, and instruction. Indra is often portrayed as needing the help of other deities or even humans to defeat the demons. He likewise receives advice from others about new spiritual practices and realizations.[2]

These narratives are diverse and complex, and have numerous meanings. It is clear that they generally have the import of demonstrating the superiority of various later metaphysical and soteriological conceptions by "overcoding" Indra and his cult.[3] Similar subordinations between Śiva, Viṣṇu, and Devī are common in later Hindu narratives.[4]

Important for our present inquiry is that some of these narratives also contain instructions in what we might call religious and philosophical psychology. In the context of claims that Indra's importance was previously overestimated—by Indra himself along with his devotees—some of the myths describe his humiliation as a valuable lesson regarding the personality problems of "grandiosity," "pride," or "egotism." As such, these narratives illustrate how various traditions view pride, and so on, within their respective soteriologies and metaphysics.

The VAP and VAPV pick up this motif to contextualize their exposition of the monistic Śaiva philosophy of absolute "egoity." I will briefly summarize three accounts of Indra's instruction through humiliation, all of which *probably* preceded our texts. It is not clear that any of these particular narratives were of direct concern to the monistic Śaiva authors. My intention is only to illustrate the broad problematic that the Śaiva authors address.

The *Chāndogya Upaniṣad* on Transcending the Reflected Identity of the Body

Our oldest example is the classic story of the instruction of Indra about the Self (*ātman*) by the creator God Prajāpati in the *Chāndogya Upaniṣad.*[5] While this account addresses Indra's pride only by implication, it has fascinating psychological features, including its approach to the body and reflected identity. The narrative begins with a proclamation by Prajāpati:

> The Self, which is free from evil, ageless, deathless, sorrowless, hungerless, thirstless, whose desire is the Real, whose conception is the Real—He should be searched out, Him one should desire to understand. He obtains all worlds and all desires who has found out and who understands that Self.[6]

Both the other gods and the demons (*asura*) hear this announcement and decide to seek the Self. Indra from among the gods and Virocana from the demons go to Prajāpati. They pay him the respect appropriate for a spiritual preceptor and live with him chastely for many years. Finally, they are allowed to inquire of Prajāpati about the Self that he had described.

Then follows a long and tortuous pedagogical process in which Prajāpati responds to his students' confusions with trickery. Prajāpati first asserts that: "That Person who is seen in the eye—He is the Self (Ātman) of whom I spoke. That is the immortal, the fearless. That is Brahma."[7] Śaṅkarācarya, the circa eight century Advaita Vedāntin philosopher, in his commentary explains that Prajāpati was in this statement referring to the Seer (*draṣṭṛ*) known by yogis who have detached themselves from sense experience. However, Indra and Virocana misunderstood him to be referring to the person *reflected* in the eyes of others. According to Śaṅkara, this error accounts for their ensuing question and then Prajāpati's response.[8]

Indra and Virocana ask: "But this one, sir, who is observed in water and in a mirror—which one is he?"[9] Prajāpati, humoring them in their delusion, indicates that "The same one, indeed, is observed in all these."[10] He asks them to look at themselves in a plate of water, and to determine whom they see; and then to dress nicely and ornament themselves, and to investigate again. Prajāpati approves of their conviction that their reflected bodies are the Self: "That is the immortal, the fearless. That is Brahma."[11] However, as they leave, he says to himself that they have not found the true Self, and that those holding such a view will perish.

Virocana is satisfied that the body that he identified through reflections is the true Self, and he teaches this to his fellow demons. The narrator remarks that those who hold such a doctrine (that the body is the Self) and do not properly practice religion are for this reason described as demonic (*āsura*).[12]

Indra, however, begins to consider that the body is vulnerable to injury and will ultimately perish. He realizes that it therefore cannot be the immortal Self proclaimed by Prajāpati, and he returns to his teacher for more years of probationary service and instruction. In the course of this, Prajāpati misleads Indra twice more, first suggesting that the Self is the subject of dreams and then that it is that of deep sleep. Indra realizes that the former cannot be the true Self because not only happiness but also unhappiness and even apparent death occur in dreams. Likewise, he decides that the Self cannot be the one in deep sleep because that state is itself like annihilation.[13]

Prajāpati finally reveals the truth:

> O Maghavan, verily, this body (*śarīra*) is mortal. It has been appropriated by death (Mṛityu). [But] it is the standing ground of that deathless, bodiless Self (Ātman). Verily, he who is incorporate has been appropriated by pleasure and pain. Verily, there is no freedom from pleasure and pain for one while he is incorporate. Verily, while one is bodiless, pleasure and pain do not touch him.[14]

According to Prajāpati, the bodiless true Self is the witness and agent of the corporeal faculties of seeing, smelling, speaking, hearing, and thinking.[15]

However, reiterating his earlier statement that the one realizing the Self satisfies all desires, he describes its disincarnate pleasures in paradoxically carnal terms:

> That serene one (*samprasāda*), when he rises up from this body (*śarīra*) and reaches the highest light, appears with his own form. Such a one is the supreme person (*uttama puruṣa*). There such a one goes around laughing, sporting, having enjoyment with women or chariots or friends, not remembering the appendage of this body.[16]

Prajāpati's teaching must be understood against the background of Indra's renown in the Veda for his martial valor. It would have been a very challenging and humbling lesson for the heroic deity to stop identifying with his body. It is not clear how literally we should take Prajāpati's description of the pleasures of the Self. In any event, although the repudiation of the body and its reflections disagrees with later tantric traditions, this text anticipates those traditions in including omnipotence and the enjoyment associated with that in self-realization.

Although we will focus on the dialogical engagement of Hindu with Western ideas in chapter 4, we may presently observe a remarkable parallelism between this text's theme of mirrored identity and the Western accounts of Narcissus and narcissism. Actually, there would be a basis in Freudian theory for interpreting Prajāpati's second and third deceptive teachings as continuing the same problematic. Both the wish fulfillments of dreams and the contentlessness of deep sleep could be viewed as further stages of narcissistic, or, if you will, "demonic" or "Virocanistic" self-absorption.[17] As we shall see, psychoanalysis also interprets narcissism to be the reality underlying spiritual realizations of a monistic and omnipotent Self.[18]

The Govardhana Story in the *Bhāgavata Purāṇa*

One of the most famous episodes of Vaiṣṇava mythology is the story in the *Bhāgavata Purāṇa* of Kṛṣṇa lifting Mount Govardhana.[19] Kṛṣṇa in this story is notably described as having "the nature of time (*kāla*) and acting to destroy the pride of Śakra [Indra]."[20] We are reminded of Kṛṣṇa's famous identification of himself as time in the course of his awesome revelation of his universal form in the *Bhagavad Gītā*.[21] This aspect of Kṛṣṇa makes obvious the essential finitude of all creatures and terrifies them.

In the *Bhāgavata* account, Kṛṣṇa sees that the cowherds in the land of Vraja are preparing to worship Indra as the god of rain. Kṛṣṇa argues that this is wrong, claiming that Indra has no control over the great determinants of human life. He persuades them instead to worship three other subjects: cows, Brahmans and Mount Govardhana. When they follow his advice, Kṛṣṇa himself appears as the mountain and consumes the offerings to it.

Indra is infuriated and actually accuses both Kṛṣṇa and the cowherds of pride. He then attempts to annihilate them by creating a deluge from clouds ordinarily released only at the time of cosmic dissolution. He follows the storm in, riding on his elephant mount, Airāvata.

Kṛṣṇa, however, proclaims that he will thwart Indra's pride and his presumption of being the Lord of the universe, and acts to protect the people and the cows of Vraja. He lifts up Mount Govardhana with one hand to serve as an umbrella over the creatures, and holds it that way for a week. Indra is finally humiliated and surrenders to Kṛṣṇa, begging for forgiveness and extolling him at length:

> You are the father, the preceptor and the supreme ruler of (all) the worlds. You are the Time-Spirit that cannot be easily set at naught and that hold the scepter of sway (over the universe). It is for the good of the world that You carry on Your sport in embodied forms assumed at will, curbing the pride of those who fancy themselves to be the rulers of the world. Fools like me, who regard themselves as rulers of the universe, speedily shake off that pride on seeing You undaunted even in times of danger and, rid of their haughtiness, take the path of Devotion trodden by righteousness.[22]

The thematic relations to the VAP and VAPV are obvious. Indra is cured of pride and the presumption of being Lord of the universe by an *avatāra* of the actual Lord of the universe. Also notable are Indra's association with the elephant, Airāvata, and Lord Kṛṣṇa's demonstration of his superiority by his power over mountains.[23]

Indra and the Ants in the *Brahmavaivarta Purāṇa*

Another myth of Indra being cured of his pride, the story of Indra and the ants in the *Brahmavaivarta Purāṇa,* was made famous in the West by the early twentieth century Indologist Heinrich Zimmer.[24] I will mention only some of the prominent episodes of this rather complex narrative.

Before the part of the story recounted by Zimmer, Indra's pride has already led him into a lot of trouble, from which he should have learned his lessons. He had alienated his priest and guru Bṛhaspati by his discourtesy. For seducing the wife of the sage Gautama he was punished to have one thousand vaginas on his body for a year. Because he killed his new priest, Viśvarūpa, Viśvarūpa's father Tvaṣṭṛ invoked to rise against him none other than the Vedic demon Vṛtra. Having defeated Vṛtra, he was fiercely pursued by the terrifying figure Brahmahatyā, the female personification of the sin of killing a Brahman. Finally, Indra had to beg for the forgiveness of Bṛhaspati and obtain his help in overcoming Brahmahatyā.

Nevertheless, Indra becomes inflated again, and begins to make grandiose and oppressive demands of the divine architect Viśvakarman for the reconstruction of his heavenly city. It becomes necessary for Viṣṇu to incarnate himself as a Brahman boy and visit Indra. The boy makes a backhanded complement that no Indra before has constructed such a great city. He continues to shock and humiliate Indra by informing him that he is only one of an infinite number of Indras. Indras have been born, lived, and died in uncountable parallel universes over uncountable cosmic cycles. In the course of their conversation, a long column of ants appears. The boy explains that each of the ants had at one time been an Indra.

Then a mysterious old ascetic appears whom Zimmer identifies as Śiva. This man has a circle of hairs on his chest. He explains that he is pursuing asceticism rather than the life of a householder because his life is short. Every time an Indra passes, one hair is pulled out. When they all are removed, he will die.

All this overwhelms Indra. He halts his construction plans and decides to become an ascetic. However, Bṛhaspati assists Indra's wife in persuading Indra to remain with her. The lesson Indra finally learns has some similarity with that of the *Bhagavad Gītā*. He will continue his worldly duties with a proper sense of his role in the cosmic scheme, and with the ascetic's detachment from the vanities of life.

Volumes could be written about the mythic backgrounds to the framing narrative of the VAP and VAPV.[25] My purpose has only been to situate the teachings of our texts in the context of instructions of Indra on his problem of pride. As we will see in the next chapter, the VAP and VAPV give such instructions a new twist. Virūpākṣa does not teach Indra to abandon his corporeal form that appears in reflections, by identifying with abstract consciousness, or to surrender in devotion. Virūpākṣa teaches him contemplations to transform his grandiosity into genuine omnipotence.

Chapter 3

The Odd-Eyed One's Teachings on the Tantric Self and its Universal Body

The VAP and VAPV follow the basic monistic Śaiva mythico-ritual pattern described in chapter 1. That is, they endeavor to lead Indra and us readers to the recognition of our identity with the omnipotent Virūpākṣa/Śiva by revealing our possession of his Śakti. While this realization confers a great variety of benefits, the texts extol two overlapping ones as the highest, becoming the guru of the universe, and performing Śiva's five cosmic acts.[1] Those acts are:

1. Creation of the universe at the beginning of each cosmic cycle.
2. Preservation of the universe.
3. Destruction of the universe at the end of each cycle.
4. Bringing about the delusion of creatures that leads them to suffer in *saṁsāra.*
5. Graciously liberating creatures from delusion and suffering, which is essentially the same as being the guru of the universe.

The text and commentary make extensive use of the concepts and vocabulary of the Pratyabhijñā system. In a couple places, Vidyācakravartin goes so far as to assert that the texts are propounding an inference for the sake of others.[2] However, the VAP and VAPV do not engage in the same technical investigations of epistemology and ontology as do the original Pratyabhijñā works. Here the mythic problem of the instruction of Indra on pride provides a setting for a rigorous contemplative regimen founded on the Śaiva philosophical psychology of egoity and the body.

The Transformation of Embodiment

The broadest framework organizing the contemplations of the VAP and VAPV focuses on the transformation of the sense of embodiment. As explained in chapter 1, this transformation is one of the common monistic Śaiva "codes" for the mythico-ritual process of possessing Śakti, and can be described equally as a universalization of the human body and a corporification of the universe. At the very beginning of his instruction, Virūpākṣa explains the reason his power is superior to that of Indra:

> Well, this is [our] point of disagreement: I [recognize that I] have the nature of consciousness [and that] this universe, beginning with the void state and ending with the earth, is my body. This [fact that the universe is one's body] is proven because [the universe] is perceptible, like the fleshly body.[3]

The "void state" (*śūnyapada*) mentioned by Virūpākṣa in this context refers to the "Śiva principle" (*śivatattva*), the first emanation from the "Supreme Śiva" (*paramaśiva*), in which he bifurcates himself from Śakti. This is understood as a mode of consciousness abstracted from all action and experiential contents; it is also homologized with noncognitive states such as deep sleep.[4] Thus, Virūpākṣa affirms that his body extends from the beginning of the emanatory process and the most rudimentary forms of consciousness through all the contents of immanent experience.

In this statement Virūpākṣa is clearly alluding to the assertion of the ninth century monistic Śaiva contemplative manual, the *Śiva Sūtra:* "The perceptible [universe] is [one's true] body. Through the concentration of the fluctuating mind [*citta*] within the heart, one experiences both the perceptible as well as sleep [which is deep and void of contents, as one's own body]."[5] As I mentioned earlier, according to the VAP and VAPV, one of the greatest benefits of Śiva-identity is becoming guru of the universe. Vidyācakravartin reiterates near the end of the text that such a guru is precisely one who is not embodied in a particular, limited body, but rather the universe.[6]

Virūpākṣa explains that the root cause of Indra's and our predicament is simply the misidentification of our true body:

> Having departed from the body that is the universe, one's I-hood becomes confined to a particular body that is a portion

> of that [universal one]. [Unenlightened] people are as if dead while living, as if their throats were gasping for breath.[7]

Whereas the Śaiva sage is liberated while living, the bodily finitude of our life in *saṁsāra* is a kind of living death.

The Lord explains to Indra the great power accruing from the proper identification of one's body:

> [You] whose I-am-ness refers to the [fleshly] body can, through mere intention, strike [your] two insentient arms together. Just so, [I, whose I-am-ness] refers to the universe can, through the force of that [intention, strike together] even two mountains.[8]

The contemplative agenda presented in the Śaiva texts differs markedly from that in the instruction of Indra in the *Chāndogya Upaniṣad.* Now Indra's sense of embodiment must not be negated but rather vastly increased and universalized.

Expansion of I-am-ness

How does one cultivate a sense that one's body is not any particular body, but rather everything? The VAP and VAPV explain the modus operandi of embodiment-transformation using other homologous codes for Śakti possession. The most philosophically and psychologically illuminating of these, because it directly addresses the fundamental problem of Indra's pride, is the Pratyabhijñā theory of egoity. This theory constitutes the other predominant framework of contemplation in the texts, and gives them much of their intellectual force.

One of the key terms that the texts utilize in explaining the contemplative process is mentioned in the verse just quoted, that is, "I-am-ness" (*asmitā*). This term, which apparently was first introduced by the *Yoga Sūtra,* is formed by combining the conjugated verb *asmi,* "I am," with the suffix, *-tā,* indicating an abstract condition. It thus signifies the abstract condition of positing one's identity as "I." Other terms that the VAP and VAPV use either synonymously or in close functional relationships with I-am-ness, are "pride" or "self-conception" (*abhimāna,* which is used in a cognate participial form to describe Indra as originally presuming that he is the Supreme Lord[9]); "I-hood" (*ahaṁtā*), and "I-concept" (*ahaṁkāra*).

Yoga Sūtra 2.3 classifies "I-am-ness" as one of the five spiritual "afflictions" (*kleśa*).[10] It is a basic expression of the misidentification of the self (*puruṣa*) and matter (*prakṛti*).[11] This misidentification, which is also understood as misidentification with one's reflection in matter, causes suffering in *saṁsāra* and must ultimately be eliminated through discriminative knowledge. Although I-am-ness is present in a higher form of meditative enstasy with objective support (*samprajñāta samādhi*), it is transcended in meditative enstasy without support (*asamprajñāta samādhi*).[12]

As explained in chapter 1, the monistic Śaivas do not conceive egoity, referred to by I-am-ness and the other terms, as an affliction to be eliminated. Like other Hindu tantric traditions, they also disagree with the *Yoga Sūtra*'s negative assessment of the identification of consciousness with its contents. They view the Self and nature not as distinct realia but rather as *continuous,* since the former emanates the latter. The VAP and VAPV thus equate the various terms for egoity with other codes for emanatory Śakti, such as self-recognition (*pratyavamarśa,* and so on), Supreme Speech (*parāvāk*), universal agency (*kartṛtā*), and agential self-determination (*svatantratā*).[13]

For Virūpākṣa and Vidyācakravartin, the proper understanding of egoity is paramount to the transformation of the experience of embodiment. They analyze six features of experience to which an unenlightened person commonly applies his or her sense of I-am-ness: (1) One identifies with possessions, that is, external objects such as a house or land, in conceptions such as "I am prosperous." (2) One identifies with the fleshly body in observations such as "I am lean." (3) There is identification with the sense organs in experiences such as "I am relishing." (4) There is identification with the inner organ or mind[14] in experiences such as "I am happy." (5) "I am breathing" expresses identification with the vital breath. (6) One also identifies with apparently noncognitive states such as deep sleep in experiences such as "I am void."[15]

The Śaiva practitioner must expand this sense of I-am-ness to include the entire universe. As Vidyācakravartin explains:

> Contemplate this consciousness of I-am-ness that is well known in the six conditions for the entire course. That is, firmly recognitively synthesize this eternally pure recognition [of I-am-ness]—as in the six conditions—everywhere, regarding everything, beginning with [the emanated, lower] Śiva[16] and ending with the earth. Then you will have the recognition of the universe as your body.[17]

Possession of Wheels of Śaktis

Some of the contemplative schemes in the VAP and VAPV directly advert to the most basic monistic Śaiva mythico-ritual act of possessing Śakti. Thus, there are contemplations appropriated from the Krama stream of tantrism on the Self as possessing "wheels" (*cakra*) of the subordinate modalities of Śakti who emanate all features of epistemic experience:

> Consciousness should be contemplated as possessing innumerable wheels of its own Śaktis. [Those wheels of Śaktis] emanate this universe, which consists of the five sense fields, such as the visible; and takes the forms of objects of knowledge, the senses and the knower.[18]

Following the Krama tradition, the texts identify the cognitive triad of objects of knowledge, the instruments of knowledge, and the knower or agent of knowledge respectively with the symbols of the moon, the sun, and fire.[19]

Another approach is the contemplation of one's possession of Śakti as analyzed into a set of five sub-Śaktis—Illuminator, Cosmic Pulsation, Happiness, Smokey, and Omnipresent.[20] Each of these is said to perform a particular function, and to have as her effect one of the five elements. Furthermore, according to Vidyācakravartin, the possession of each of the five Śaktis enables one to perform each of Śiva's five cosmic acts. The correspondences are illustrated in table 3.1.[21]

There is only one correlation that Vidyācakravartin does not state explicitly, and which I have determined by elimination—that between Happiness, whose basic function is fulfillment, and Śiva's cosmic act of destruction. The idea seems to be based on the homology respectively between the

Table 3.1: Five Modalities of Śakti and their Correspondences

Modality of Śakti	Basic Description of Function	Elemental Effect	Act of Śiva
Illuminator	manifestation	fire	creation
Cosmic Pulsation	agitation	air	preservation
Happiness	fulfillment	water	destruction
Smokey	concealment	earth	delusion
Omnipresent	pervasion	sky (or ether)	grace

creation and destruction of the cosmos, and delusion and grace in the experience of limited subjects. That is, the entire universe will realize fulfillment in returning to its source.

Virūpākṣa concludes the discussion of the five modalities of Śakti by describing the universalization of the body in the terms of the Pratyabhijñā epistemological approach to the disclosure of Śakti. He interprets the Śakti possessed by the adept as self-recognition:

> My Śakti has the nature of recognitive apprehension. She makes [one recognize that] awareness, of which [She herself is] the integral nature, is the essential nature of the multitude of the objects of awareness. [She] makes [one recognize that] everything is my body.[22]

Linguistic Contemplations of the Odd-Eyed One

Several of the contemplations prescribed in the VAP and VAPV are formulated in terms of the linguistic theories discussed in chapter 1. Thus, some are based on the equivalence of egoity with semantically foundational Supreme Speech. Among those are contemplations on the tantric Self as possessing six "courses" (*adhvan*) of the emanation of Supreme Speech, also designated collectively as the sixfold course.[23]

The six courses are analyzed into two triads according to the root bifurcation of Supreme Speech into expressive speech (*vācaka*) and the referents of that speech (*vācya*). The triad of expressive speech comprises in descending order the increasingly concrete phonemes (*varṇa*), mantras, and words (*pada*). The three corresponding courses of referents are cosmic segments (*kalā*), cosmic principles (*tattva*), and cosmic realms (*bhuvana*).[24] This scheme is utilized as a sort of "theosophical" map of the cosmic-linguistic totality as understood by the Pratyabhijñā and Bhartṛharian philosophy of language. The student contemplates all the courses as emanating from his or her own I-hood.[25]

On the basis of the equation of I-hood with Supreme Speech, Virūpākṣa and Vidyācakravartin likewise follow Abhinavagupta in propounding a theosophical etymology of the word "I" (*aham*) itself. According to this etymology, the word is formed by a procedure of abbreviation (*pratyāhara*) used by Pāṇini in his linguistic rules. Following this procedure, a set of phonemes is designated by its first and last members. Now, in the traditional Sanskritic list of all phonemes, *a* is the first and *ha* is the last. These make up the *aha* of *aham*. Thus, "I" as Supreme Speech encompasses within itself all meaningful sounds that constitute mantras as well as ordinary speech.[26]

Vidyācakravartin further explains that *aha* is by itself a noun stem, which requires declension for verbal usage. According to this view, the final *-m* of *aham* is the required declensional termination.[27] Now, graphemically the *-m* in Sanskrit can be represented by a dot, called a *bindu,* above the previous letter.

Bindu, which literally means "drop" or "dot," has rich and complex significations in the history of tantric and other South Asian religious traditions.[28] In the VAP and VAPV, it is often treated as another equivalent for I-hood as Supreme Speech and self-recognition, and may be translated as "germinal essence."[29] David White has argued that this term originally, and later often implicitly, refers to the male sexual fluid, or combined male and female fluids, offered and ingested in Kaula sexual rituals.[30] While such a meaning is not explicit in the VAP and VAPV, it is difficult to prove whether or not it is implicit. In any event, the explanation of the termination of *aha* with the final *bindu, -m,* further substantiates that the I is the source of all language and referents of language.

Besides those founded on the semantics of Supreme Speech, other contemplations in the VAP and VAPV invoke the distinctive monistic Śaiva approaches to more commonly recognized grammatical structures. The texts do not enter into a technical discussion of the Pratyabhijñā theory of noun-verb relations, which I have described as a "mythico-ritual syntax of omnipotence." However, they do advert to that theory in equating I-hood with universal agency (*kartṛtā*) and agential self-determination (*svatantratā*).[31] They also refer in various places to the determinative role of the agent's intention (*icchā*).[32]

Virūpākṣa and Vidyācakravartin devote more sustained attention to Abhinavagupta's theory of grammatical persons.[33] They endeavor to lead students to the discovery of the absolute form of the I as underlying and constituting the limited I as well as You and He/She/It. As Vidyācakravartin explains:

> The three [grammatical] persons are referred to by disjunctive designations as "He," "You," and "I." . . . None of these are external to me who have the nature of recognitive apprehension and who, as inclusive of them, am the Great Person. . . . The first and other [grammatical] persons are exclusive of each other. However, their creation and destruction depend upon

me who have the nature of recognitive apprehension. They are experienced upon the background that is myself, as identical with myself. Thus they are not external to me.[34]

There appears a differentiated form "I," which is the contrary of both of them [He and You]. Like "He" and "You," that is a differentiated portion, a particular aspect of myself. It is not I, that is, not my ultimate form. The reason for this is that [my] eternal form [is as described in the statement, in 3.22] "I am unitary." That is, I am eternally an unlimited and unitary compact mass of awareness.[35]

The Subsumption of Difference and Sequence

In the passage just quoted, the description of the Great Person, the I in its higher nature, as a unitary compact mass (*ekaghana*) of awareness and as inclusive (*anuvṛtta*) rather than exclusive (*vyāvṛtta*), articulates another important practical principle informing the contemplations of the VAP and VAPV—which may be described as the "subsumption" of difference and sequence.[36]

While this principle reflects some influence of Krama, "Sequence," tantrism, it may be understood more broadly as an expression of one of the perennial quests of religious philosophy, for a monistic Ultimate that is simple and indissoluble and therefore above the temporal contingencies of transformation and decay.[37] Monistic philosophies are of course themselves highly diverse in methods and conclusions, as is evinced in South Asia in the differences between various Upaniṣadic speculations, Advaita Vedānta, the antisubstantialism of Mādhyamika and other Buddhist interpretations of dependent origination, and Hindu and Buddhist tantric monisms.

Monistic Kashmiri Śaivism utilizes its religious and intellectual resources to formulate a distinctive approach to a "substantialist" monism. Advaita Vedānta, to mention an alternative, teaches the negation of the diverse, contingent and temporary, on the basis of criteriology indebted to both the Upaniṣadic revelation and the Buddhist doctrine of dependent origination. All that is left is *ātman/brahman* as an incorporeal substratum.

For monistic Śaivism, however, the integral or complete (*pūrṇa*) and paradoxically dynamic unity of Śiva-Śakti subsumes multiplicity and sequence within itself. Śaiva writers articulate this subsumption in diverse ways through the various "secondary codes" for the mythico-ritual process, for example, in terms of the body, reflection, mantras, *maṇḍalas,* the Pratyabhijñā epistemology, metaphysics, linguistics and psychology, and so on. In various doctrinal and practical spheres, they pursue categories and corresponding modes of experience that are more and more inclusive or continuous rather than exclusive and sequential.[38]

The VAP and VAPV themselves propound the contemplative subsumption of difference and sequence in numerous ways. Aside from the approach to the I, You, and He/She/It as grammatical persons, some contemplations in these texts are formulated in the more epistemological terms of subjects and objects. For example, the VAP and VAPV discuss subjects and objects as designated by "I" and "this"—which, it will be recalled, are according to the Pratyabhijñā identified in the Pure Wisdom of emanation with the apposition "I am this." As Vidyācakravartin explains with regards to the framework of subsumption, on the one hand:

> There is reciprocal exclusions [between instances of] the presentation "this," as is illustrated by the observation "This is blue and this is yellow." When that [exclusion] does not arise, there do not appear manifestations of objects such as blue.[39]

On the other hand, "the presentation 'I' is inclusive [of manifestations of different objects, as is illustrated by the statement] 'I know both blue and yellow.'"[40]

Vidyācakravartin likewise argues that it is only due to association with differentiated objects of experience that there is the false appearance of differences between individual subjects:

> There may be this objection: [The cognition that] "I am a subject here and now" refers to sequence of both place and time. How can there be unity? In response to this doubt, Virūpākṣa] explains that "there is no sequence in it of either place or time." That is, in this awareness, there is no sequence due to differentiation of either place or time. . . . What we call differentiation is exclusiveness. Nondifferentiation is inclusiveness. Objects of consciousness are differentiated by both place and time. Consciousness is the [inclusive] substratum of that differentiation. The delusion that consciousness is itself differentiated is predicated upon those objects that are merely its accidental qualifications.[41]

The Śaiva practitioner reverses the delusion. The expansion of the recognitive synthesis of differentiated objects reveals both that one is the universal subject, Śiva, rather than a particular subject; and that the universe is one's body:

> This fact [that the universe is one's body] is proven in everyone's direct experience [if that is understood properly]. When one attends to a particular and distinct object of knowledge, for example [a color] such as blue or yellow, then one becomes an individual subject, that is, a delimited awareness. The delimitation of one's awareness is the adventitious qualification of it by the differentiated object of knowledge. However, when one recognitively synthesizes everything in its universal nature [*sāmānyato*], then one [recognizes oneself to be] consciousness, that is, unlimited awareness. This is because it is impossible for the one who illuminates [limiting conditions] such as place and time to be limited by [those conditions such as] place and time. Therefore, at that time [when one perceives everything in its universal nature, one recognizes that] the universe is one's body.[42]

Elsewhere, they describe a similar subsumption of what are ordinarily understood as the discrete types of experience—perception, memory, and recognition—along with the objects of those experiences. All these are absorbed in the recognitive apprehension of the unitary and nonse-quential Self.[43]

The contemplative subsumption of sequence is elaborated in an interesting though rather complex and difficult manner in the VAP and VAPV 3.32–37. I will explain what I understand of the process.[44] At the most basic level, this section presents a contemplation of a hierarchy of five progressively internal, inclusive, and nonsequential essential natures.

This begins with the standard epistemic triad of South Asian philosophy—object (*jñeya*), knowledge (*jñāna*), and the limited subject or epistemic agent (*jñātṛ*).[45] As the texts explain, the internal and less sequential essential nature of the object of knowledge is knowledge itself, and the internal and less sequential essential nature of knowledge is the limited knower. Then the texts proceed further to state that the internal and less sequential essential nature of the knower is unitary consciousness (*citir ekā*), which they also identify with Śakti and recognitive apprehension (*pratyavamarśa*). Then they state that the (higher) "I," which they also identify with awareness (*prakāśa*), is the internal and less sequential essential nature of that consciousness or Śakti.[46]

The rationale for the identification of the I/awareness as the encompassing essential nature of consciousness/recognition/Śakti is that the former is the pure unity within which the latter occurs. As Vidyācakvartin elucidates:

> Consciousness is defined as recognitive apprehension. When that aspect of recognitive apprehension submerges [back into its internal essential nature], there remains only the I, having the nature of abstract awareness. . . . I, who have reached the summit, am alone the reality. There is "no other," that is, there is nothing that may be distinguished from myself [as a higher and more internal essential nature].[47]

The progressive subsumption of epistemic entities discussed so far is represented in figure 3.1.

FIGURE 3.1: Progressive Subsumption of Epistemic Entities

Object → Knowledge → Knower → Consciousness (Śakti) → I

At the next level of complexity, this fivefold scheme of increasing nonsequentiality is analyzed into a new threefold one—as sequential, sequential-cum-nonsequential, and nonsequential. Although the first three members (the epistemic triad of object, knowledge and knower) have already been described as increasingly nonsequential, they are now all classified as sequential in comparison to the latter two categories that overcome the distinctions of ordinary experience.[48]

In this new threefold analysis, Virūpākṣa and Vidyācakravartin clearly have in mind the correlations of sequence, sequence-cum-nonsequence, and nonsequence with a basic cosmological triad of Trika Śaivism: human, Śakti and Śiva. It would seem that they intend to subsume the standard epistemic triad within the first stage of the Trika triad, as identifying the structures of ordinary human cognition. The threefold analysis of the fivefold scheme may be clarified by table 3.2.

TABLE 3.2: Threefold Analysis of Sequentiality in Fivefold Scheme

Sequential (Human)	Sequential-cum-Nonsequential (Śakti)	Nonsequential (Śiva)
Object → Knowledge → Knower →	Consciousness →	I

The contemplation begins to convolute when Virūpākṣa and Vidyācakravartin make associations between the items in the standard epistemic triad and other items or sets of items. These associations consist of observations of similarities between items and prescriptions for the contemplation of their ultimate identities.[49] Therefore, I will interpret them as homologies rather than mere analogies. The first two homologies are fairly straightforward. The knower is said to be like the higher I. This is not hard to understand, as such a notion underlies the whole monistic Śaiva program for the expansion of human into divine egoity. Knowledge is then said to be like Śakti. That is also comprehensible insofar as knowledge is a capacity exercised by a knower.

More challenging is the interpretation of Virūpākṣa's assertion that the object is "like the triad."[50] From the previous two comparisons, it may be reliably inferred that he is homologizing the object with the entire lower epistemic triad. However, Vidyācakravartin's interpretation further complicates things. He explains that the triad homologized with the object includes the higher homologues paired with the knower and knowledge, that is, respectively the I and Śakti. What about the object in the epistemic triad that as a whole is homologized with the object? Vidyācakravartin pairs that with "other objects."[51] Table 3.3 represents these associations.

It is significant that, when all homologies are included in the equation, the lowest member of the original fivefold scheme—the object—subsumes all other members with their higher degrees of inclusiveness or nonsequentiality. It thus comprehends itself, again comprehending all items including itself, with a recursiveness somewhat like a Möbius strip.[52] It is illustrative of the monistic Śaiva approach to the reduction of all things to the emanating Śakti of the Self/Śiva that the most immanent and sequential in a sense subsumes the transcendent and nonsequential. We are

TABLE 3.3: Homologies between Items of Epistemic Triad and Those of Fivefold Scheme

Epistemic Triad	Homologues
Knower	I
Knowledge	Śakti
Object	a. Knower and I b. Knowledge and Śakti c. Other Objects

reminded of Flood's explanation, quoted in chapter 1, of how the human body is homologous with the entire cosmic hierarchy. Virūpākṣā and Vidyācakravartin emphasize that one should contemplate the identity of the homologized terms without conceptual construction (*vikalpa*).[53]

Contemplations of Specific Cosmic Agencies and Yoga Discipline

The VAP and VAPV also teach a number of contemplations to achieve more limited yogic proficiencies (*siddhi, vibhūti*). These are among the topics presented in the fourth book of the texts. Vidyācakravartin calls that section the Book on Powers (*vibhūtiskandha*), apparently on the model of the third section, the Book on Powers (*vibhūtipada*), in the *Yoga Sūtra.*

In fact, the contemplations described by the VAP and VAPV have a clear resemblance to the practices of discipline (*saṁyama*) described in the corresponding section of the *Yoga Sūtra.* The *Yoga Sūtra* describes this sort of discipline as the focusing of concentration (*dhāraṇa*), meditation (*dhyāna*), and enstasy (*samādhi*) on a single object.[54] In so doing one gains knowledge and power over that thing.[55]

Virūpākṣa and Vidyācakravartin formulate the procedure in terms of the monistic Śaiva understanding of egoity. One identifies one's I-hood or I-concept with a specific cosmic agency, for example, a deity, a heavenly body, the ocean, submarine fire, lightning, a cloud, a cave, a forest, or one of the five elements. And one is thereby enabled to perform its respective karma and gain its results.[56]

The *Yoga Sūtra* does not criticize the cultivation of these proficiencies per se, but emphasizes that liberation comes only when one has achieved detachment from them.[57] The Śaivas also maintain that the powers achieved by identifying with the various cosmic agencies are not the ultimate power.[58] However, they do not advocate the renunciation of power itself. Rather, the lower powers are consolidated and subsumed—or, we might say, overcoded—within the absolute power gained through corporifying the universe. As Vidyācakravartin explains:

> [The yogin] himself exists in the forms of entities such as the sun. Due to weakness of recognitive apprehension, he is as if differentiated. Through strong recognitive apprehension, the subliminal tendencies for the delusion of differentiation are removed. One then exists as identical with the universe. [One

> recognizes that] all proficiencies are eternally established as one's own. Through the firmness of one's recognition, they accomplish their purposeful actions. Those who desire all-embracing proficiency [recognize that they] have the essential nature of perfectly complete, supreme awareness, which is the essential nature of the universe. Thus their contemplation of identity with the sun, and so on is undeviating. They bring [this contemplation of identity with the sun and other entities] to its completion, that is, the contemplation of their identity with the universe. This is what is the gurus explain.[59]

Pedagogical Outcome

The text concludes by reporting a successful outcome of Virūpākṣa's instruction of Indra. Indra abandoned the spiritual taint of presuming "I am the king of heaven," and truly became the Supreme Lord who is the guru preceptor of the universe.[60] Vidyācakravartin emphasizes that in this realization the dichotomy of teacher and disciple is overcome:

> Śiva, who is the glorious and venerable preceptor, Lord Virūpākṣa, stood before him as the one who was enlightening him. Having thus been enlightened, [Indra] saw himself as him. This is because it is impossible that [Indra] could be other than Śiva, in the sense of being separate from his guru. There is not the slightest difference of degree between the knowledge of the enlightened and the enlightener. Rather, it has been established, without defects, that: I, perceptibly, am none other than the Supreme Lord, who is the guru of this universe.[61]

Chapter 4

Comparative Reflections
Cosmic Narcissism and Divine Self-Satisfaction

Monism, Mysticism, and Omnipotence

In this chapter, I will provide some suggestions about a comparative philosophical interpretation of the monistic Śaiva teachings presented in the VAP and VAPV. My intention is not just to *apply* Western ideas, taken as normative, to the explanation of the Sanskrit texts. Now the hermeneutic circle, in my view, entails that integral to all interpretations of culture is a component of evaluation, or hierarchization, on the basis of the scholar's own conceptual and axiological positions. There is no neutral exegetical standpoint that avoids this evaluation, in philology, history, postcolonial research, or any other specialized discipline of cultural theory. The varieties of cultural relativism reductionistically contextualize and thus subordinate all nonrelative claims, and even agnosticism subordinates those who believe they know something.[1]

Philosophy, or comparative philosophy as it is called in cross-cultural studies, may be understood as an open-ended effort to make the inevitable evaluation—whether favorable, unfavorable, or both—as much as possible dialogical and reflexive, rather than dogmatic or insidious.[2] I will accordingly identify discussions in the West that seem analogous and relevant to the Śaiva teachings, and then reflect on possibilities for genuine agreement as well as mutual challenge. In that way, I wish to create a kind of dialogue. The ultimate goal is to facilitate a critical response to the subject, whatever that may be.

In my previous work, I have endeavored to defend the Pratyabhijñā epistemology and metaphysics of divine self-recognition, along with analogous moments in Christian philosophical theologies of logos, from the Church Fathers through Bernard Lonergan. Among the many disagreements between these traditions, I focused on that between Utpaladeva and

Abhinavagupta's view that humans can fully possess divine self-recognition and the common Christian standpoint that they may at the most participate in it only partially.

I have supported the Pratyabhjñā view that God and creatures are identical primarily on the basis of an idealistic position found in both the Śaiva and Western theories: Whether creation is conceived as ex nihilo or through emanation, in terms of Pratyabhijñā epistemology and ontology, Bhartṛharian linguistics, Platonic idealism, Thomist theories of the act of the divine intellect, or Hegelian logic and phenomenology, the original essence and ground of the intelligibility of all things is founded in the contents of divine subjectivity. Bishop Berkeley articulated an important aspect of the logic underlying this strategy with his formula *esse est percipi.* The *identification* within these theories is hard to delimit, and in the West has persisted in tension with monotheistic dualism.[3]

Engagement with the VAP and VAPV leads to a similar problematic, but from the perspectives of philosophical psychology and ethics. The path to empowered monistic Śaiva identity taught by the Odd-Eyed One elicits questions pertaining to the topic of the relations of the Self and the Other or Others. We are reminded of the ethical and theological arguments of thinkers such as Martin Buber and Emmanuel Levinas that differences between individuals and between individuals and God are the basis of their relationships, and that these are obstructed by monistic "mysticism" and metaphysics.[4]

In the field of mystical studies proper, R. C. Zaehner and Arthur Danto are well known for arguing similar viewpoints.[5] Recently Jeffrey J. Kripal has demonstrated the historical backdrop of these and related arguments in the Orientalist dichotomy between the Christian, modern, rational, and ethical West and the mystical, backwards, and unethical East. Kripal repudiates the colonialist implications of such arguments, and affirms that monistic mysticism may provide genuine ontological insights. Nevertheless, he endeavors further to advance the case for the nonethical character of monistic mysticism on the bases of cultural psychology, embodiment theories, environmentalism, and evidence of ethical scandals of spiritual teachers of Asian religions in the West.[6]

Such questions would seem especially pertinent in the case of monistic Śaivism because this tradition is not only monistic but also pursues powers culminating in omnipotence through transgressive practices that are in some respects antinomian. Powers may be used in ways harmful to others and tantric transgressiveness may likewise be unethical. In monistic Śaivism, Otherness is itself ultimately subsumed within Śakti.

The Cultural Legacy of Narcissism: Human and Divine

Paramount to Western understandings of the problem of Self and Other is the long history of discussions of self-love, self-admiration, or "narcissism." The reader may recall that, according to the ancient legend, Narcissus was unable to love others because of his fierce pride, and that he perished grasping for his own alluring reflection in a pool of water. Narcissus's treatment of others is epitomized in the fate of the nymph Echo. She had previously been cursed with the inability to speak for herself and was able only to repeat the final words of others. When Narcissus does not reciprocate her love, her body withers away and her bones turn into stone. She finally can only echo or sonically reflect Narcissus's proclamations of his increasingly desperate self-infatuation.[7]

Since ancient times, numerous interpretations have been written of the ethical problems caused by Narcissus's pride.[8] This moralistic legacy continues in contemporary psychoanalytic theories of problems of narcissistic individuals in developing healthy "object" relations, as well as social critiques of the contemporary culture of narcissism.[9] Before proceeding further, however, we must situate these ethical concerns within a yet broader historical tradition of theological and anthropological discourse.

As Paul Zweig observes in *The Heresy of Self Love,* Western philosophy and theology since the Hellenistic period—including Platonism, Hermeticism, Gnosticism, and Judeo-Christian thought—have frequently described God as creating the world along with human beings in his own image. Just as God is often understood as recognizing himself through his creative act in the logos, he also in a sense loves himself in loving creation.[10]

In my understanding, this notion is entailed by the conceived perfection and self-sufficiency of the divine. God inherently contains everything admirable and desirable, and is accordingly self-satisfied. Likewise, everything that God creates and values must reflect something in himself or herself, whether creation is through emanation or ex nihilo. In the following passages, Plotinus describes the One's self-love and consequent self-emanation:

> Lovable, very love, the Supreme is also self-love in that He is lovely no otherwise than from Himself and in Himself. Self-presence can hold only in the identity of associated and associating; since, in the Supreme, associated and associating are one, seeker and sought one—the sought serving as Hypostasis and substrate of the seeker—once more God's being and his seeking are identical.[11]

> He is borne, so to speak, to the inmost of Himself in love of that pure radiance which He is, He Himself being that which He loves.[12]

Thomas Aquinas explains the Christian cosmogony:

> Everyone desires the perfection of that which is willed and loved by him for its own sake. For the things that we love for their own sake we want to be most perfect, and always to become better and be multiplied as much as possible. But God wills and loves His essence for its own sake. Now, the divine essence cannot be increased or multiplied in itself, as is manifest from what has been said; it can be multiplied solely according to its likeness, which is participated by many. God, therefore, wills the multitude of things in willing and loving His own essence and perfection.[13]

Meister Eckhart describes God's creation of and relation to creatures again in more monistic terms:

> When God made man, he put into the soul his equal, his active, everlasting masterpiece. . . . Blessed, blessed be God that he does work in the soul and that he loves his work! That work is love and love is God. God loves himself and his own nature, being and Godhead, and in the love he has for himself he loves all creatures, not as creatures but as God. The love God bears himself contains his love for the whole world. Now I shall say what I never said before. God enjoys himself. His own inner enjoyment is such that it includes his enjoyment of all creatures not as creatures, but as God. His own inner enjoyment includes everything.[14]

As Zweig observes, Western traditions have generally admonished against the human presumption to be like God in his self-love; Christians identify that with original sin.[15] Out of a sense of "creatureliness," the human being must efface his or her own will: "For the only virtue the good Christian must traditionally seek is to become less and less himself, so that God, through his act of personal self-effacement, may delight more purely in his own image."[16] Nevertheless, Zweig argues, human narcissism in its very religious and ethical ambiguity has been a great resource for cultural creativity in the West. This is epitomized in fascination with the biblical figure Simon Magus, prototype of the Faust legends:

> Simon's immense "pride" never ceased to fascinate Christianity for he embodies one of the permanent temptations of the Christian mind: the irrepressible desire to wield for oneself those powers of divinity that are revealed to a man who has opened the right doors in his spirit.[17]
>
> Faust's lust for power represents one of the constant passions of the European psyche: the longing for a final, all-powerful solitude to which the world itself must submit. Faust, like Simon the Gnostic, wanted to become the god of a universe which mirrored his most hidden potentialities.[18]

According to Zweig, narcissism has been the basis of a Western tradition of what he describes as "subversive individualism" or "subversive egotism":

> It is a tradition of heroic self-scrutiny and self-affirmation in the face of great odds. The subversive "egotist" responds to authority by disqualifying it, drawing out of his own idiosyncrasy another, better authority before which all else must give way. In its most extreme form, this attitude is not only anti-authoritarian, it is antisocial.[19]

Zweig maintains that this broad tradition is exemplified in ancient Gnosticism and Hermeticism, medieval Christian mysticism, traditions of courtly love, Romanticism, German idealism, and contemporary popular culture.

In my opinion, Zweig's thesis is highly illuminating, but there are problems with it as thus formulated. While it may be that the cultural movements he mentions tend toward the subversion of norms predicated on the broad category of human "creatureliness," I do not believe that they should all be described as expressions of *individualism.*

Thus, in classic Neoplatonic and medieval Christian spirituality, it is through the very effacement of individuality that one realizes or participates in divine self-love. Plotinus, for example, deplores the person who does not immediately trace the beauty reflected in the world to its transcendent source as perishing like Narcissus gazing in the water.[20] It is by the surrender of the narcissism inherent to love in immanent, embodied experience that the aspirant comes to experience the nonindividual self-love of the One, a realization that Julia Kristeva has described as "Narcissan."[21]

Bernard of Clairvaux likewise describes the Christian mystical quest as involving self-surrender in order to participate in divine self-love:

> Since Scripture says that God made everything for himself (Prv 16:4; Rev 4:11), there will be a time when he will cause everything to conform to its Maker and be in harmony with him. In the meantime, we must make this our desire: that as God himself willed that everything should be for himself, so we, too, will that nothing, not even ourselves, may be or have been except for him, that is according to his will, not ours. The satisfaction of our needs will not bring us happiness, not chance delights, as does the sight of his will being fulfilled in us and in everything which concerns us.[22]

Christian mystics often describe this ecstatic process as inspiration by and participation in the Holy Spirit, who constitutes the love between God the Father and God the Son. Bernard's friend William of St. Thierry thus explains that the human soul desires "that very fullness—the fullness of the Holy Spirit who is the unity and the love of the Father and the Son," and accordingly to "be dissolved and be with Christ."[23] He identifies this process with the Pauline experience of grace:

> When the spirit of man deserves to be drawn to him, spirit to Spirit, love to Love, then human love becomes in a certain manner divine; from then on, when man loves God, man is at work, but it is God who works. Not Paul, but the grace of God with him.[24]

The great Flemish mystic John Ruusbroec similarly recounts that the devotee whose "spirit has been raised above itself and been made one with the Spirit of God," thereby "savors and sees—without measure, like God himself—the riches which it has itself become in the Unity of the living ground where it possesses itself in accordance with the mode of its uncreated being."[25] Ruusbroec emphasizes the self-effacement prerequisite for the experience, as well as the monotheistic distinction preserved between the soul and God:

> In our state of emptiness, in which we are one with God in his love, there begins a superessential contemplative experience which is the highest anyone could express in words. This is a dying life and a living death, in which we go out of our own being into our superessential beatitude. . . . There we are one with him in love, though not in being or nature. Rather, we are blessed—and blessedness itself—in God's essential being, where he enjoys both himself and all of us in his sublime nature.[26]

I believe that it was in Renaissance Humanism and Hermeticism that the medieval mystical quest became combined with more individual "narcissistic" concerns for personal identity and agency in the body, relationships, and creative achievements, as well as magic.[27] The tradition of narcissistic, subversive individualism or egotism identified by Zweig became prominent in later Romantic and popular movements—from Jean Jacques Rousseau through the contemporary culture of hedonic, psychological, and spiritual self-fulfillment.

Is the monistic Śaiva quest for omnipotent divine egoity a species of subversive individualism? The subversion of norms that delimit agency for the sake of symbolic and ritual purity is often basic to the tantric quest, although actual transgressions vary greatly in nature and degree. And certainly, tantric practitioners who pursue limited "magical" powers may do so for their own individual benefit. However, this sort of nonideological individualism typifies pursuits of self-interest that are commonplace in every culture.[28]

Many tantric texts, including the VAP, VAPV, and other monistic Śaiva works, propound methods for the achievement of limited powers side by side with methods for the realization of salvation. Nevertheless, as explained, monistic Śaiva texts generally represent the pursuit of salvation as far more valuable. Thus, Vidyācakravartin advocates the consolidation of limited powers within the omnipotence coming from identification with Śiva.[29]

We have seen that the VAP and VAPV, like other Pratyabhijñā-inspired tantric traditions, do not prescribe the surrender or negation of ordinary egoistic identity. Even though the ego is not effaced, it is nevertheless not elevated with its prima facie characteristics. The various contemplative codes presented in chapter 3, from the expansion of I-am-ness to the subsumption of difference, transfigure the ego into its essential nature as perfect I-hood by *deindividualizing it.* Monistic Śaivism following Utpaladeva and

Abhinavagupta might initially appeal to individual motivations for power. However, such motivations are subsumed by identification with the supra-individual, cosmocratic egoity of God.

Psychoanalytic Theories of Narcissism

It is with trepidation that I even mention the word psychoanalysis in a study of a Hindu tradition, after all the controversy over Jeffrey J. Kripal's *Kālī's Child,* with accusations of Orientalism and right-wing fundamentalism being exchanged by those on each side of the debate.[30] However, the rich contributions of psychoanalysis to Western discourse on pride and narcissism should not be ignored. Again, my goal here is not to *apply* psychoanalysis to Hinduism, but rather to suggest possibilities for a dialogue with some of its ideas.[31]

Sigmund Freud propounded the standard psychoanalytic interpretation of various mystical experiences of unity as a regression to a primary narcissism in which an infant feels all of its needs supplied by its caretaker/mother. He first suggested this in his dialogue with Romain Rolland about the mystic's unitive "oceanic feeling."[32] Freud explains Rolland's persistent oceanic feeling:

> Originally the ego includes everything, later it separates off an external world from itself. Our present ego-feeling is, therefore, only a shrunken residue of a much more inclusive—indeed, an all-embracing—feeling which corresponded to a more intimate bond between the ego and the world about it. If we may assume that there are many people in whose mental life this primary ego-feeling has persisted to a greater or less degree, it would exist in them side by side with the narrower and more sharply demarcated ego-feeling of maturity, like a kind of counterpart to it. In that case, the ideational contents appropriate to it would be precisely those of limitlessness and of a bond with the universe—the same ideas with which my friend elucidated the "oceanic" feeling.[33]

The VAP and VAPV also use the metaphor of the ocean in various ways to describe the ultimate unity of multiplicity, but this is very common in both South Asian and Western traditions and I do not want to base any conclusions on it.[34]

There is clear evidence that Freud would interpret the tantric quest for empowerment likewise as regression to primary narcissism. Freud uses the same theory to explain the megalomania and withdrawal from object cathexes of the schizophrenic as well as ostensibly primitive peoples'

> over-estimation of the power of their wishes and mental acts, the 'omnipotence of thoughts,' a belief in the thaumaturgic force of words, and a technique for dealing with the external world—'magic'—which appears to be a logical application of these grandiose premises.[35]

Freud's theory of narcissism has been developed by a number of later psychoanalytic theorists, and has also been applied in very different ways to South Asian religious and "shamanic" traditions by Sudhir Kakar, Jeffrey Moussaieff Masson, and others.[36]

Jacques Lacan directed psychoanalytic attention back to the experience of reflected identity in narcissistic processes. He posited a narcissistic "mirror stage" of early psychological development that begins with the infant's recognition and enjoyment of its image in mirrors as well as in the pleased eyes of others. According to Lacan, the narcissistic enjoyment of such self-reflections is the basis for the child's formation of a cohesive sense of "I" and of its body amid the confusion of disjointed psychological and physical experiences.[37] We recall Indra and Virocana's initial and ostensibly mistaken discovery of the Self as the reflected image of the body.[38]

Now, for Lacan, this mirror identity is the beginning of a pervasive *alienation* that becomes encoded in the socially mediated, linguistic-symbolic order. Paradoxically, however, the alienated self does not have any substantial existence. As a corrective to narcissistic mirroring, Lacan formulates a desubstantialized subjectivity interpreted in the dialectic between desire and interpersonal relations in the structures of the symbolic order.[39] Lacan's approach to subjectivity would give him even greater reason than earlier psychoanalytic theorists to interpret the monistic Śaivas' socially subversive expansion of mirroring, I-am-ness or body-sense to encompass the universe as a pathological exercise in megalomania.[40]

Lacan's theory of the mirror stage was taken up by Donald W. Winnicot,[41] and later came to inform the self psychology of Heinz Kohut. Among classic psychoanalytic theories, Heinz Kohut's account of transformations of narcissism would seem to have the most promise for a sympathetic approach—for he accepts narcissism as constitutive of a psychotherapeutically viable self.[42] Kohut compares the stage of primary narcissism to an exaggerated sense of bodily control:

> The baby originally experiences the mother and her ministrations, not as a you and its actions, but within a view of the world in which the I-you differentiation has not yet been established. Thus, the expected control over the mother and her ministrations is closer to the concept a grownup has of himself and of the control he expects over his own body and mind than to the grownup's experience of others and of his control over them.[43]

As the child develops, explains Kohut, the primal narcissism is fragmented into two configurations: The first is a sense of a "grandiose self." This is manifest in the "mirror transference," in which one expects others to reflect one's heightened self-esteem.[44] Persistent processes of mirroring, as described by Lacan, along with fantasies of exaggerated power or omnipotence would be classified within this constellation.

The second is the "idealized parental imago," correlated with the "idealizing transference," in which one ascribes all narcissistic perfection to another.[45] Psychoanalytic interpretations of Hindu devotion to gurus have made use of Kohut's and related understandings of idealization. Citing Kohut, Kakar thus describes the process of self-effacement and identification with the guru in the Radha Soami movement:

> The whole transformation has its roots in, and is a replication of, psychic events in that early period of childhood when the child, in the face of the many narcissistic hurts and disappointments that the ending of infancy brought in its wake, sought to recapture his early feelings of "greatness" through a new route, where he projected this greatness onto the idealized image of a parent and then partook of it himself by setting up a configuration in the psyche: "You are great but I am a part of you."[46]

We recall the emphasis on the final identity between Virūpākṣa and Indra in the VAP and VAPV. In the monistic Śaiva metaphysics, however, Virūpākṣa is supposed to have been a full incarnation of the true Self as Śiva.

According to Kohut, in proper psychological development the grandiose self is transformed into a realistic and constructive sense of self-esteem, and the idealized imago is internalized and integrated as a healthy ego ideal or superego.[47] Kohut further describes a higher transformation of narcissistic energy attained by persons of exceptional psychological health, particularly great mystics and poets, which he calls "cosmic narcissism." The motivating factor in these people's more deeply working through the narcissistic transferences is *the realization of their finitude, especially their mortality.*[48] Again, we have seen that in the Śaiva and other Indra stories, the transformations of Indra's grandiosity begin with his humiliations and continue through his self-effacement, surrender, or deindividualization.

Cosmic narcissism is then realized as a higher, nongrandiose identification with the universe and all its beings, integrally and genetically linked to empathy. Kohut explains this as an enduring psychological achievement deriving from primary narcissistic energy:

> Just as the child's *primary empathy* with the mother is the precursor of the adult's ability to be empathic, so his *primary identity* with her must be considered the precursor of an expansion of the self, late in life, when the finiteness of individual existence is acknowledged. The original psychological universe, i.e., the primordial experience of the mother, is "remembered" by many people in the form of the occasionally occurring vague reverberations known by the term "oceanic feeling." . . . The achievement—as the certainty of eventual death is fully realized—of a shift of the narcissistic cathexes from the self to a concept of participation in a supraindividual and timeless existence must also be regarded as genetically predetermined by the child's primary identity with the mother. In contrast to the oceanic feeling, however, which is experienced passively (and usually fleetingly), the genuine shift of the cathexes toward a cosmic narcissism is the enduring, creative result of the steadfast activities of an autonomous ego, and only very few are able to attain it.[49]

In his references to the "autonomous ego" and "participation" in the supraindividual, Kohut reveals a typical Western monotheistic presumption that such unitive experiences fall short of a realization of absolute identity.[50] It is possible that Kohut would classify monistic Śaiva experiences of full identity with Śiva, and the achievement of his omnipotence by possessing his Śakti, as expressions of the grandiose self rather than cosmic narcissism.

However, as already suggested, though monistic Śaiva teachings might initially appeal to individual desires for power, they require the deindividualization of the ego in its identification with Śiva's higher, universal egoity.[51] While Kohut would not have accepted the possibility of omnipotence, there may nevertheless be some agreement between his developmental model and the program of the VAP and VAPV.

Constructive Dialogical Proposals

Classic psychoanalysis rests on very different epistemological and metaphysical premises than monistic Kashmiri Śaivism as well as the other religious worldviews that have been mentioned in this Introduction. Psychoanalysis is typically atheistic or agnostic, and bases its explanations on biological or quasibiological motivations and familial and social factors of psychological development. Kohut's methodology accordingly could not provide an epistemological or metaphysical rationale for the empathic identification with the universe.[52] How may his theory be mediated with monistic Śaiva and other religious thought?

William B. Parsons has suggested in his *The Enigma of the Oceanic Feeling* that a basis for dialogue between psychoanalysis and mystical traditions may be found in psychoanalytic conceptions of developmentally primal or archaic forms of intuitive knowledge.[53] He observes the backgrounds to Kohut's understanding of the child's primary empathy in Freud's notion of an unconscious form of communication remaining from earlier stages of human evolution. According to Freud, this mode of communication is still evinced in the cooperation of insect colonies, mob excitement, and alleged telepathic phenomena.[54]

Parsons argues that such conceptions may be further advanced with Arthur Deikman's use of ego psychology to describe a process of "deautomatization" in mystical experiences. According to Deikman's theory, mystical experiences may recover a valid primal cognition of unity. Such a primal cognition is ordinarily occluded by the developmental "automatization" of cognitive processes, which select, limit, and organize stimuli.[55] Parsons's suggestions are provocative for showing that there are aspects of psychoanalytic understandings of the childhood roots and transformations of narcissism that may be compatible with the articulation of religious epistemological and metaphysical claims.

I am not aware of any monistic Śaiva or other traditional religious theories with significant analogies to Kohut's account of narcissism in early psychological development. However, I do not think that the Śaiva or other religious modes of thought need be opposed in principle to his psychoanalytic explanation—which has a strong evidential basis—provided that it is not applied reductionistically. Moreover, although lacking the psychoanalytic developmental perspective, there has certainly been a great deal of traditional religious concern with the psychology of pride or grandiosity, as we have observed in the stories of the instruction of Indra, the monistic Śaiva theory of egoity, and the history of Western discussions of narcissism.

My constructive suggestions are founded on the premise, which some would consider grandiose, that the Pratyabhijñā arguments as interpreted in my *Rediscovering God* are basically valid. This premise may be formulated in pluralistic terms:[56] There is a religious Ultimate Reality, which the Śaivas know as Śiva with his integral emanatory Śakti. He, she, or it creates and controls the cosmic process through self-recognition, originary Speech, agency, and so on. This is substantively the same Ultimate Reality known in Christian philosophical theologies of logos (as well as many other religious traditions, in ways that are not being considered here), although there are many deep and consequential disagreements about its nature, how it is revealed, and its requirements of us. Moreover, the Śaivas are right that we are, in our deepest nature, identical with that Reality.[57]

On this basis, I propose that there is a substantial commonality of insight between the Pratyabhijñā theory of egoity articulated in the VAP and VAPV, Western notions of divine narcissism, and Kohut's theory. If we are all a monistic Ultimate that creates the world, it would seem appropriate for us to feel a cosmically narcissistic, empathic identification with that world. Robert K. C. Forman has argued that a "knowledge by identity," transcending the intentionality of ordinary cognition, typifies the epistemic character of various monistic and unitive mystical experiences.[58] I suggest that an analogous "cathexis by identity" typifies what Abhinava calls the self-relishing (*svātmāsvāda*) or satiating self-repose (*svātmāviśrānti*) of one who has recognized his or her identity with the Ultimate.

Paul Ricoeur has endeavored to mediate Freudian understandings of the unconscious, identification and sublimation, with his own hermeneutics of religion, morality, and art, in terms of a dialectic between archaeology and teleology.[59] Combining the religious metaphysics and the developmental notions discussed here, I suggest that the experience of divine self-satisfaction or narcissism is the telos of human narcissistic libido. This telos may be prefigured in an intuitive knowledge intrinsic to childhood narcissism along the lines suggested by Parsons. And in all our egoistic striving we may be searching for the metaphysically foundational, perfect self-sufficiency or contentment of divine consciousness. According to the monistic Śaivas, Indra was not entirely misguided in his presumption to be the Supreme Lord. He only had to learn how properly to realize that status.

This leads to the question of how to account for the divergence between the program for the universalization or deindividualization of egoity in Utpaladeva, Abhinavagupta, and later monistic Śaivism, and practices for its negation, subjugation, or surrender in other South Asian and Western religious traditions. I believe that a constellation of factors led the Pratyabhijñā to distinctive insights into the religious significance of egoity.

Among such factors is the conception by the monistic Śaivas, along with various Śākta and Vaiṣṇava tantric traditions, of the Ultimate Reality as both monistic and theistic. Contrary to more impersonal varieties of monism, the aspirant in such traditions identifies with an Ultimate that has some kind of personality and ego. Monotheists from Abrahamic traditions such as Meister Eckhart and al-Hallaj found trouble by gravitating too closely to monism.

Also important is the monistic Śaiva traditions' strategy of subsuming or overcoding tantric pursuits of limited powers within the omnipotence of identification with Śiva as the possessor of Śakti. As we have seen, this strategy paradoxically affirms individual "egoistic" or "selfish" motivations while exploiting and deindividualizing them for a soteriological realization. What might be called a "scale of transformation"[60] is thereby established between the human ego and that of Śiva.

This scale of transformation is itself informed by the broader tantric themes of Śakti's simultaneous transcendence and immanence, and the ritual subversion of norms of purity. The monistic Śaivas, like many other tantrics, view immanent experiences that are normally binding as media for the revealing of his Śakti (*śaktyāviṣkaraṇa*). One's ego is transformed into God's ego, and one's body into the universe as God's body—in the same manner as physical and aesthetic pleasures are transfigured into Śiva's bliss, argument is transformed into good reasoning (*sattarka*), and conceptual constructions are by such reasoning submitted to a subversive "purification" (*vikalpasaṁskāra*) to embody the Pure Wisdom that one is the emanator and controller of the world.

Other important factors are the inspiration, brilliance, and efforts of writers such as Utpaladeva and Abhinavagupta to explain monistic Śaiva experience, doctrine, and practice, as well as the stimulation they gained from the rich religious and philosophical culture of medieval Kashmir.

A psychoanalytic scholar of the sort who is incredulous toward religious and metaphysical claims would perhaps view the Śaiva theory of egoity, as well as my dialogical suggestions, as extravagant rationalizations of narcissistic regression. Those of other monistic and nonmonistic religious traditions would likely suggest alternative ways of relating pride or narcissism and spiritual bliss. For example, Buddhists sympathetic with some of the suggestions about psychology might prefer to talk of the noncontingency of nirvāṇa, while eschewing claims of its egoity, self-sufficiency, or metaphysically foundational character. Regardless of one's interpretive perspective, I believe that engagement with the Pratyabhijñā teachings of the VAP and VAPV illuminates and calls for further investigation into the rich dialectical relationships between religious conceptions of the Ultimate, human identity, pride or narcissism, and embodiment.

The Guru's Ethical Concern with Universal Redemption

Pace earlier and contemporary Western criticisms, there is abundant evidence for the compatibility, and frequent affinity, between monistic religions and ethics. Most Hindu, Buddhist, and Taoist monisms articulate strong concerns with ethics within their distinctive metaphysical and axiological frameworks. The same is true of monistic Kashmiri Śaivism and related tantric traditions.[61]

Doctrines such as the Advaita Vedāntin and Buddhist distinctions of ultimate and provisional truth relegate unity and the differentiations involved in ethical relations to separate spheres of explanation. Even when unity in some sense negates difference, various sorts of ethics are maintained in practical life, along the lines of what G. William Barnard advocates as a "both–and" rather than an "either–or" logic.[62] Monistic Śaivism mediates unity and difference in threefold, fivefold, and several other hierarchies of emanating categories. And, as we will discuss further, this emanationism, which subsumes rather than negates, provides further metaphysical support for the ethical valuation of immanent experience.

Reminding one of the bodhisattva ideal in Mahāyāna and Vajrayāna Buddhism, monistic Śaiva authors affirm that great compassion—which includes empathy—applied in efforts to free other suffering creatures, is integral to the soteriological realization.[63] As observed in chapter 3, the two highest expressions of power according to the VAP and VAPV are becoming "the grace-bestowing guru, the eminent preceptor, of the entire universe,"[64] and performing the five cosmic acts of Śiva (creation, preservation, destruction, delusion, and grace).[65] It is arguable that the theodicean scheme of the five acts transcends considerations of morality.[66] In any event, the separate and redundant thematization of grace as embodied in the guru indicates its preeminent value for the texts as a liberative teaching.[67]

Utpaladeva proclaims his purpose for creating the Pratyabhijñā system with the first verse of his *Īśvarapratyabhijñākārikā:* "Having somehow been caused to attain servitude to the Great Lord and desiring the benefit of humanity, I am establishing the recognition of Him, which is the cause of obtaining all prosperity."[68] Servitude (*dāsya*) is a term for high spiritual realization, understood in this system as the recognition of identity with Śiva.[69] Utpaladeva is stating that he is creating the system in order to lead humanity to the same recognition and ensuing absolute felicity that he himself has experienced. In his short autocommentary on the same text, he elaborates that he created the Pratyabhijñā system because he was ashamed that he alone was fortunate, and so that by leading humanity to recognition he would gain complete satisfaction.[70]

It is interesting that Abhinavagupta engages in a justification for the identification of the benefit of others as a purpose. It is a purpose, he asserts, because it conforms to the classic definition of purpose in the *Nyāya Sūtra* as "that object aiming at which a person acts."[71] He argues that "there is not a divine curse such that a purpose is only the advantage of oneself and not the advantage of others."[72]

Abhinava interprets the term "humanity" in Utpala's verse as indicating "those who are afflicted by incessant birth and death" and who "as objects of compassion, should be helped."[73] He emphasizes that Utpala has made no restrictions regarding caste for following the system.[74] Abhinava further argues in his commentary on *Bhagavad Gītā* 9.33–34 that God saves low castes, women, and animals, and strongly criticizes commentators who will not accept this.[75] In his *Tantrāloka* Abhinava also advises that one must not regard or treat any fellow Śaivas differently due to caste, but must rather view them all as identical with Śiva.[76]

Elsewhere in the *Tantrāloka* Abhinava explains that ordinarily people are occupied with their own activities and do not make any effort for others. However, those who have destroyed all taints of worldly existence and are perfect in their identification with Bhairava are occupied only with the benefit of humanity.[77]

Ethics in Monistic Śaiva Spiritual Praxis

In the fifteenth chapter of the *Tantrāloka,* Abhinava expounds on the basis of earlier tantric precedents a series of eight groups of eight practical rules (*samaya*) for Śaiva initiates, many of which bear upon ethics. To mention some examples, what should not be said includes that which is untrue and harmful. That from which one should refrain includes the injurious, touching another's wife, arrogance, deceit, and cursing others with evil sprits, poison, and sickness. Besides the guru, guru's family, scripture, and so on, the class of those that are to be venerated includes women. Beings for which there should be satisfaction include the destitute, the afflicted, one's parents, the multitudes of living beings, and birds. What one should strike includes passion, aversion, displeasure, timidity, envy, and conceitedness—along with those who break or do not follow the rules! Those who should be confounded include the cruel, those full of enmity, the treacherous, the evil, and those who create obstructions.[78]

Furthermore, I observe that monistic Śaiva scholastic texts, including the VAP and VAPV, follow Sanskritic traditions of what might be called "discursive ethics." The original Pratyabhijñā verses and commentaries are rigorously structured according to the sixteen Nyāya categories pertaining to philosophical discussion, the most widely accepted Sanskritic standards for philosophical discourse.[79] Abhinava's hierarchical ranking of alternative traditions according to their approximation to the realization of monistic Śaiva empowered identity itself rests on the validity of the Pratyabhijñā system. The importance of this discursive ethics for the Pratyabhijñā writers is evinced in the construal of the fundamental monistic Śaiva mythico-ritual act of possessing Śakti as itself a Nyāya inference for the sake of others, as explained in chapter 1. As likewise mentioned, the VAPV interprets the VAP as following the inference for the sake of others. It is on the basis of this discursive ethics that the monistic Śaiva claims we have discussed are in principle open to further questioning and dispute.

The Dialectic of Transcendence and Immanence in Contemporary Religious Metaphysics: Ongoing Creative Syntheses

Finally, with regard to the ethical import of the monistic Śaiva religious vision, I reiterate an observation that I have made in other writings: Many contemporary retrievals of monistic Śaivism follow one of the common strategies for making traditional religions relevant to present concerns.[80] In the last few centuries, modernistic opponents have frequently argued that traditional religions are too "otherworldly," and therefore incompatible with increasingly "this-worldly" values, including science and technology, social and political progress, worldly comforts, liberated sexuality, and the environment. In response, there have been many efforts to retrieve varieties of religious metaphysics that emphasize the simultaneous transcendence and immanence of the Ultimate Reality—including the process theories of Teilhard de Chardin, Alfred North Whitehead, and Charles Hartshorne; the hermeneutics of Mircea Eliade, Paul Ricoeur, and David Tracy; the Heideggerian theology of John Macquarrie; and new interpretations of Taoism and Confucianism.

The same agenda is evinced in much contemporary interest in monistic Śaivism and other forms of tantrism by both Indians and non-Indians, for example, Gopinath Kaviraj, Swami Lakshman Joo, and Sir John Woodroffe. Sri Aurobindo's well-known philosophy of the Supermind also unites what is basically a tantric metaphysics with contemporary values of social and cultural development. Rita Dasgupta Sherma has also argued for the ecofeminist value of monistic Śaiva and Śākta conceptions of Śakti.[81] While one must always exercise interpretive caution, I believe that it is not anachronistic but rather faithful to the monistic Śaivas' own concerns with universal felicity to be hopeful about the viability of their philosophy of empowered identity for addressing contemporary religious and ethical concerns.[82]

Chapter 5

On the Translation

L. D. Barnett published the first contemporary edition of the VAP verses alone, in 1908.[1] The first edition of the VAP with the VAPV was that published by T. Ganapati Śāstrī in 1910.[2] Gopinath Kaviraj largely duplicated this version with minor changes in the edition in his 1970 anthology *Tantrasaṁgraha.*[3] I have been collecting manuscripts of the texts and will consider publishing a new edition of them in the future, if that seems warranted. This translation largely follows the edition of Kaviraj in *Tantrasaṁgraha,* with occasional reference to that of T. Ganapati Śāstrī.

There exists one other attempted translation of the VAP and VAPV, by Henri Lenaerts, in his 1971 Ph.D. thesis at Banaras Hindu University.[4] This is actually a rough and problematic paraphrase, and I have not made significant use of it in the present translation.

While the meaning of the VAP and VAPV is often straightforward, there are also many obscure points. Some of these pertain to the texts' references to esoteric tantric symbolism and ritual. Others may be due to problems in the manuscripts. Therefore, there are likely points that I have misunderstood.

The translation of these texts presents challenges that are common with many *śāstras.* The sentences are often longer and more convoluted than is acceptable in contemporary English. This is particularly the case in the VAPV, where sentences combine glosses of individual words with interpretations of the import of entire verses. For this reason, I have often divided Sanskrit sentences into two or more English sentences.

Conversely, for assistance in following the ideas, I have divided the continuous commentary into paragraphs. Likewise, I have rendered abstract constructions into simple and direct forms. For example, I translate *akramatā me* (VAP 3.33) as "I am without sequence," rather than "There is nonsequentiality of me." My goal has been to be as literal as possible within the limitations of readable English.

To increase readability, I have also endeavored to avoid using Sanskrit terms in the translation as much as possible. The reader may find the original Sanskrit expressions for a number of terms in the index. A few key Sanskrit terms are kept in brackets so that the reader may trace their uses throughout the texts. On some occasions, I have also noted original Sanskrit terms and phrases in the notes, for the benefit of Sanskritists.

Though the designation of Virūpākṣa's teachings as a *pañcāśikā* indicates that they constitute fifty verses, they actually amount to fifty-three. According to Vidyācakravartin, the first and last verses are not counted because they are, respectively, the introduction and conclusion. He suggests that verse 4.50 is also not counted because it is incidental.[5]

It is unknown when the VAP was divided into the four present books.[6] I have followed the convention in Śāstrī and Kaviraj's editions of not beginning verse numbers anew with each book, but rather continuing them successively. For example, verse 1.8 is followed by 2.9.

Part II

Translation of the Virūpākṣapañcāśikā with the Commentary of Vidyācakravartin

Book 1

Introduction

> Homage to Śambhu, whose body is the universe, who shines in unity with the universe, who has eternal recognitive apprehension,[1] and whose [yogic] proficiency[2] is the universe.[3]
>
> I am commenting upon the *Fifty Verses* propounded by Virūpākṣa, which are a summary of the established facts that comprise the Doctrine of Consciousness.

The only pleasure of the glorious Lord, the Supreme Śiva is bestowing grace on the universe. Once, in sport, he assumed a body [in this world].[4] His name was glorious and venerable Lord Virūpākṣa. Wandering about, on a certain occasion he came upon the Lord of the [lower] gods [Indra]. [Indra] had presumed himself [*abhimanyamānam*][5] to be the Supreme Lord, and was holding a fight between rutting elephants. Then [Virūpākṣa], through his mere intention, exhibited before that [Indra] a fight between two great mountains! This spectacle was more marvelous [than the elephant fight]. It quelled [Indra's] presumption of being the Lord. [Indra] became completely amenable [to being given spiritual instruction]. Thus [Virūpākṣa] to enlighten him revealed this text consisting of fifty verses, which is a summary of all the facts that comprise the Doctrine of Consciousness.

The first and last verses in this [text] are the introduction and the conclusion. The verse that [in the Sanskrit] begins "of Śuka, Vāmadeva" [4.50][6] is incidental. Thus [these three verses] are not included within the instruction. Fifty verses remain. Therefore, this text is a collection of fifty verses.[7]

The first book consists of seven verses, beginning with "the point of disagreement" [verses 2–8]. One [ordinarily] experiences the universe to be external to one's body. [This book] demonstrates by arguments that [the universe actually] is one's body.

The second book consists of thirteen verses, beginning with "has the nature of recognitive apprehension" [verses 9–21]. [This book] demonstrates thoroughly that the universe [besides being one's body] is identical with awareness, in order to remove the delusion that there is a difference between the body and the one who possesses the body.[8]

[Through the arguments in the first two books] the identity [of the universe] with awareness is recognized. There must not be any errors regarding this [identity] such as a doubt as to its possibility or a misunderstanding of it.[9] Thus the third book, which consists of nineteen verses beginning with "I am unitary and have the nature of unsetting awareness" [verses 22–40], elaborately explains the modes of its recognitive apprehension.[10]

The fourth book consists of eleven verses beginning with "established within myself" [verses 41–51]. It first explains the modes of experience that belong to those who are not enlightened, those who are enlightened, and so on.[11] Then it explains the way by which one may display the higher and lower proficiencies. Finally, it explains the great proficiency.

Thus this text has four books. Its details will be explained in the appropriate contexts.

Notes

1. *pratyavamarśa.* See the explanation of the terminology of the Pratyabhijñā philosophy of recognition on p. 137, n. 42.

2. *Siddhi* literally means accomplishment or attainment, and has a variety of secondary meanings. Its meaning relevant to the present context is that of power attained through yogic practices. This text claims that such *siddhis* are innate and need only be awakened to be used. I have used the gloss "proficiency" as including the significance of both achievement and innateness.

3. *Viśvasiddhaye* could also be taken as "who has all *siddhis.*" I believe that the present translation best coheres with the themes of the text.

4. Because God is self-sufficient, and his actions thereby transcend comprehensible purposes, they are frequently described in Hindu traditions as a kind of sport or play (*līlā*).

5. The prefix *abhi-* with the verb root *man* generally means "conceive," "believe," or "desire." In a more technical philosophical and theological sense it refers to conceiving or presuming one's personal identity, particularly in a deluded, egoistic manner. Indra and the readers' *abhimāna,* "pride" or "egoistic identity"—which will also be explained with terms such as "I-am-ness" (*asmitā*) and "I-hood" (*ahaṁtā*)—is the central problem of the VAP and the VAPV. Other

forms of conceiving and desiring, when designated here with *abhi-man,* are also understood as affected by egoistic thinking. In this translation, I indicate in brackets whenever verbs or nouns derived from *abhi-man* are used. As explained in the Introduction, in the Pratyabhijñā tradition followed by the VAP and VAPV the aim is not to eliminate egoism but rather to disclose its proper deindividualized or universalized application. Abhinavagupta thus explains both bondage and liberation as kinds of *abhimanana* in IPV 2.3.17, 2:143–144.

6. The VAPV is following a common Sanskritic practice of identifying sections of a text by the first words of verses. I am indicating the corresponding book and verse numbers in brackets.

7. Vidyācakravartin has attempted to explain why the text of "Fifty Verses" (*pañcāśikā*) actually has fifty-three verses.

8. That is, the first book demonstrates that the universe is one's body. However, people frequently make various kinds of distinction between their conscious selves, or an ostensible universal Self, and their bodies. The second book eliminates such false distinctions.

9. *asambhāvanāviparītabhāvanā.*

10. The third book expounds a variety of metaphorical, philosophical and theosophical frameworks for contemplations through which one can experience the self-recognition of Śiva/awareness. Vidyācakravartin suggests that the realization of these various modes (*prakāra*) of self-recognition thoroughly establishes one within it.

11. According to Vidyācakravartin's introduction to book four, there are five kinds of subject: the unenlightened, the almost enlightened, the enlightened, the almost completely enlightened, and the completely enlightened.

VERSE 1

I will now expound the text. [The author] prepares the setting[1] to introduce the text:

> **1.1. Virūpākṣa displayed the battle of the two mountains. Having been asked, he then explained the seed[2] of his innate proficiency to that Indra who had enjoyed the fight of rutting elephants.**

[Virūpākṣa is described in the verse] as "having been asked" [about the seed of his proficiency]. For this reason it must be inferred that Indra [who posed the question] has experienced a gracious descent of Śakti.[3] Therefore, he is worthy to receive instruction about reality. Thus [Indra's] eligibility is indicated.[4] "He . . . explained" means that [Virūpākṣa] began to perform a verbal initiation.[5]

Notes

1. Literally, he prepares the seat. Vidyācakravartin invokes a metaphor of sitting down for instruction.

2. The word translated as "seed" is *bīja.* In tantric traditions, *bīja* also signifies the essential, seminal component of a mantra. Here it refers to the seminal cause of Virūpākṣa's proficiency. On the concept, see Hemendra Nath Chakravarty, "Bīja," in *Kalātattvakośa,* general editor, Kapila Vatsyayan, vol. 1, *Eight Selected Terms,* ed. Bettina Baumer (Delhi: Indira Gandhi National Centre for the Arts, 1992), 117–133.

3. *śaktipāta.* In the monistic Śaiva traditions, the Lord's bestowal of grace is described as a descent of his Power.

4. Eligibility (*adhikāra*) is a basic issue addressed at the beginning of Sanskrit religious and philosophical texts. The commentator suggests that a desire to understand the source of Virūpākṣa's omnipotence indicates that one has received God's grace, and is thus eligible.

5. *śābdīṁ dīkṣā.* Just as Indra's curiosity indicates that he is a recipient of divine grace, so he is initiated through philosophical instruction. The implication is that this text will also provide a verbal initiation to the reader. This understanding resonates with Utapaladeva and Abhinavagupta's conception of the Pratyabhijñā system simultaneously as a publicly intelligible philosophical discourse and a gnoseological reenactment of tantric praxis.

VERSE 2

[Virūpākṣa] first propounds a syllogism that is established through five parts.[1] This demonstrates that the universe, although [ordinarily] conceived to be different from one's body, [actually] is one's body.

> **1.2. Well, this is [our] point of disagreement: I [recognize that I] have the nature of consciousness [and that] this universe, beginning with the void state[2] and ending with the earth, is my body.[3] This [fact that the universe is one's body] is proven because [the universe] is perceptible, like the fleshly body.[4]**

With the address "Well" [Virūpākṣa] gets the one being taught [Indra] to turn toward him.[5] [He explains that] "this is [our] point of disagreement": You, presuming yourself [*abhimāninā*] to be an individual subject, understand this universe—beginning with the void state and ending with the earth—to be external to your body. I, who [recognize that I] have the nature of consciousness, understand it to be my body. Thus the subject of debate is whether the universe, beginning with the unsupported[6] and ending with the earth, is my body.

The reason for this [the inference that the universe is the body, is stated] "because it is perceptible."[7] For you, who are delimited as an individual subject, your body is the fleshly body because it is perceptible. Similarly, for me, who [recognize that I] am unlimited consciousness, the universe is my body because it is perceptible. The inferential application is implied. [Virūpākṣa] recognitively synthesizes that and concludes the proof by saying that it "is proven."[8]

This fact [that the universe is one's body] is proven in everyone's direct experience [if that is understood properly]. When one attends to a particular and distinct object of knowledge, for example [a color] such as blue or yellow, then one becomes an individual subject, that is, a delimited awareness. The delimitation of one's awareness is the adventitious qualification of it by the differentiated object of knowledge. However, when one recognitively synthesizes everything in its universal nature,[9] then one [recognizes oneself to be] consciousness, that is, unlimited awareness. This is because it is impossible for the one who illuminates[10] [limiting conditions] such as place and time to be limited by [those conditions such as] place and time.[11] Therefore, at that time [when one perceives everything in its universal nature, one recognizes that] the universe is one's body due to its being perceptible. If it were not so [that one is such a consciousness], then even the fleshly body could not be the body of the individual subject because it would not be perceptible.[12]

This is the gist: The definitive characteristic of the individual subject is its particular [objects of knowledge]. When there is the dissolution of those [particular objects into their universal nature], you will [recognize that you] have the nature of consciousness and have the universe as your body.[13]

Notes

1. Vidyācakravartin is stating that the verse articulates the classic Nyāya inference for the sake of others (*parārthānumāna*), which has five parts. In his Pratyabhijñā commentaries, Abhinavagupta explains that the Pratyabhijñā system gains its power to lead humanity toward the recognition of Śiva through following this inferential method. See Lawrence, *Rediscovering God*, 48–57. The VAP and VAPV appear to me to present not so much a series of contemplations that are simultaneously technical philosophical syllogisms—as contemplations (focused on egoity and the body) that are *based on* the Pratyabhijñā arguments. While Vidyācakravartin's interpretations of the structures of the inference thus do not

have the same demonstrative force as Abhinavagupta's, they do bring out some of the rationales in the text's program of contemplation. Another distinction is that, whereas the inference exposited by Abhinavagupta is for the thesis that one is Śiva, that identified by Vidyācakravartin in this verse is for the thesis that the universe is one's body. I think that this divergence is more rhetorical than substantive, as the result in both cases is identity with the omnipotent Śiva. The relation between the two formulations will be further clarified in the following notes to this verse. Vidyācakravartin's interpretation of VAP 2.18–19 as an inference for the identity of the student with the germinal essence is closer to Abhinavagupta's formulation. See p. 88, nn. 2, 7.

2. *śūnyapada.* On the concept of *śūnya,* "void," see Introduction, p. 26 and p. 144, n. 4.

3. As explained in the Introduction, within the range of monistic Śaiva concepts and techniques of the body, central is its significance as a code for Śakti. The practice of revealing Śakti, divine self-recognition, and so on, thus becomes the disclosure of one's universal body.

4. The assertion that the universe is the body because it is "perceptible" (*dṛśyatvāt*) alludes to *Śiva Sūtra,* 1.14, 15: "The perceptible [universe] is [one's true] body" (*dṛśyaṁ śarīram*). On the concept of the "perceptible," also see below, p. 66, nn. 7, 12. Both *Śiva Sūtra* 1.14 and VAP 1.2 are quoted in MMP, 29, 73.

5. That is, he gets Indra to pay attention. The student must sincerely and devoutly face the guru to receive instruction.

6. Here "unsupported" (*anāśrita*) is being used as a synonym for void (*śūnyapada*) in the verse, referring to the emanated, lower Śiva category. On that category, see below, p. 69, n. 4.

7. The reason (*hetu*) is supposed to adduce a property in the inferential subject (*pakṣa*) that is invariably concomitant with that which is to be established regarding it. For example, one may infer fire on the hill for the reason that there is smoke there. Virūpākṣa and Vidyācakravartin claim that the fact that the universe is perceptible is the reason proving that it is the body. For Abhinavagupta, Śakti is herself the reason in the inference that one is Śiva. It may seem, prima facie, that the class of the perceptible is too wide in its concomitance. One does not normally understand everything that is seen as one's body. I have argued that Utpaladeva's and Abhinavagupta's idealistic arguments on epistemology and ontology in effect constitute reasons for the reason that is Śakti. Lawrence, *Rediscovering God,* 102. The ensuing discussion in the VAP and VAPV clarifies the Pratyabhijñā idealism presupposed by their contemplative program. Thus, whereas perceptibility (*dṛśyatva*) is an indication of illusion in Advaita Vedānta, here it is an indication of one's Power and Lordship.

8. Virūpākṣa puts together the components of the syllogism in reaching the conclusion. In Indian philosophy, inference as an interpretation is viewed as having a recognitive structure. This is evinced particularly in the fourth step, the application (*upanaya*), which affirms that the subject falls within the concomitance between the reason and that which is to be established. For example: The hill,

because it has smoke on it, has fire on it. The application in this case would be that the universe, because it is perceptible, is the body. The application is often described by such terms as recognitive synthesis (*anusaṁdhāna, pratisaṁdhāna*) and recognitive judgment (*liṅgaparāmarśa*). See Lawrence, *Rediscovering God,* 76, 205 n. 46.

9. *sāmānyato.* On this concept, see p. 67, n. 13.

10. *prakāśaka.*

11. To use David Tracy's terms, because the Self/Śiva is the transcendental "limit of" the "limits to" ordinary experience—such as place and time—it cannot itself be limited. Also see the explanations of the Self/Śiva as lacking sequences of place and time in VAP and VAPV 2.12, and of place and time as generated from his Śaktis in VAP and VAPV 3.25.

12. Vidyācakravartin is adverting to the Pratyabhijñā idealistic epistemology of emanating consciousness/self-recognition as the only way of successfully understanding perceptibility. This passage is discussed in the Introduction as an illustration of the general program in the VAP and VAPV of the subsumption of difference and sequence.

13. The idea is that when one perceives everything in its universal (*sāmānya*) nature, rather than as particulars (*viśeṣa*), one also perceives everything as one's body. The cultivation of such universal cognition is another important theme in monistic Śaiva spiritual teaching, and may be understood within the broad program of the subsumption of difference. Thus, the Spanda tradition teaches the contemplation of the encompassment of "particular cosmic pulsations" (*viśeṣa spanda*) within the "universal cosmic pulsation" (*sāmānya spanda*). In the Pratyabhijñā system, the recovery of transcendental recognition is likewise conceived as a recovery of the immanent universal and complete (*pūrṇa*) aspect of all objective categories. Lawrence, *Rediscovering God,* 96–97. On this theme, also see below the explanation of the germinal essence as the corporification of the particularized object of knowledge, the means of knowledge and the knower, VAP and VAPV 2.15, and the description of recognitive apprehension as burning up the same three particularizations and leaving universal awareness, VAP and VAPV 3.29.

VERSE 3

There may be this objection: The mere fact that [something] is perceptible is not a reason [that establishes that it is] the body. It must also be experienced as "I." The fleshly body is experienced as "I." However, the universe is experienced as "this." So how can the proposition be proven? [Virūpākṣa] answers:

1.3. I-am-ness[1] is observed in the six conditions "I am prosperous," "I am lean," "I relish with the senses," "I am happy," "I am breathing," and "I am void [of experience]."[2]

Prosperity is a quality that refers to objects such as a house and a field. Leanness [is a quality] that belongs to the [fleshly] body. Relish [is a quality] of the sense organs such as the eye. Happiness [is a quality] of the inner organ [the mind].[3] Breathing [is a quality] that pertains to the vital air.[4] Voidness [is a quality] of the condition of deep sleep, which is a synonym for Māyā.[5] "I-am-ness" is observed in these six conditions which comprise objects and so on. The conception of "I" [*ahamabhimāna*] is established by your own experience.

Thus one does conceive as "I" [*ahamabhimāna*] even objects that one understands [*abhimite*] to be external to the [fleshly] body. Therefore, the object [which typifies the universe as an ostensibly separate "this"] is also the body, because it is perceptible.

When they are not conceived as "I" [*ahamabhimāna*], even the fleshly body and the senses are not [understood as] the body. Therefore, the objection raised, that there is I-am-ness in the fleshly body and thisness in the thing that is external to that [fleshly body], is a mere delusion resulting from a lack of recognitive apprehension of that [I-am-ness]. This is the meaning.[6]

Notes

1. *asmitā.* On this term, see the Introduction, pp. 27–28. As explained with regard to the related term, *abhimāna,* the goal in the present system is not to eliminate but rather to expand and universalize the prima facie conception of identity.

2. *śūnya.* The void is conceived as a mode of subjectivity without any cognitive contents. One may "experience" the void in deep sleep as well as in some kinds of meditative enstasy. The commentary takes *śūnya* in this verse as referring to the state of deep sleep.

3. *Antaḥkaraṇa* can be taken as "mind" in the broad sense including emotions. See below, VAPV 1.7 and p. 73, n. 5.

4. *vāyoḥ.*

5. The nescience of deep sleep is homologous to cosmic illusion.

6. The gist of this discussion is that people actually identify themselves with a variety of observable things besides their fleshly bodies. One who believes "I am prosperous" identifies himself or herself with his or her belongings. Our various self-identifications should be expanded into the realization that everything observable is our body. Cf. IPK and IPV 3.1.8, 2:232–235 on the delusory identification with the body and other limited conditions.

VERSE 4

There may be this objection: Even though I-am-ness is observed in those six particular conditions, which comprise objects, and so on, it is not [observed] everywhere. [Virūpākṣa] answers:

1.4. I-am-ness is well known [in the six conditions just mentioned, which comprise] objects, the [fleshly] body, the senses, the intelligence, the breath and mental arrest.[1] The one who contemplates this consciousness [that I am] for the entire course[2] has [the realization of] the universe as his body.

I-am-ness is well known in the six [conditions mentioned, which] comprise objects, and so on. [This I-am-ness] can belong only to consciousness. It could not belong to the individual subject, because that [individual subject] is submerged when in the void state.[3]

Contemplate this consciousness of I-am-ness that is well known in the six conditions for the entire course. That is, firmly recognitively synthesize this eternally pure recognition [of I-am-ness]—as in the six conditions—everywhere, regarding everything, beginning with [the emanated, lower] Śiva[4] and ending with the earth. Then you will have the recognition of the universe as your body. Thus is the explication.

According to the stated position, that I-am-ness within the six conditions belongs only to consciousness and not to the individual subject. That consciousness has the nature of unlimited awareness. It is impossible that I-am-ness could belong only to a particular aspect [of that consciousness] rather than to the entirety of it. With a firm conviction, recognitively apprehend that eternally established I-am-ness of consciousness everywhere. Then you will recognize it as eternally established that the universe is your body. That is the purport.

Notes

1. *Nirodha,* "mental arrest," in the *Yoga Sūtra* refers to the suppression of mental activity. See YS 1.2, 9; 1.12, 46; 1.51, 132; 3.9, 286. Here the arrest of mental activity is being correlated with the void mentioned in the previous verse.

2. *akhile 'dhvani.* This refers to the important doctrine of the six "courses" (*adhvan*) of emanating Speech, also designated collectively as the sixfold course. See the Introduction, pp. 13, 30.

3. As the individual subject is not experienced in the void state, there must be a deeper subjectivity that is aware of that state. This same point regarding deep sleep was frequently made by Ramana Maharshi.

4. The name Śiva has two principle meanings in this system. It designates the ultimate deity, sometimes also called Paramaśiva, "the Supreme Śiva," or Parameśvara, "the Supreme Lord," with whom the adept endeavors to identify. Śiva also refers to one of the lower cosmic principles (*tattva*) emanated by the Supreme Śiva. I will indicate in brackets when the second meaning is intended. (Neither should be confused with another emanated cosmic principle, Sadāśiva.)

VERSE 5

There may be this objection: The stated position is that it is established that all people have the universe as their body. However, this is not what is observed. I-hood is [commonly observed to be] restricted to the fleshly body. Thus one is justified by direct perception to conceive one's identity [*abhimantṛtva*] as the fleshly body. How could [one be justified to conceive one's identity] otherwise? [Virūpākṣa] answers:

> **1.5. Having departed[1] from the body that is the universe, one's I-hood becomes confined to a particular body that is a portion of that [universal one]. [Unenlightened] people are as if dead while living, as if their throats were gasping for breath.[2]**

"From the body that is the universe" means from the universe, beginning with [the emanated, lower] Śiva, which is one's [actual] body. "Having departed" means that, although one has not actually departed from that reality, one has apparently departed from it. That [apparent departure is] due to a lack of recognitive apprehension of oneself.

"One's I-hood becomes confined to a particular body that is a portion of that [universal one]" means: One comes to have a firm conviction about one's I-hood as referring only to one particular body that exists within that [universal body], for example, the body of a god, human or lower animal.

Therefore, "people are as if dead while living, as if their throats were gasping for breath." This means that the multitude of creatures, though living, are really as good as dead. There is no denying this.

The cause [of that spiritual death] has been determined to be Māyā, which is defined as the lack of recognitive apprehension of oneself. When one attains that recognitive apprehension, then one [recognizes that one] is none other than Śiva, who has the universe as his body.

NOTES

1. This word *utkramya* literally means "having risen above." In the context of religious practice, the verbal and nominal derivatives of *ut-kram* refer to the process of the yogin leaving the fleshly body by an ascent of vital energy out through the *brahmarandha cakra.* I use the expression "having departed" here to avoid the connotation that leaving the universal body is a journey to a higher state. In terms of spiritual value, it is more of a descent. For background, see YS 3.39, 357; and Teun Goudriaan, "Some Beliefs and Rituals Concerning Time and Death in the Kubjikāmata," in *Selected Studies on Ritual in Indian Religions: Essays*

to D. J. Hoens, ed. Ria Kloppenborg (Leiden: E. J. Brill, 1983), 92–117. (I learned the latter reference from White, *Kiss of the Yoginī,* 326, n. 53.)

2. The expression *jīvanmṛta,* "dead while living," inverts the notion of *jīvanmukta,* "liberated while living," to emphasize the irony of the human situation. What we normally call life is a death to our true life. The *jīvanmukta,* on the other hand, lives the true life while participating in the death we normally call life. Shashibhusan Dasgupta paraphrases a Nāth text: "Where an ordinary man lives (in his physical form) the yogin is dead—and where there is the death for all (in the physical form) there is no death for the yogin." Dasgupta, *Obscure Religious Cults,* 220.

VERSE 6

Such being the case, it follows that:

> **1.6. [You] whose I-am-ness refers to the [fleshly] body can, through mere intention, strike [your] two insentient arms together. Just so, [I, whose I-am-ness] refers to the universe can, through the force of that [intention, strike together] even two mountains.[1]**

You, "whose I-am-ness refers to the [fleshly] body," that is, who suppose yourself [*abhimāninas*] to be an individual subject, can through mere intention strike your two hands together. Similarly, I, who have the nature of consciousness and whose I-am-ness refers to the universe can, through nothing other than the force of intention, strike two mountains together.

You have [1] a firm conviction that "I" refers to the [fleshly] body, and [2] an intention. Those [two factors] alone cause your hands to strike together. There is no other cause. Similarly, I have [1] a firm conviction that "I" refers to the universe and [2] an intention. Those [two factors] cause the two mountains to strike together.

Therefore, you lack Lordship because your conviction has diminished that "I" refers to the universe. However, through firmness of that [conviction], your Lordship, which is [in reality] established eternally, will be revealed. That is the meaning.

Note

1. Indra's powerful arms and other limbs are a frequent theme in his mythology. In more metaphysically elaborated interpretations they are identified with features of the cosmos; Indra is also seen as the animating power in human arms. See Choudhuri, 20–21, 27, 29, 32, 142. For the VAP, this will be true of Indra only when he is enlightened.

VERSE 7

There may be this objection: We do not observe that mere I-am-ness along with intention accomplish the striking of the hands. On the contrary, [the striking of the hands is accomplished] only when [I-am-ness and intention] are accompanied by a constellation that consists in the impulsion of the [various elemental factors of the human being, such as] the germinal essence, breath, and so on. Therefore, how can what has been claimed be possible? [Virūpākṣa] answers:

> **1.7. Possessing[1] the germinal essence, breath, Śakti, the mind, the collection of senses and the [fleshly] body, contemplate I-hood as impelling all of them.**

The germinal essence is the subtle conception of I that precedes the arising of the particular conceptions of the individual subject and the means of knowledge.[2] [The subtle conception of I] flows from its own ecstasy[3] and is universal in nature.[4]

Breath [*prāṇa*] is the vital breath [*asu*], which is the cause of the activation of the inner organ in the forms of the conception of limited personal identity [*abhimāna*], determinate ascertainment, and so on [the mind].[5]

By the word Śakti the intelligence and the I-concept are to be understood. This is because conceptions such as that of one's identity [*abhimāna*] and ascertainment have the nature of Śakti.[6]

Possessing these six entities beginning with the germinal essence, contemplate I-hood as impelling all of them, that is, activating[7] them through the majesty of your slightest touch. [In effect, in ordinary unenlightened experience] you contemplate with a firm conviction I-hood as possessing and impelling] your [fleshly] body. You should in the same way contemplate [I-hood as possessing and impelling] all of these [six entities]. Then you will realize as yours such eternally established proficiencies. That is the meaning.

NOTES

1. The word, translated as "possessing," is *āviśya,* from the prefix *ā* and the verb root *viś*. Derivatives of *ā-viś* and related *sam-ā-viś* can also mean "enter into," "submerse oneself into," and "possess." The backgrounds to this concept lie in notions of spirit and deity possession. Such ideas are developed in the descriptions of three mystical *samāveśas,* "possessions" or "submersions" in *Śrī Mālinīvijayottara Tantram,* ed. Madhusudan Kaul Shastri (Delhi: Butala & Company, 1984), 2.21–23, 9. In the VAP, as in other monistic Śaiva texts, there is a blending of the

ideas of the adept *possessing* realia and *being possessed by them.* For discussions of this concept, see Navjivan Rastogi, "The Philosophy of Krama," 2:367–383; Sanderson, "Maṇḍala and Āgamic Identity," 176–177; Raffaele Torella, "Introduction" to *The Īśvarapratyabhijñākārikā of Utpaladeva,* xxxii–xxxv; Loriliai Biernacki, "*Samāveśa,*" in "Taboo and Orthodoxy: Making Tantra Respectable in 11th Century Kashmir" (Ph.D. diss., University of Pennsylvania, 1999), 14–59; Marcy Alison Braverman, "Totally Soaked: Immersion (*samāveśā*) and Intoxication of Devotion (*bhaktyunmāda*) in the Nondual Śaiva Yoga Traditions of Kashmir" (Ph.D. diss., University of California, Santa Barbara, 2002); and Frederick M. Smith, *The Self Possessed: Deity and Spirit Possession in South Asian Literature and Civilization* (New York: Columbia University Press, 2006).

2. On the term *bindu,* "germinal essence," see Introduction, p. 31. Vidyācakravartin's interpretation of *bindu* in this verse articulates its significance as one of the chief codes in the VAP and VAPV for the ultimate state of I-hood or self-recognition. The same significance is clearly evinced in VAP 2.15. One may question, however, whether Virūpākṣa is actually using the term *bindu* in that sense in the present verse. Why would he teach that one should contemplate I-hood as impelling the ultimate I-hood? One possibility is that he is using *bindu* here, contra Vidyācakravartin's interpretation, in a different sense to refer to a limited constituent of the unenlightened human personality. Another possibility, which I favor, is that he is teaching how one may expand one's prima facie sense of I-hood to comprehend its full metaphysical reality. In possessing the ultimate *bindu,* the limited I-hood would be realized actually to be that *bindu.* (Cf. the remarks on Vidyācakravartin's interpretation of the term Śakti in this verse below, p. 74, n. 6.) Also important in tantric theosophical contemplations is the graphemic significance of *bindu* as the dot above the line in Sanskrit scripts that indicates the *anusvāra,* a final nasal sound created through *saṁdhi*; as well as the untransformed *-m* sound. See the discussion of the formation of the word *aham,* "I," below, VAP and VAPV 2.9–10.

3. My translation of *svarasavāhinī* as "flows from its own ecstasy" is influenced by the translation of *svarasodita* as "rising out of its own ecstasy," in *Īśvara Pratyabhijñā Kārikā: Verses on the Recognition of the Lord,* trans. B. N. Pandit (Delhi: Motilal Banarsidass, 2004), 1.5.13, 62. Besides alluding to Utpaladeva's verse, Vidyācakravartin's use of the expression *svarasavāhinī* anticipates Virūpākṣa's more thorough allusion in his description of consciousness in VAP 2.9.

4. *sāmānyabhūta.*

5. According to Sāṁkhya, the inner organ (*antaḥkaraṇa*) includes intelligence (*buddhi*), the I-concept (*ahaṁkāra*), and the mind (*manas*). The first two are respectively correlated with the functions of determinate ascertainment (*adhyavasāya*) and egoity (*abhimāna*), and the latter with the focusing of attention, or intentionality (*saṁkalpa*). See the discussions of the terms in Karl H. Potter, ed., *Encyclopedia of Indian Philosophies,* vol. 4, *Sāṁkhya,* ed. Gerald James Larson and Ram Shankar Bhattacharya (Delhi: Motilal Banarsidass, 1987).

6. That is, these conceived faculties and functions of the inner organ are expressions or manifestations of Śakti. Note that Vidyācakravartin, contrary to his approach to *bindu* in the verse, is interpreting the word Śakti as signifying only limited aspects of the personality generated by Śakti, rather than Śakti in her ultimate metaphysical nature.

7. *parispandayantīm.*

VERSE 8

There may be this objection: I-hood is manifested through mere contemplation. However, one does not [thereby] experience oneself to be endowed with such lofty qualities as Lordship and [universal] agency.[1] Therefore, how are such proficiencies possible? To remove this doubt, [Virūpākṣa] explains:

> **1.8. The wise verily say that Lordship, [universal] agency, agential self-determination,[2] and being of the nature of consciousness[3] are synonyms for I-hood.**

That very I-hood that has been recognized by you is Lordship, [universal] agency, agential self-determination, and consisting of consciousness. Every excellence in proficiencies [that is described] in the religious literature,[4] such as Lordship, and so on, consists of nothing but I-hood. Thus Lordship, and so on, are synonyms [for I-hood].

Therefore the doubt arising from the lack of experience of I-hood as Lordship, and so on, has been dispelled. Inasmuch as one has a firm recognition [of that I-hood], one displays one's eternally established powers such as Lordship, [universal] agency and so on. This is what is expressed by the verse. Thus Śiva.

NOTES

1. *kartṛtā.* This word refers to the cosmogonic and all-controlling agency of Śiva. See the discussion of the monistic Śaiva approach to agential syntax in the Introduction, pp. 14, 31.

2. *svatantratā.*

3. *citsvarūpatā.*

4. *śāstreṣu.*

Thus ends the first book of the *Virūpākṣapañcāśikā* with the commentary, which demonstrates that the universe is one's body.

Book 2

The first book has demonstrated that the universe is one's body. Now begins the second book. [This book demonstrates that] the universe has the nature of awareness, to refute the delusion that there is a difference between the body and the one who possesses the body.

VERSE 9

In this regard [there may be the objection]: Through the dissolution of particulars such as the individual subject, [there is the realization of] consciousness that is universal and flows from its own ecstasy.[1] That [universal consciousness] is not experienced as "I." Therefore, how can it be said to be I-hood? [Virūpākṣa] answers this doubt:

> **2.9. That consciousness has the nature of recognitive apprehension, flows from its own ecstasy, is Supreme Speech,[2] and comprises the collection of phonemes as abbreviated into the first and the last.[3] [That consciousness] is in reality I-hood.[4]**

[The assertion that consciousness] "has the nature of recognitive apprehension [*pratyavamarśātmā*]" means that it has the nature of recognitive judgment [*vimarśātmā*].[5] That [consciousness] is properly referred to with [the pronoun] "that,"[6] in the sense of something observable, because it is proven to everybody through their own experience. Consciousness is the abiding of the sentient being in its essential nature when there is the dissolution of all colorations by objects of consciousness.[7] [The assertion that that consciousness] "flows from its own ecstasy" means that it bursts into manifestation[8] continuously because it has no obstructions.

That [consciousness] is Speech because it consists of recognitive apprehension.[9] However, it shines[10] as illuminating [everything as comprised within] its own essential nature. It does not have the form of [Speech at lower levels] such as Seeing, which [illuminates objects that] are distinguished from its essential nature.[11] On the contrary, it is Supreme [Speech]. As it is said in the scriptural tradition: "It is self-luminous; inner, subtle Speech; and undying."[12] It comprises the phonemes because it has the nature of pure Speech. Following the method of abbreviation, that I-hood is explained to comprehend all the phonemes, from the phoneme *a* to the phoneme *ha*. Such I-hood is not merely that [limited identity that deluded people] conceive as "I."[13]

Notes

1. In his characterizations of consciousness as universal (*sāmānyarūpā*) and flowing from its own ecstasy (*svarasavāhinī*), Vidyācakravartin is linking the present verse with his explanation of *bindu* in VAPV 1.7.

2. See the Introduction on philosophical and contemplative aspects of the monistic Śaiva understanding of the principle "Supreme Speech," which they derive from Bhartṛhari.

3. *ādyantapratyāhṛtavarṇa.* Virūpākṣa is giving an occult etymology of the word *aham,* "I," from its constituent phonemes. On this interpretation, see the Introduction, pp. 13, 30–31. Bhāskararāya in his *Yoginīhṛdayasetubandha,* 109–110, quotes different sources on this summation from *a* to *ha.* Likewise, see *The Hevajra Tantra,* ed. and trans. David L. Snellgrove (London: Oxford University Press, 1959).

4. Virūpākṣa's verse closely corresponds to Utpaladeva's explanation of consciousness in IPK 1.5.13, 1:250:

> *citiḥ pratyavamarśātmā parā vāksvarasoditā*
> *svātantryametanmukhyaṁ tadaiśvaryam paramātmanaḥ*
>
> Consciousness has the nature of recognitive apprehension; it is Supreme Speech; it has risen out of its own ecstasy; it is agential self-determination; and it is therefore the chief Lordship of the Supreme Self.

As already noted, I am following B. N. Pandit, trans., *Īśvara Pratyabhijñā Kārikā,* 1.5.13, 62, in glossing *svarasoditā* as "risen out of its own ecstasy."

5. This is a simple gloss of a term by a cognate synonym.

6. *asau.*

7. *citiḥ vigalitacetyoparāgā cetanasya svarūpeṇāvasthitiḥ.* It seems that Vidyācakravartin here alludes to the YS 1.2–3, 9–16: *yoga cittavṛttinirodaḥ. draṣṭuḥ svarūpe'vasthānam.* "Yoga is the arrest of mental fluctuations. Then there is the abiding of the cognizer in its essential nature."

8. *sphurad.*

9. The Pratyabhijñā follows Bhatṛhari in viewing recognitive apprehension (*vimarśa, pratyavamarśa,* and so on) as an intrinsically linguistic process, deriving from the monistic essence of language.

10. *prakāśanāt.*

11. The monistic Śaiva traditions since Somānanda interpret Bhartṛhari as positing four descending cosmic levels of language. According to this interpretation, the highest level is Supreme Speech, which is identical with the Trika Goddess/cosmic level Supreme (*parā*). The Śaivas locate below Supreme Speech Bhartṛhari's levels of "Seeing" (*paśyantī*), "Intermediate" (*madhyamā*), and "Gross" (*vaikharī*). On the debate about whether Bhartṛhari intended to posit a Supreme level above Seeing, see Gaurināth Śāstrī, *The Philosophy of Word and Meaning: Some Indian Approaches with Special Reference to the Philosophy of Bhartṛhari,* Calcutta Sanskrit College Research Series, no. 5 (Calcutta: Sanskrit College, 1959). According to the Śaivas, even Seeing involves some degree of the duality between language and objects that becomes increasingly concrete in the lower stages.

12. This verse is quoted in the commentary of *Vākyapadīya of Bhartṛhari, kāṇḍa* 1, ed. K. A. Subramania Iyer (Pune: Deccan College, 1966), 1.134, 219. Bhartṛhari actually seems to use the verse to describe *paśyantī*. The idea that the monistic Ultimate Reality in its self-luminosity (*svaprakāśatva*) transcends the subject-object and language-object dichotomies comes from the Upaniṣads.

13. Abhinavagupta explains in his commentary on Utpaladeva's original verse, at IPV 1.5.13, 1:253–254:

> It is the life of language sounds of the realm of *Māyā,* such as [the phoneme] "*a,*" and so on, which have their reference fixed through convention. It is called Supreme because it is the inner foundation of recognitive apprehensions such as "This is blue" and "I am Caitra," and because it is complete. It is called Speech because it speaks the universe by means of recognitive apprehension. For this reason, " out of its own ecstasy," that is, in the form of consciousness, and as resting in itself—it is the "arisen" that is, always unset, eternal "I."

VERSE 10

There may be this question: That which is called I-hood is the quality of the I. Who or what is it that is experienced as other [than oneself]? [For example, there may be someone else] who is different from [one's own] consciousness that has the nature of recognitive apprehension, but who can also be designated [by himself or herself] as "I."[1] [Virūpākṣa] responds:

> **2.10. That awareness is the Self of the universe, which is able to manifest both itself and that which is [apparently] other.[2] It is explained to be a unitary "I." I-hood is its abstract condition as such.[3]**

Awareness is capable of manifesting "itself," that is, as abstract awareness. [It is also capable of manifesting] that which is [apparently] other, beginning with recognitive apprehension [reified as a distinctive epistemic faculty] and ending with [objects of experience such as the color] blue.[4]

That [awareness] is the Self of the universe, including both what is conscious and what is unconscious. It would be impossible for differentiating factors such as place and time to find a place within that Self. Therefore, the noble scriptural traditions[5] teach that it is the "I," which is "unitary," that is, without a second. I-hood is nothing other than the abstract condition of that [awareness] which has just been explained. It has the nature of recognitive apprehension.

This is the purport: That awareness manifests the object of knowledge, beginning with recognitive apprehension [reified as a distinctive epistemic faculty] and ending with blue. It is solely of the nature of knowing and is endowed with all knowledge. It cannot [properly] be designated as either self or other, because those [when conceived as distinct entities] are both objects of knowledge.[6] It is impossible [to apply to that awareness] means of knowledge, which make distinctions. Therefore, it is entirely unitary.

The scriptural traditions explain that [awareness] as "I" [*aham*] through abbreviation as the phonemes "*a*" and "*ha*." In this regard, although the stem "*aha-*" is meaningful, there cannot be verbal usage with a stem alone. Therefore, in usage it is combined with the termination [*-m*], as "*aham*."[7] When that [*aham*] is [understood] in the state of a cause, then its abstract nature as recognitive apprehension, becomes apparent. That [abstract nature as recognitive apprehension] is called "I-hood" [*ahaṁtā*].

Notes

1. Vidyācakravartin raises the possibility of other selves as an example of the generic category of the other.

2. Virūpākṣa again alludes to Utpaladeva: "There is only the awareness of one's Self as oneself and others" (*prakāśa evāsti svātmanaḥ svaparātmabhiḥ*). *Ajaḍapramātṛsiddhi,* 13, 5. This verse is frequently quoted in the Pratyabhijñā literature, for example, IPV 1.1.3, 1:64; 1.1.4, 1:76; 1.5.3, 1:208; and IPVV 1.1, 1:97. Also see the discussion of the identity of the grammatical persons below, VAP and VAPV 3.23–24.

3. Virūpākṣa is explaining the suffix *-tā* attached to *aham,* which signifies an abstraction. VAP 2.10 is quoted by Bhāskararāya, *Yoginīhṛdayasetubandha,* 21–22, 109; and Naṭanāndanātha in his *Kāmakalāvilāsacidvallī,* 1.3, 17.

4. Vidyācakravartin takes the verse as describing all manners of self-differentiation of awareness (*prakāśa*). One may be surprised to see recognitive apprehension (*pratyavamarśa*), which is generally taken as integral to awareness (*prakāśa*), included in such self-differentiation along with ordinary objects of experience. Vidyācakravartin is referring to such recognitive apprehension as is artificially discriminated from its monistic essence.

5. *sannāgameṣu.*

6. The self in unenlightened experience as well as its polar other are both defined as limited objects of knowledge by their very distinction from each other.

7. Graphemically, *bindu* is the dot added to *aha-* to represent the final *-m* that makes *aham.*

VERSE 11

There may be this objection: The object of knowledge is referred to as "this." The subject who has the I-notion is referred to as "I." Then there is also awareness, which has just been explained. Thus we have three. How can what was stated about them be demonstrated?[1] [Virūpākṣa] answers:

> **2.11. That [awareness] has two presentations.[2] One, which is differentiated, is referred to as "this." The other, which is undifferentiated, is referred to as "I." The first appears in the aspect of the object of consciousness as that which is manifested. The other appears in the aspect of consciousness as that which manifests.**

"That" refers to awareness, which has been explained. It has "two presentations." Those are its qualities. One of these is "differentiated," that is, involves reciprocal exclusion [between its various instances]. It is referred to as "this." The other is undifferentiated, that is, inclusive of [the diverse manifestations referred to as] "this."[3] The presentation "this" appears in the aspect of the object of consciousness as that which is manifested. The presentation "I" appears in the aspect of consciousness as that which manifests.

Indeed, there is reciprocal exclusion [between instances of] the presentation "this," as is illustrated by the observation "This is blue and this is yellow." When that [exclusion] does not arise, there do not appear manifestations of objects such as blue.[4]

However, the presentation "I" is inclusive [of manifestations of different objects, as is illustrated by the statement] "I know both blue and yellow." The unitary substratum of the presentation of those [objects, appears] in the aspect of consciousness as that which manifests.

NOTES

1. That is, picking up from VAP 2.10, how can awareness appear as both self, referred to as "I," and other, referred to as "this"?

2. *prathā.*

3. Vidyācakravartin here introduces the important dichotomy between: (A) what is inclusive or continuous (*anuvṛtta*), and the corresponding abstract

condition of inclusiveness or continuity (*anuvṛtti*) (B) what is exclusive or discontinuous (*vyāvṛtta*) and the abstract condition of exclusiveness or discontinuity (*vyāvṛtti*). In Pāṇinian grammar, the former refers to the inclusiveness of scope or continuity of application of earlier rules over subsequent rules. In this text, it refers to the manner in which higher cosmic principles comprehend and pervade lower ones, in a manner reminiscent of the Upaniṣadic cosmic thread. Likewise, exclusiveness refers to the fragmentation of emanated entities from each other. These categories are further correlated respectively with the possession and lack of sequence (*krama*). See below, VAP and VAP 2.12, and p. 81, n. 1, as well as the general discussion in the Introduction on the subsumption of difference and sequence.

4. *na hi . . . nīlādāvābhāsyatā prakāśate.*

VERSE 12

Since that is established, therefore:

> **2.12. As the Self, that [awareness] is unitary, because there is no sequence in it of either place or time.[1] However, as associated with objects of consciousness that are differentiated from each other, that [awareness] is the substratum of differentiation.**

As the Self, that awareness is unitary, that is, without anything second to it. Awareness and the subject are not two.

There may be this objection: [The cognition that] "I am a subject here and now" refers to sequence of both place and time. How can there be unity? In response to this doubt, [Virūpākṣa] explains that "there is no sequence in it of either place or time." That is, in this awareness, there is no sequence due to differentiation of either place or time. This is the reason: [That awareness is] "associated with objects of consciousness, which are differentiated from each other." Objects of consciousness are differentiated, for example, in the manner "This is blue and this is yellow." Awareness is "associated with," and thus inclusive of [such differentiated objects of consciousness, as might be expressed], "I know blue and yellow."

He drives home this very point [in his statement] "However . . . that [awareness] is the substratum of differentiation." That is to say, that [awareness] is the substratum of the differentiation that is the quality of objects of consciousness. What we call differentiation is exclusiveness. Nondifferentiation is inclusiveness. Objects of consciousness are differentiated by both place and time. Consciousness is the [inclusive] substratum of that differentiation. The delusion that consciousness is itself differentiated is predicated upon those objects that are merely its accidental qualifications.

NOTE

1. In monistic Śaiva philosophy, as in Bhartṛhari, sequence (*krama*) is a basic expression of the fragmentation of the unitary Ultimate into limited entities that are exclusive of each other. Whereas time and place are usually conceived as the most fundamental expressions of sequence, there are also references to sequences of qualities and nonspatiotemporal cosmological principles. The goal is always contemplatively to subsume sequential conditions into the nonsequential.

VERSE 13

The position stated has clarified that there is no difference in essential nature between awareness and the subject. Now [Virūpākṣa] argues that the object also, when properly elucidated, should not be understood as different from awareness:

> **2.13. Its body is the sky[1] of consciousness. In that, it which is like the ocean of milk, creates and destroys the universe through the conjunction and disjunction of the waves of its Śaktis.**

"It" is awareness. "Its body" is its essential nature. That [body] is "the sky of consciousness," that is, a background that consists of undifferentiated consciousness. In that [sky of consciousness] it "creates," that is, manifests the universe, beginning with [the emanated, lower] Śiva. [It creates] through the "conjunction . . . of its Śaktis," that is, through directing them toward the cognition of specific objects. [Its Śaktis] are rays of its splendor taking the forms of Khecarī and so on.[2] It "destroys," that is, withdraws [the universe] through the "disjunction" [of those Śaktis] from cognized objects. Similarly, the ocean, "through the conjunction . . . of the waves," creates surf, foam, and so on. And it withdraws [surf, foam and so on] through the disjunction [of the waves].

Prior to the cognition of entities such as [the emanated, lower] Śiva, there is only consciousness, which is like the sky. When it desires to manifest [those entities], it creates through the conjunction of its Śaktis in the succession[3] of Khecarī, Gocarī, and so on. [The conjunction of its Śaktis] is the extroversion of them to bring about particular effects.

When reality is recognitively apprehended, [consciousness] withdraws through those [Śaktis]. [Those Śaktis] had fallen to become the differentiations of consciousness that constitute each particular thing. [Consciousness] dissolves them successively back into their causes.[4]

To firmly convince [his audience] that neither Śaktis nor the universe exist externally to awareness, [Virūpākṣa] uses metaphors: He describes awareness as the ocean and Śaktis as waves, with the implication that the universe is surf, and so on. Thus the universe with its parts as well as Śaktis which are the cause of that [universe], when recognitively apprehended, are established to be nothing but awareness.

Notes

1. *Gagana,* which can mean "void" as well as "sky," is an important metaphor in both Hindu and Buddhist tantrism. Also see the following note, n. 2.

2. From Vāmeśvarī emanate Khecarī (who moves in the sky, i.e., *kha* or *gagana*), Gocarī, Dikcarī and Bhūcarī. Representative discussions of this pentad of Śaktis are found in Kṣemarāja, *Pratyabhijñāhṛdayam: The Secret of Self-Recognition,* ed. and trans. Jaideva Singh (Delhi: Motilal Banarsidass, 1980), 12, 81–83; and idem, *Spandasaṁdoha,* ed. Mukunda Ram Shastri (Bombay: Shri Venkateshwar Steam Press, 1917). See the analysis in Rastogi, "Dynamic Absolutism vis-à-vis Pañcavāha and Pīṭhaniketana," in "Philosophy of Krama," 2:645–677.

3. *krama.*

4. *karaṇalayakrameṇa.*

VERSE 14

No object of knowledge, or anything else, is separate [from awareness]. Only awareness subsists as the essential nature of everything. By means of the arguments that have been propounded, consciousness has been recognized. One should accordingly contemplate [that consciousness] with a firm conviction, to remove the subliminal tendencies for the delusion that objects of knowledge, or anything else, are different [from awareness or consciousness]. [Virūpākṣa] explains:

> **2.14. Consciousness should be contemplated as possessing innumerable wheels of its own Śaktis.[1] [Those wheels of Śaktis] emanate this universe, which consists of the five sense fields, such as the visible; and takes the forms of objects of knowledge, the senses and the knower.**

This universe takes the forms of objects of knowledge, the instruments that establish those [that is, the senses], and the knower. Considered properly, it consists of the five sense fields, such as the visible. This is how: The visible sense field becomes an object of knowledge. Then the eye establishes the cognition of that [object of knowledge], and takes on its character.[2] Then the individual subject appropriates its visible form. It is similar with taste and [the other sense fields].

Consciousness should be contemplated in this way: It possesses "innumerable wheels of its own Śaktis," that is, a multitude of diverse rays of splendor. Those "emanate," that is, operate as "this universe that takes the forms of objects of knowledge, the senses and the knower." The infinity of things [arise] in that way. Because there are an infinity [of things], contemplation is difficult. For that reason [Virūpākṣa] has refuted the delusion that these things are different from consciousness.[3]

Notes

1. *anantasvaśakticakrā*.
2. That is, it comes to be affected by or to reflect that object of knowledge.
3. One will not be distracted by the multiplicity of things when one firmly understands that they are identical with consciousness.

VERSE 15

[Virūpākṣa] has [in 2.14] epitomized the universe as fivefold, and he has established that it has the nature of consciousness. He now epitomizes it as threefold, for the sake of easy contemplation. He [again] teaches that it has the nature of consciousness:

> **2.15. The object of knowledge, the senses and the knower[1] are [respectively] symbolized by the moon, the sun and fire. The germinal essence consists in the corporification of their manifestations.[2] [That germinal essence] has the nature of recognitive apprehension, and is the sole life-breath[3] of the six courses.**

The object of knowledge is symbolized by the moon because its form is external. The senses are symbolized by the sun because they are both external and internal. The knower is symbolized by fire because its essential nature is internal and unitary. This universe is threefold. There is nothing outside [these three categories].

The "corporification of their manifestations"—that is, of the object of knowledge and so on—is the manifestation that is common to them[4] when their distinctions, as the object of knowledge, and so on, have dissolved. That [common manifestation] consists in their recognitive apprehension. It is called the germinal essence.

The germinal essence is also the "sole life-breath of the six ways." This means that it is the essential nature [of the six ways] because it is the cause of their origin and fruition.

Considered properly, the three divinities conceived [*abhimāninīnām*] as the moon, and so on [the sun and fire], are actually the triad of the object of knowledge, and so on [the senses and the knower]. Their true forms are not their sportive appearances,[5] corporeal forms, discs, and so on. Discs and so on are [actually] objects of knowledge. It is impossible that the [true forms of the] senses and the knower [are objects of knowledge].

The object of knowledge and the rest are [ordinarily] experienced with their own distinctive characteristics—that is, as the object of knowledge and so on. The germinal essence is the experience of them without those distinctive characteristics.[6] [The germinal essence] is the "life-breath" [of the six ways]. That is, the six ways are the germinal essence's secondary transformations.

Notes

1. I am here glossing *bhogya* and *bhoktṛ*, respectively, as "the object of knowledge" and "the knower." The root of these words, *bhuj*, could be more literally translated with terms of broader significance as "enjoy" or "experience." However, the derivatives of that root in the VAP and VAPV receive their coherent meaning within the ongoing discussion of the factors of knowledge (usually referred to with derivatives of *jñā*, "know"). I have opted for a single rendering for the sake of clarity.

2. *bhānapiṇḍa.* The VAP with its program of corporification is overcoding a Trika appropriation of a Krama tantric scheme of contemplation. In this contemplative scheme, the object of knowledge, the means of knowledge, and the knower are respectively identified with the moon, the sun, and fire, and the former are "absorbed" into the latter. See TA and TAV, 4.122ff., 3:740ff.; 5.19ff., 3:945ff. This triad indexes phases of cycles of Kālīs that are absorbed in the goddess Kālasaṁkarṣiṇī, "the Shortener/Destroyer of Time."

3. *prāṇa.*

4. *sāmānyātmakam.*

5. *līlā.*

6. See VAP and VAPV 1.2, and p. 67, n. 13, on the corporification of all things through seeing them in their universal nature; and VAP and VAPV 3.29, on recognitive apprehension as burning up the particular object of knowledge, means of knowledge and knower, and leaving universal awareness.

VERSE 16

To further clarify, [Virūpākṣa] explains:

2.16. Indeed, when it is manifest, this universe consists of objects. [Nevertheless] it constantly depends upon that [ger-

minal essence]. When it is unmanifest, it has the nature of Śakti and submerges back into that [germinal essence].

This universe has two forms—gross and subtle.[1] The gross is said to be that which is manifest. The subtle is said to be Śakti. In this regard, the manifest universe "consists of objects." "[Nevertheless] it constantly depends upon that [germinal essence]." That is, it always, in the conditions of origination, and so on [that is, persistence and withdrawal], depends upon the Śakti of the germinal essence. However, when [the universe] is unmanifest, it has the nature of Śakti and submerges back into that [germinal essence].

One may experience the universe, in whatever way it exists, in either its gross or subtle forms. However, in no case could it be external to consciousness, which has the nature of recognitive apprehension. Similarly, waves, and so on, could not be external to water. That is the meaning.

Note

1. On the gross (*sthūla*) and the subtle (*sūkṣma*), see Hemendra Nath Chakravarty, "Sthūla-Sūkṣma-Para," in *Kalātattvakośa,* vol. 4, *Manifestation of Nature: Sṛṣṭi Vistāra,* ed. Advaitavadini Kaul and Sukumar Chattopadhyay (Delhi: Indira Gandhi National Centre for the Arts, 1999), 275–316.

VERSE 17

Different people conceive and meditate upon consciousness in various ways to achieve diverse proficiencies. However, that upon which they meditate is nothing other [than that consciousness]. [Virūpākṣa] explains:

2.17. The learned analyze this [consciousness/germinal essence] as sixteenfold, ninefold, sixfold, and threefold. Thus it is symbolized by a variety of contemplative supports,[1] and produces manifold proficiencies for those who seek those proficiencies.[2]

This germinal essence, the nature of which has been established, is "symbolized by a variety of contemplative supports." That is, it is interpreted as symbolized by different [sets of] contemplative supports as sixteenfold and so on. Therefore [the germinal essence] "produces manifold proficiencies." That is, as secondarily qualified by diverse contemplative supports, [the germinal essence] produces a variety of proficiencies.

"Those who seek those proficiencies," are practitioners.[3] They "analyze . . . [the germinal essence] as sixteenfold." That is, they contemplate it with reference to sixteen contemplative supports as having a sixteenfold nature. Similarly [they analyze the germinal essence as] ninefold, sixfold, and threefold. These analyses of that [germinal essence] as sixteenfold by association with sixteen contemplative supports, and so on, are secondary qualifications of it. This is because it is impossible for there to be differentiation in the essential nature [of that germinal essence].

This is the import of [Virūpākṣa's] reference to [practitioners as] "those who seek those proficiencies": The [highest, quintessential] proficiency is the recognition of the essential nature of that [germinal essence]. Those who meditate with a diversity [of contemplative supports] are limited yogins who have not attained [that quintessential proficiency]. Those who have attained it[4] do not worship in such a manner. Their only relish is that of liberation while living, which may be defined as the firmness of the realization that consciousness is a unity. They incessantly worship consciousness in oneness with it.

Notes

1. There are discussions pertaining to the differentiation of contemplative supports (*ādhārabheda*) in the *Netra Tantra,* the *Mālinīvijaya Tantra,* and the *Tantrāloka.*
2. *setsyantaḥ.*
3. *sādhakāḥ.*
4. *siddhāḥ.*

VERSES 18–19

[Virūpākṣa] now uses two verses to explain the inferential concomitance with the existence of the germinal essence and the inferential exclusion by its nonexistence. [He supports this explanation with the well-known example] of the sun and the world-egg.[1] He thus demonstrates [the identity of the subject with the germinal essence, as may be expressed] "You verily are that."[2]

> **2.18. The threefold Speech, consisting of word, *mantra* and phoneme, is a minute part[3] of recognitive apprehension. The [threefold] referent-object consisting of cosmic realm,[4] cosmic principle and cosmic segment[5] is correspondingly [a minute part] of awareness, which has that [recognitive apprehension] as its essential nature.[6]**

2.19. That Supreme Sun enlivens the world-egg by the force of its possession of it. [That world-egg would] be dead without it [the Supreme Sun]. Do you not see that [Sun] in the highest heaven?[7]

There is no grammatical agreement between "recognitive apprehension" and "which."[8] Thus awareness is referred to [in the second sentence] as possessing an essential nature.[9] It has already been established that awareness possesses an essential nature. That essential nature was explained to be recognitive apprehension, referred to as "I-hood."

[Each of the two triadic subsets of courses, namely,] phoneme, word, and *mantra;* and cosmic principle, cosmic realm, and cosmic segment[10]—is a "minute part," that is, a mere aspect [respectively, of recognitive apprehension and awareness]. [The first subset is categorized as] having the form of speech, [and the second is categorized as] having the form of the object. [Together, the two] triads make up the sixfold course.

The Supreme Sun is that awareness that has already been recognitively apprehended as that "which has [that recognitive apprehension as its] essential nature." It is the Supreme Sun because it illuminates[11] the lower sun of this world.[12]

How is it like the sun? The world-egg would be "dead," that is, unmanifest[13] "without it [the Supreme Sun]," that is, without its extroversion as the universe. "By the force of its possession" means by its power[14] for this extroversion. It thereby "enlivens," that is, manifests[15] the universe, beginning with [the emanated, lower] Śiva. That Sun, which is such, is [said to be] "in the highest heaven" because [that heaven in which it resides] is different from the physical heaven.

Do you not see [that Sun] in the Supreme Space that is the heart?[16] With the interrogative particle[17] he makes a rhetorical negation, which implies the affirmative. He thereby removes [the delusion that the Supreme Sun] is not [actually] perceived throughout the three times [past, present and future].[18]

That Sun has the nature of awareness. It is Supreme because it enlivens the world-egg which [would otherwise be] dead. You always see that in the heart, which is the locus of its manifestation, and which is referred to by the term "highest heaven." This is because, without seeing it, it would be impossible to see anything else. That unlimited awareness of yours is [in the ordinary deluded condition] experienced in the heart as limited. [However, by this discussion you] are made to recognize that "You verily are that" [unlimited awareness].

NOTES

1. In Sanskritic philosophies, concomitance (*anvaya*) and exclusion (*vyatireka*) are categories pertaining to the formulation of *inductions*. Such inductions are in turn integral to most Sanskritic philosophical understandings of the syllogism. Most of these syllogisms involve a deductive application of a predicate (*sādhya*) to a subject (*pakṣa*) on the basis of a reason (*hetu*). The standard example is the inference that there is fire on the hill for the reason that there is smoke there. The reason identifies a property in the subject *that is known inductively to accompany the predicate.* This induction is stated in the third step of the inference, the "general principle with exemplification" (*udāharaṇa*). In the inference of fire from smoke, the induction is that wherever there is smoke there is fire. The concomitance is that fire is always present where smoke is present, and the exclusion is that smoke is absent wherever fire is absent.

2. This argument that the subject is identical with *bindu*/consciousness (*citi*), instantiates in special terms the inference of Utpaladeva and Abhinavagupta's Pratyabhijñā works that the individual is identical with Śiva. See VAP and VAPV 1.2 and pp. 65–67, nn. 1, 7, 8, as well as n. 7 below.

3. *kaṇa.*

4. After being used once in the verse to refer to the course, "word," the term *pada* is used again (rather than the usual *bhuvana*) to refer to "cosmic realm." This is likely because of the syllabic limitations of the verse.

5. The two triads of courses are here presented in ascending order from gross to subtle or ultimate.

6. VAP 2.18 is quoted in MMP, 27, 70.

7. In this verse one may discern the syllogism noted by Vidyācakravartin. In the Pratyabhijñā writings of Utpaladeva and Abhinavagupta, the reason that an individual is Śiva is that a person possesses Śakti, that is, the Power/Consort by which Śiva emanates the universe. Śakti in turn is philosophically explained as various modes of the *dependence* of all experiences and things on the subject (epistemologically interpreted in terms of transcendental recognition and ontologically in terms of agency). The present verse likewise claims that the subject must be the monistic germinal essence/consciousness (*citi*) because the universe ultimately depends on it.

8. That is, although in VAP 2.18 *vimarśasya* and *yasya* are adjacent and in the same case, they are not to be taken together. My translation places "which" in a second sentence.

9. *dharmin.*

10. Vidyācakravartin here presents the courses in an odd order that is neither ascending nor descending, and in which the elements of the triads do not properly correspond.

11. *prakāśakatvāt.*

12. In the South Asian context, the metaphor of the Ultimate Reality as the highest sun, which illuminates the ordinary sun is Vedic and Upaniṣadic. See *Kaṭha Upaniṣad,* in Śāstrī, *Upaniṣatsaṅgraha,* 5.15, 9. The same verse is also found in *Muṇḍaka Upaniṣad,* ibid., 2.2.10, 18; and *Śvetāśvatara Upaniṣad,* ibid., 6.14, 140. *Kaṭha Upaniṣad* 5.15 is translated by Hume, 358:

> The Sun shines not there, nor the moon and stars,
> These lightings shine not, much less this (earthly) fire!
> After Him, as He shines, doth everything shine,
> This whole world is illumined with his light.

We are also reminded of Plato's famous analogy of the Good with the sun, and description of the Good as the source of the illumination of the sun. *Republic,* trans. Paul Shorey, in *The Collected Dialogues of Plato,* ed. Edith Hamilton and Huntington Cairns (Princeton: Princeton University Press, 1989), 6.508–509, 743–745; 7.514–517, 747–750.

13. *Nimiṣitam* literally means "having the eyes shut." This is a technical concept in monistic Kashmiri Śaivism. *Nimeṣa,* "eye-shutting," refers to Śiva's/consciousness's nonmanifestation of the cosmos; and *unmeṣa,* "eye-opening," refers to his manifestation of it. See Vasugupta, *Spanda-Kārikās: The Divine Creative Pulsation* (with the *Spandanirṇaya* of Kṣemarāja), ed. and trans. Jaideva Singh (Delhi: Motilal Banarsidass, 1980), 1.1, 5.

14. *mahimnā.*

15. *unmeṣayati.*

16. On the important symbolism of the heart in the monistic Śaiva traditions, see Paul Eduardo Muller-Ortega, *The Triadic Heart of Śiva: Kaula Tantricism of Abhinavagupta in the Non-Dual Shaivism of Kashmir* (Albany: State University of New York Press, 1989); and the articles of Javier Ugaz Ortiz, "The Symbolic Meaning of Light and Its Relation to Heart in the Śivaism of Kāśmīr and Vedānta," *Orientalia Lovaniensia Periodica* 14 (1983): 275–292; "Triangle and Triad and Their Relation to 'Heart' in the Śivaism of Kāśmīr and Śaktism," *Orientalia Lovaniensia Periodica* 17 (1986): 209–231; and "A Hermeneutics of the Symbolism of the Interior Domain (*Guhā* and *Hṛdguhā*) in Abhinavagupta's Śivaism and Vedānta," *Orientalia Lovaniensia Periodica* 19 (1988): 157–188.

17. *kim.*

18. There is a reference here to the doctrine of self-luminosity (*svaprakāśatva*). We are always aware of our true nature as Śiva, the germinal essence, and so on. Spiritual teaching only removes the delusion that we are not aware of this. See Lawrence, *Rediscovering God,* 45–48, 56–57.

VERSE 20

[Virūpākṣa] elaborates that the one who has recognized [identity with awareness] is the creator of the universe:

> **2.20. He, by himself, churns the ocean of milk that is the sky of consciousness with the Mandara[1] that is intention. He thereby, through the waves of his Śaktis, brings up the moon that is called the world-egg.**

"By himself" means through nothing but agential self-determination. "With the Mandara that is intention" means with the mountain that has the nature of the will to manifest. With that he churns the ocean that consists of unlimited consciousness, that is, he leads it to extroversion toward its effect [the universe]. "Through the waves of his Śaktis" means through the waves in the form of his Śaktis, Khecarī and the rest. Thus he brings up the moon that is called the world-egg.

This is the meaning: You have been made to recognize yourself as awareness. [That awareness], through the force of its will, manifests the universe which is not different from itself upon the background that is itself.

NOTE

1. This is the mountain that the gods used to churn the ocean of milk in the myth of Viṣṇu's tortoise incarnation. The mountain was supported on the back of the tortoise. There is a great mixture of metaphors in this verse. This mythical action is invested with rich meanings in monistic Śaiva practices, from sexual rituals through interiorized operations of the vital breath. It is also associated with the friction of fire sticks in the Vedic ritual. See Silburn, 41–46.

VERSE 21

[Virūpākṣa] analyzes the divisions of the world-egg. Then he explains that [that world-egg] is attached to the background that is one's Self, which is the witness of [all] one's experience:

> **2.21. The world-egg has four divisions—Śakti, Māyā, matter, and earth.[1] Each division, again, is also manifold. All that is established in me.**

Śakti is the germinal essence. She is a cause, [reference to which] also implies its effect, that is, the pure course.[2] Māyā [is also a cause, reference to which implies its effect, that is] the mixed course.[3] Matter [likewise, is a cause, reference to which implies its effect, that is] the impure course.[4] Earth [again, is a cause, reference to which implies its effect, that is] that which is gross, such as experienced objects and the [fleshly] body.[5] Thus the world-egg has four divisions. Each of its divisions also contains cosmic realms, and so on.

"All that is established in me," that is, exists in the supreme awareness. The expression "established" is not intended to signify that which is past [as would be translated "was established"]. The establishment [of all things within me] pertains to all three times [past, present and future]. Thus Śiva.

Notes

1. The fourfold world-egg is discussed in a number of monistic Śaiva works. According to this scheme, there are four concentric eggs or spheres: the Śakti egg contains the Māyā egg, which contains the matter egg, which in turn contains the earth egg. Abhinavagupta treats this in various places. See *The Paramārtha-Sāra of Abhinavagupta with the Commentary of Yogarāja,* ed. J. C. Chatterji (Srinagar: Kashmir Pratap Steam Press, 1916), 4, 9–12. Also see the discussion, which observes precedents in the *Mālinīvijaya Tantra,* in Flood, *Body and Cosmology,* 122ff.

2. *śuddhādhva.* In this and the following two sentences, Vidyācakravartin presents a different application of the term *adhvan,* "course," to delineate a Trika hierarchy of three levels of the emanation of cosmic principles (*tattva*). To constitute the fourfold egg, this triad is followed by the fourth item, earth.

3. *miśrādhva.*

4. *śuddhetara.*

5. *Bhogāyatana* is a technical philosophical term for the fleshly body, as the locus that receives experience. Vidyācakravartin employs the same term to refer to *aṅga* in VAPV 3.37.

Thus ends the second book of the *Virūpākṣapañcāśikā* with the commentary, which demonstrates the unity of awareness.

Book 3

This work has so far demonstrated on the basis of both direct experience and reasoning that the Self is the essential nature of the universe. The determined fact that the Self is the essential nature of the universe must not be obscured either by doubt as to its possibility or misunderstanding.[1] Thus [Virūpākṣa] begins a third book [to eliminate such doubts].

Note

1. *asambhāvanayā viparītabhāvanayā vā.*

VERSE 22

One may [mistakenly] conceive that there is a distinction between the locus and that which is located in the statement "[All that] is established in me" [2.21]. [Virūpākṣa] removes [this error] by explaining that, to the contrary:

> **3.22. I am unitary and have the nature of unsetting awareness. I am established within lights and darknesses. And lights and darknesses are [established] within me who am unitary.[1]**

I "have the nature of unsetting awareness," that is, consist of awareness that is eternally arisen. I am "unitary," that is, without a second. I am established within lights, that is, what are ordinarily conceived [*abhimatānām*] as lights, including faculties such as the intelligence and [apparently external] lights such as the sun. Since I shine as them,[2] I am their inner nature. In the same manner, since I shine[3] as darkness, I am established as internal to darknesses such as the germinal essence,[4] Māyā and so on. This is the meaning: I, who have the nature of awareness, am established as internal [to every light and darkness]. Therefore, light can shine as light and darkness as darkness.

Those lights and darknesses are [likewise] established as internal to me. I have the nature of awareness and am entirely unitary. I burst into manifestation[5] as the universe that comprises both existence and nonexistence. Thus there is no scope for any objection that there is a distinction [between the locus and the located]. That is the purport.

NOTES

1. Besides articulating the ancient theme of the Self as the light of the world, Virūpākṣa may here be alluding specifically to Abhinavagupta, *Parātrīśikā Laghuvṛtti,* ed. Jagaddhara Zadoo Shastri (Srinagar: Research and Publication Department, Jammu and Kashmir Government, 1947), benedictory verse 1, 1:

> *yatra tejasi tejāṁsi tamāṁsi ca tamasyalam/*
> *tejāṁsi ca tamāṁsyetadvande jyotiranuttarm.*

Muller-Ortega, 204, translates:

> Where all splendors are in the light
> And all darknesses in the dark
> brilliant light and gloomy darkness!
> I praise that transcendent light.

2. *prakāśamānatvena.*
3. *prakāśamānatvāt.*
4. Why is the germinal essence described as a darkness? Perhaps Vidyācakravartin is just emphasizing its transcendent aspect. Rastogi has suggested to me that he is here referring to a Śaivasiddhāntin understanding of the germinal essence as closely related to Mahāmāyā.
5. *sphurāmi.*

VERSE 23

[Virūpākṣa] has established that there is no difference between consciousness on the one hand and, on the other, the generic subject and the object of knowledge. He now demonstrates that there is also no difference between the three types of manifestation [of individualized subjects], "He," "You," and "I."

> **3.23. The three [grammatical] persons are distinguished from each other as first, middle, and last. However, they are not external to me who am the Great Person and have the nature of recognitive apprehension.[1]**

The three [grammatical] persons are referred to by disjunctive designations as "He," "You," and "I." Thus they are "distinguished from each other," that is, they are exclusive of each other, "as first, middle, and last." None of these are external to me who have the nature of recognitive apprehension and who, as inclusive of them, am the Great Person. That is, there is no reality other than myself.

[Again,] the first and other [grammatical] persons are exclusive of each other. However, their creation and destruction depend upon me who have the nature of recognitive apprehension. They are experienced upon the background that is myself, as identical with myself. Thus they are not external to me.

Note

1. See the discussion of the monistic Śaiva theory of grammatical persons in the Introduction. Note that in Sanskrit theory the designations and the order of the grammatical persons are different than those in contemporary linguistics. That is, "He/She/It/They" is called the first person, and "I/We," the last person. What we call the second person is termed the middle person in Sanskrit.

VERSE 24

There may be this objection: You distinguish yourself as [the Sanskrit last person expressed] "I," as opposed to the first and middle persons. However, you [claim that you] have the nature of unlimited awareness. Since you thus [with the pronoun "I"] make a distinction [between yourself and the other persons], how can there be unity? [Virūpākṣa] answers:

> **3.24. Here [in ordinary unenlightened experience] there appears a differentiated form, "I," that is exclusive of "You" and the rest ["He," "She," and "They"]. These differentiated portions [of the Self] are not the eternal [Self explained in the statement in 3.22] "I am unitary. . . ."**

"Exclusive of 'You' and the rest ['He,' 'She,' and 'They']" means exclusive of the middle and the first persons. Thus there appears a differentiated form "I," which is the contrary of both of them. Like "He" and "You," that is a differentiated portion, a particular aspect of myself. It is not I, that is, it is not my ultimate form. The reason for this is that [my] eternal form [is as described in the statement] "I am unitary." That is, I am eternally an unlimited and unitary compact mass of awareness. The unitary essential nature of awareness is unlimited. Thus it is eternally my true essential form. The form [delimited by the Sanskrit last-person pronoun] "I" is adventitious because it is distinguished [from the other grammatical persons], that is, "He," and so on. It is only a particular aspect [of the true Self]. That is the meaning.

VERSE 25

Thus the subject, distinguished as an individual, is an aspect of myself. Similarly the object of knowledge, distinguished as a particular, is the emanation of my Śaktis. [Virūpākṣa] explains:

> **3.25. Places such as the sky and the earth and times such as day and night are the emanations of my two Śaktis that act to manifest and conceal the multitude of things.**

Sky and earth are places. Day and night are times. This pair of objects of knowledge [place and time] embraces all other objects of knowledge. They are the emanations of my two Śaktis that manifest and conceal the multitude of things.

The manifestation and the concealment of the entire collection of things are nothing but my two Śaktis. Indeed, the manifestation of things is nothing but the conjunction of my Śaktis. The concealment [of things] is nothing but the disjunction [of my Śaktis]. This was explained previously in "It . . . creates and destroys . . . through the conjunction and disjunction of the waves of its Śaktis" [2.13].[1]

Thus [place and time] are the emanations of the two Śaktis of the manifestation and the concealment of things. [Place and time] are established through the opposition of existence and nonexistence.[2] They do not exist as external to myself.[3] That is the meaning.

Notes

1. Making things rather convoluted, Vidyācakravartin is here identifying the two Śaktis said in this verse to manifest and conceal things with the mechanisms for the same described in VAP 2.13, respectively, the conjunction and disjunction of Śaktis. Perhaps his idea is that two Śaktis are responsible for the general processes of conjoining and disjoining Śaktis.

2. Place is the identification of *where* things do and do not exist, and time is the identification of *when.*

3. The true Self as God is the inclusive source of both place and time, and is thus not delimited by them, as has already been observed by Vidyācakravartin in VAPV 1.2.

VERSE 26

[Virūpākṣa] elaborates by providing details about other activities [of the Lord's Śaktis] that are implied by [the reference in 3.25 to the two activities of] manifestation and concealment:[1]

> **3.26. In concealment there is Smokey. In fulfillment there is Happiness. In manifestation there is Illuminator. In agitation there is Cosmic Pulsation.[2] In pervasion there is Omnipresent. Those are [my] five Śaktis.**

In the beginning there is my Śakti called Smokey. In "fulfillment," that is, flourishing, there is [my Śakti] called Happiness. In manifestation there is [my Śakti called] Illuminator. In agitation, that is, cosmic pulsation, there is [my Śakti] called Cosmic Pulsation. In pervasion there is [my Śakti] called Omnipresent. Those are my five Śaktis.

NOTES

1. See table 3.1 on the homologies made in VAP and VAPV 3.26–27 between Śaktis, their basic functions, elemental effects, and Śiva's cosmic acts.

2. *parispandā.* With the feminine ending, Virūpākṣa is referring to a goddess called Cosmic Pulsation.

VERSE 27

Since Śaktis are imperceptible, their natures are known from their effects. With this understanding, [Virūpākṣa] explains those [Śaktis] by reference to their principal effects:

> **3.27. Smokey is manifest in the earth, Happiness in water, Illuminator in fire, Cosmic Pulsation in the air, and Omnipresent in the sky. The universe is pervaded by those [Śaktis].[1]**

Since it is so [that the Śaktis are manifest in this encompassing collection of effects], the universe consisting of the six courses is "pervaded by," that is, comprehended within my five Śaktis beginning with Smokey. Thus it should be understood that [Virūpākṣa] has demonstrated that: [I] who have the nature of consciousness eternally perform the five cosmic acts. [The correlations between the activities of the five Śaktis just described and the five cosmic acts] are as follows: Manifestation is creation. Agitation is preservation. Withdrawal and concealment have already been indicated by their respective designations.[2] Pervasion is grace.

Notes

1. Cf. VAP and VAPV 4.47 on the proficiencies gained through the I-hood respectively possessing each of the five elements.

2. Actually, VAP and VAPV 3.26–27 have not mentioned the term "withdrawal" (*saṁharaṇa*) until now. It is evident that Vidyācakravartin is correlating withdrawal with the activity of the Happiness (*hlādā*) Śakti—that is, fulfillment (*puṣṭi*). Happiness is ordinarily experienced when the purpose of an action has been fulfilled. The idea in the present context is that the entire universe reaches satisfaction in returning to its source. Cf. the discussion of the identification of cosmogony and teleology in monistic Śaiva metaphysics, and an analogous tendency in some Western theories, in Lawrence, *Rediscovering God,* 98–102.

VERSE 28

Thus [my Śaktis through their various activities] such as manifestation accomplish this universe. However, through the mere touch of the Śakti of recognitive apprehension [this universe] again becomes a unitary ocean of awareness. [Virūpākṣa] explains this with four verses beginning with ". . . of which [She herself is] the integral nature . . ." [3.28] and ending with "Just as . . . entirely possessed . . ." [3.31].

> **3.28. My Śakti has the nature of recognitive apprehension. She makes [one recognize that] awareness, of which [She herself is] the integral nature, is the essential nature of the multitude of the objects of awareness. [She] makes [one recognize] that everything is my body.**

"My Śakti has the nature of recognitive apprehension [*vimarśarūpā*]" means that this consciousness [of mine] has the nature of recognitive judgment [*pratyavamarśarūpinī*].[1] "[She] makes [one recognize] that everything is my body" means that [She] establishes that the universe, beginning with [the emanated, lower] Śiva and ending with the earth, is identical with myself.

What [else should be said] about that [Śakti/consciousness]? [Vidyācakravartin explains:] "Awareness" is the consciousness that is the unitary essential nature of cognition. [Such awareness] is that "of which [Śakti is herself] the integral nature." That is, [awareness] is the substratum or background upon which [its own integral] nature [namely, Śakti, accomplishes] creation, destruction, and so on [the other cosmic acts].

[Virūpākṣa also states that] "She makes [one recognize that] awareness . . . is the essential nature of the multitude of the objects of awareness." This means that she definitively establishes that [awareness] is the real essential nature of the multitude of the objects of knowledge. In other words, she demonstrates on the strength of one's own experience that awareness remains unsublated until the end, as the essential nature of this entire multitude of objects of knowledge.

Thus my Śakti, who is consciousness and who has the nature of recognitive apprehension, establishes that the entire course, beginning with [the emanated, lower] Śiva, belongs only to me.

Note

1. This is a gloss of a term by a cognate synonym.

VERSE 29

For it is thus:

> **3.29. The flame of the fire that is my recognitive apprehension burns up everything that comprises the knower, knowledge and the object of knowledge; and leaves white ashes that have the nature of awareness.**[1]

"The flame of the fire that is my recognitive apprehension" is this recognitive apprehension that is experienced as pervading everything. That is, it is a flame that pervades all the courses. My recognitive apprehension as such "burns up everything that comprises the knower, knowledge and the object of knowledge." That is, it destroys in that very instant the particular aspects [of myself] such as the knower and so on.

[As a consequence], it leaves "ashes," that is, power-ashes[2] that are only existence.[3] [Those ashes/existence] "have the nature of awareness," that is, they consist of awareness in its universal nature.[4] [Likewise,] they are "white," that is, unsullied by the afflictions or what not.[5] For they are a compact mass[6] of inartificial bliss. That is, [my recognitive apprehension] makes those [the knower, knowledge, and the object of knowledge] into a unitary ocean [of awareness].

Notes

1. Burning, now taken up in VAP and VAPV 3.29–31, is an important literal and metaphorical theme in the tantric ritual process of purification. Burning

and also sprinkling are essential to the purification of the elements (*bhūtaśuddhi*) preparatory for worship and, more generally, characteristic of interiorized ritual practices. The two themes are treated together below, VAP and VAPV 4.51.

2. *vibhūti*. In his gloss Vidyācakravartin is making a pun, as *vibhūti* can mean both power/Lordship and the ashes, indicating that Lordship, with which Śiva and his devotees smear their bodies. Cf. the internalized interpretation of burning the universe to ashes in consciousness at TA 4.116–117, 3.735.

3. *sanmātrā*.

4. *prakāśasāmānyātmakam*. He is distinguishing awareness as a universal from the limited knower, knowledge, and object of knowledge, which are particulars. Cf. VAPV 1.2, with p. 67, n. 13; and VAPV 2.15, on the corporification of all things through seeing them in their universal nature.

5. The *Yoga Sūtra* presents the classic treatment of spiritual afflictions (*kleśas*). See YS 2.2–3, 139–140.

6. That is, an unbreakable realization.

VERSE 30

There may be this objection: It is proper that the recognitive apprehension [of the Self] immediately leads to the destruction of differentiation between the aspects [of the Self] that are objects of knowledge. However, some differentiation between those aspects that are individual knowers never ceases. Recognitive apprehension is an action. The agents [who perform] that [action, must be] differentiated from each other. [Virūpākṣa] answers:

> **3.30. When [everything that comprises the knower, knowledge, and the object of knowledge] has been [only partially] consumed by a weak fire of my recognitive apprehension, there [remains] a delusional appearance of the multitude of individuals. That [delusional appearance of the multitude of individuals] appears like ashes that contain charcoal.**

[The subject of the first clause, namely] everything that comprises the knower, knowledge, and [the object of knowledge] has already been stated [in 3.29]. [Here Virūpākṣa supposes that that] "has been [only partially] consumed by a weak fire of my recognitive apprehension." That is, there remains differentiation of the aspect "I," [as might be expressed] "I have recognitively apprehended." One has been possessed[1] by my recognitive apprehension. However, that [recognitive apprehension] does not shine fully[2] as Śakti, which is a fire [that consumes all differentiations].

Therefore, there is an appearance "of the multitude of individuals." That is, there is the conception [of a limited] "I" distinguishing [each] of the multitude of individual subjects. What [else should be said] about that [appearance of the multitude of individuals]? It is "delusional," that is, obscured by reason of its differentiation. Although objects of knowledge have been withdrawn, an aspect of objectivity still remains. "That [delusional appearance of the multitude of individuals] appears like ashes that contain charcoal." That is, it is experienced like a heap of ashes within which remains subtle charcoal.

NOTES

1. *ākrānta.*
2. *anatiprakāśita.*

VERSE 31

[Virūpākṣa] explains what to look for if the fire is intense:

> **3.31. Just as a forest, city, and so on, are entirely possessed by fire, so the universe [is entirely possessed] by me. [Thereby] having shaken off manifold diversity, [the universe] indeed assumes a unitary form.**

"By me" means by the one who has the essential nature of recognitive apprehension, which solely consists in the withdrawal of all diversity. "The universe" is that which begins with [the emanated, lower] Śiva and ends with the earth. "Entirely possessed" means recognitively apprehended without a remainder. This is just like when a forest, city, and so on, are entirely possessed by a fire. "Manifold" means multifarious. "Diversity" means mutual distinction. "Having shaken off [this manifold diversity]" means having submerged into myself. "Assumes a unitary form" signifies that [the universe] becomes a unitary compact mass of awareness. With the word "indeed," he points out that this is established in everyone's experience [if they discern it properly].

VERSE 32

[Virūpākṣa] has explained that, when the universe is totally possessed by recognitive apprehension, there is a lysis of all delusions of multiplicity. He now meticulously describes that way toward the total possession [of the universe]:[1]

3.32. Knowledge is the internal essential nature of the object of knowledge. The knower is [the internal essential nature] of that [knowledge]. The unitary consciousness is [the internal essential nature] of that knowledge that has [been properly contemplated and therefore recognized in its internal] form as the knower.[2] I am [the internal essential nature] of that [unitary consciousness]. There is no other [more internal essential nature of myself].

According to this system, entities have two natures, the external and the internal. The first of these is gross and exclusive. It is not the true [essential nature]. The second, internal [essential nature] is subtle and inclusive. It is the true [essential nature].

This being so, the internal, true essential nature of an object of knowledge such as a pot is nothing but the knowledge "pot." This is because it is from that [knowledge] that the external form [of the pot] arises. [The external form] exists only as attached to the background that is that [knowledge]. Likewise, [the external form] dissolves back into that very [knowledge].[3]

The knower is the limited subject, that is, one who presumes an individual identity [*abhimantṛ*]. That [individual subject] is the internal essential nature of the knowledge of the pot, for in that it has its origin, existence, and dissolution.

[The statement that] "The unitary consciousness is [the internal essential nature] of that knowledge that has [been properly contemplated and therefore recognized in its internal] form as the knower" [may be explained as follows:] According to the method propounded [that is, identifying successively more internal essential natures], knowledge that is undifferentiated by objects of knowledge attains the state of a knower. Consciousness, which has the nature of recognitive apprehension, is the most internal essential nature [of that knowledge that has been recognized as the knower].

[Virūpākṣa next asserts that:] "I am [the internal essential nature] of that [unitary consciousness]. There is no other [internal essential nature of myself]." [This may be explained as follows:] Consciousness is defined as recognitive apprehension. When that aspect of recognitive apprehension submerges [back into its internal essential nature], there remains only the I, having the nature of abstract awareness. This has already been described in "It is explained to be a unitary 'I'" [2.10]. I, who have reached the summit, am alone the reality. There is "no other," that is, there is nothing that may be distinguished from myself [as a higher and more internal essential nature].

This is the purport: Immediately after an object contacts the senses, a conceptual construction arises, such as "This is a pot." Before that [construction] arises, a pot cannot be designated as a pot or as anything else. There is only knowledge, which is the internal essential nature of the object of knowledge. Similarly, the origin and destruction of knowledge depend entirely upon the knower. Thus the knower is the most internal essential nature [of knowledge]. By the same method, consciousness is [the internal essential nature] of the knower. The unitary I is the noncontingent essential nature of that consciousness. Therefore, it is indisputable that objects of consciousness, when entirely possessed by the fire of recognitive apprehension, assume oneness with awareness [a.k.a. the unitary I].[4]

Notes

1. The following section, VAP and VAPV 3.32–37, presents a complex scheme for contemplation of the subsumption of more sequential stages of a fivefold hierarchy of cognitive process into their less sequential substrata, and of homologies between various stages in the hierarchy. See the discussion of this section with tables in the Introduction, pp. 32–37.

2. *jñātṛtanoś.*

3. That is, the creation, preservation and withdrawal of the object of knowledge occur within knowledge itself.

4. All the items of the hierarchy—of the object of knowledge, knowledge, the knower, consciousness, and awareness/the unitary I—have been discussed previously, and we have been presented with contemplative reductions of various lower elements into the higher. However, only in this section are we introduced to the items as a fivefold telescoping hierarchy.

VERSE 33

Thus [Virūpākṣa] has demonstrated that the triad of the object of knowledge, and so on [the knower and knowledge] is not different from awareness. Now he explains that there is also no difference [in the ultimate perspective] between those [separate members of the hierarchy].[1]

> **3.33. I am without sequence. The knower, and so on [knowledge and the object of knowledge] are sequential. Consciousness is both sequential and nonsequential. The knower is like myself. Knowledge is like Śakti. The object of knowledge is like the triad [of the knower, knowledge, and the object of knowledge].**

[The statement] "I am without sequence" [may be interpreted as follows:] I am in my real nature abstract awareness.[2] I am absolutely without sequence in relation to the tetrad of consciousness, and so on [the knower, knowledge, and the object of knowledge], as well as in relation to myself. For, since I thread through everything, it is impossible that anything could be excluded from me.

"The knower, and so on [knowledge and the object of knowledge] are sequential." That is, the knower, knowledge, and the object of knowledge are grasped as excluding each other. Thus this triad is sequential.

"Consciousness is both sequential and nonsequential." That is, it is sequential in relation to the knower, and so on [knowledge and the object of knowledge]. However, it is nonsequential in relation to myself. Thus it has two forms.[3] These are the modes of understanding that belong to one who is enlightened.[4]

Actually, "The knower is like myself."[5] That is, since I am inclusive of the tetrad of consciousness, and so on [the knower, knowledge, and the object of knowledge], I am nonsequential. Similarly, the knower is inclusive of knowledge and the object of knowledge. Therefore, it is nonsequential in relation to both of those. It also nonsequential in relation to myself.

The statement "Knowledge is like Śakti" [may be explained as follows:] It is established that consciousness is sequential in relation to the knower, and so on [knowledge and the object of knowledge];[6] and nonsequential in relation to myself. Similarly, knowledge is sequential in relation to the object of knowledge[7] and nonsequential in relation to myself. Thus it is like Śakti.[8]

The statement "The object of knowledge is like the triad [of the knower, knowledge, and the object of knowledge]" [may be explained:] The object of knowledge is a triad comprising the knower and [its homologue,[9] that is] myself; knowledge and [its homologue] Śakti, and other objects of knowledge.[10] Thus it is like the triad.

[Virūpākṣa now explains the occurrence of sequence and the lack of sequence within the three classifications of the object of knowledge just mentioned:] The knower and myself are nonsequential. Similarly, the object of knowledge is not sequential in relation to us two. In the same manner, it is both sequential and nonsequential in relation to Śakti and knowledge. [By the same reasoning, the object of knowledge is sequential in relation to other objects of knowledge.]

However, the delusion that consciousness has the forms of both, in relation to both, has been refuted. For there is essentially no difference between the knower and myself, knowledge and Śakti, and the object of knowledge and the triad.[11]

This is the purport: In [the cognition] "This is a forest," the forest is inclusive in relation to the trees and the trees are inclusive in relation to the forest. There is no differentiation at all between them. Take the cognitions of mango and campaka.[12] The mango and campaka are inclusive in relation to the forest. That is, there is no differentiation [between them and the forest]. However, [the mango and campaka] are exclusive in relation to each other. Thus there is differentiation [between them]. Similarly, with regard to that which is being discussed: As [ultimately] awareness, there is no difference between individual things and the aggregate of them. However, [individual things] are distinct in relation to each other.

Therefore, that which is nonsequential is inclusive in relation to everything.[13] The items that have sequence or that have the two forms [sequence and lack of sequence] are exclusive. The unity of awareness is the ultimate reality. Differentiation appears only for the one who lacks recognitive apprehension.

Notes

1. This verse introduces a series of homologies between members of the fivefold hierarchy just presented, which aim ultimately to demonstrate the unity of all of them. For some reason, Vidyācakravartin has here omitted reference to the fourth item of the hierarchy, consciousness—although both the verse and his subsequent commentary include it. This verse and commentary present the greatest interpretive difficulties in the text. For some reason, the difficulties mainly relate to the term consciousness (*citi*).

2. I here follow the edition of T. Ganapati Śāstrī, 17, *niṣkṛtaprakāśa,* rather than that of Kaviraj, 14, *nikṛtaprakāśa.*

3. It is perplexing that consciousness is described in VAP and VAPV 3.32 as the unitary essential nature of the hierarchy of the object of knowledge, knowledge, and the knower; and that it is said in VAP and VAPV 3.33 to be sequential in relation to the same.

4. See the discussion of the various stages of enlightenment in VAP and VAPV 4.41–44.

5. Sthaneshwar Timalsina has suggested that the expression translated "actually" (*vastutastu*) indicates the mode of experience of the "completely enlightened" (*suprabuddha*), which is above that of the "enlightened" (*prabuddha*).

6. Again I follow T. Ganapati Śāstrī, 17, *citiḥ jñātrādyapekṣayā sakramā,* rather than Kaviraj, 14, *citijñātrādyapekṣayā sakramā.*

7. On this idea, see the quotation in VAPV 3.37, p. 110.

8. The pattern of homologizing higher and lower parts of the hierarchy, as well as other discussions in the VAP and VAPV (e.g., 4.48), indicate that Śakti is presented in the verse as an equivalent to consciousness. Likewise, Vidyācakravartin here explains Śakti as both sequential and nonsequential in the same manner that he has just explained consciousness.

9. I am using the word homologue rather than analogue, because VAP and VAPV 3.35 identifies the terms compared in VAP and VAPV 3.33.

10. The object of knowledge in this sense includes the subdivision of objects of knowledge in the ordinary sense, as well as the knower and knowledge, and their homologues.

11. This passage is quite difficult to interpret. Just previously, Vidyācakravartin has said that consciousness has two forms, sequential and nonsequential, respectively, in relation to the knower, knowledge, and the object of knowledge on the one hand, and myself on the other. Perhaps Vidyācakravartin now wishes to assert that consciousness, as an expression of the higher awareness (*prakāśa*)/I, is not bifurcated in relation to the separate components of each pair because the comparisons disclose underlying unities. Perhaps, as Rastogi has suggested, Vidyācakravartin is saying that because consciousness (referred to as Śakti) is identified with knowledge, it does not have two forms as itself and as knowledge. Perhaps we are missing the point entirely, or perhaps the text is corrupt.

12. The campaka is a tree.

13. I follow T. Ganapati Śāstrī, 18, *ataḥ sarvatrānuvṛtamakramatvam,* rather than Kaviraj, 14, *ataḥ sarvatrānuvṛtakramatvam.*

VERSE 34

[Virūpākṣa] explains this in further detail:

> **3.34. Indeed, there is no blue in [other visual objects] such as yellow. [However,] visual knowledge appears both in this [blue] and in those [other visual objects such as yellow]. Nevertheless that [visual knowledge] does not [appear in other types of knowledge such as the] auditory. [Again, however,] the knower is inclusive of both this [visual knowledge] and those [other types of knowledge such as the auditory].**

It has been stated that each object of knowledge is sequential in relation to other objects of knowledge. To illustrate this, he explains "Indeed, there is no blue in [other visual objects such as] yellow." This means: Indeed, when there is the experience of yellow, then there is no blue. Since objects of knowledge are exclusive of each other, they are likewise sequential in relation to each other.

It has also been asserted that "Knowledge is like Śakti" [3.33], that is, it is both sequential and nonsequential.[1] He illustrates this: "[However,] visual knowledge appears both in this [blue] and in those [other visual objects such as yellow]." "This" refers to blue. "Those" refers to yellow, and so on. [The statement] "Nevertheless that [visual knowledge] does not [appear in other types of knowledge such as the] auditory" [may be explained:] One knowledge is auditory, that is, hearing. Another is visual. [Knowledge] is thus both sequential and nonsequential. Therefore it is correct that "Knowledge is like Śakti."

It has likewise been said that "The knower is like myself" [3.33]. He explains that idea in the [statement in the present verse] that: "[Again, however,] the knower is inclusive of both that [visual knowledge] and those [other types of knowledge such as the auditory]." "This" refers to auditory [knowledge], and so on. "Those" refers to visual [knowledge, which has objects] such as yellow, blue, and so on.[2] Therefore, since the knower is inclusive in relation to everything, it is established that it is like myself.

Notes

1. T. Ganapati Śāstrī, 18, has *jñānaṁ śaktiriva.* This makes better sense than Kaviraj, 14, *jñānaśaktiriva.*

2. Vidyācakravartin has apparently made a slight mistake in reversing the referents of "this" and "those" in the verse.

VERSE 35

Since these facts have been determined, therefore:

> **3.35. One contemplates without conceptual construction that the knower is myself, that knowledge is Śakti, and that the object of knowledge is the triad. [These contemplations are respectively expressed:] "I am he," "That [knowledge] is that [Śakti]," and "That [object of knowledge] is the triad."**

"One contemplates without conceptual construction that the knower is myself," in the manner explained, as "I am he." That is, because one does not provide occasion for the arising of conceptual constructions, one meditates on the identity of the knower with awareness.[1] Because the subliminal tendencies for differentiation have ceased, [one maintains] an inner conviction that is firm. One thus realizes the proficiency characterized by the elimination of the delusion of differentiation between them [the knower and myself].

Similarly, "One contemplates without conceptual construction . . . that knowledge is Śakti," in the manner explained, as "That [knowledge] is that [Śakti]." That is, one firmly contemplates the nondifferentiation of Śakti and knowledge. One thereby realizes the proficiency that consists in the recognition of their nondifferentiation.

Likewise, "One contemplates [without conceptual construction] . . . that the object of knowledge is the triad," in the manner explained, as "That [object of knowledge] is the triad." It is difficult to overcome the delusion that there are differences between the object of knowledge and [1] awareness and the knower, [2] Śakti and knowledge, and [3] other objects of knowledge. [The one who contemplates as prescribed] instantly realizes the proficiency that consists in eradicating that delusion together with its root cause.[2]

[Virūpākṣa] has not employed a verb in the three sentences "I am he," "That [knowledge] is that [Śakti]," and "That [object of knowledge] is the triad."[3] [He] has disclosed that there is nothing but identity [between the items].[4] This identity of theirs is not something to be established. Rather, the preceptor's intention[5] is that, through the stated arguments, one recognizes that [identity] as eternally established.

Notes

1. Conceptual constructions (*vikalpa*) are understood to be the source of the differentiation of experience. Because one does not allow them to arise, one is able to realize the unity of the subject with Śiva/universal awareness.

2. The root cause referred to would seem to be conceptual constructions.

3. In Sanskrit these statements are made through the simple apposition of nouns in the nominative case. For example, "I am He" is expressed "*so'ham.*"

4. The idea is that the copula too much implies a process of identifying separate items. The items are actually the same.

5. *anusaṁhitam.*

VERSE 36

It is eternally the case that the knower assumes sequence only through accidental qualification. Therefore, it is eternally established that he is identical with awareness. [Virūpākṣa] explains:

> **3.36. The knower assumes exclusive appearances and becomes sequential in the flow of alternate phenomenal series.[1] As such, it is called the limited soul. From union with me, it can, like me, manifest nonsequentially.**

"The flow of alternate phenomenal series" [may be explained as follows:] Immediately after the phenomenal series of the focusing attention upon,[2] and the conceptual construction of blue, there flows the phenomenal series of the focusing attention upon, and the conceptual construction of yellow.

[The statement] "The knower assumes exclusive appearances and becomes sequential" [may be explained:] The subject has cognitions that are mutually exclusive, such as "I am the manifestor of blue" and "I am the manifestor of yellow." Therefore it is sequential. When it assumes sequence in this way, it is called the limited soul. In reality it is Śiva. It is designated as a "limited soul" only with regard to that limited duration [defined by sequence].

"From union with me" [it is recognized that] whatever sequence [accrues] to me is due only to accidental qualification by objects of knowledge. In reality, I am inclusive [and therefore undifferentiated throughout every phenomenal series, such as of] blue and yellow, because I manifest them. I always have the nature of awareness, which is inclusive of everything. Such being my nature, I am the supreme awareness. Union with me is a merging having the character of the recognitive apprehension of reality.[3]

From that [union, the limited soul] "can, like me, manifest nonsequentially." That is, just as awareness eternally shines without sequence, so also [in reality] does the individual knower. [In reality, the individual knower] shines without sequence, as identical with awareness even while in the state of knowing [alternate phenomenal series] such as of yellow, and so on.

Therefore, when one is enlightened and [thereby] has intercourse[4] with the universe, one is Śiva. However, when one has intercourse with particular objects, one is an individual subject. There persists a delusion that there are only these two forms [of knowing] and that, therefore, the subliminal tendencies of a limited soul [whose life involves constant intercourse with particular objects] will always remain.[5] [Virūpākṣa] has completely refuted that [delusion]. The stated position is that one has the essential nature of Śaṅkara even while in the condition of knowing [particular objects] such as yellow. [That Śaṅkara] has the nature of a nonsequential, perfectly complete,[6] unitary compact mass of awareness. This is the instruction.

Notes

1. *Santāna,* "phenomenal series," is a term used in Yogācāra Buddhism to refer to the coherent flow of moments of consciousness.

2. *saṁkalpa.* I am here following Gerald Larson's gloss of this term in *Encyclopedia of Indian Philosophy,* vol. 4, *Sāṁkhya,* 38.

3. The word translated as "merging" is *saṁsparśa.* This word literally means "touching," as does *vimarśa* and cognates, which I translate as "recognitive apprehension."

4. *pratiyogitva.*

5. The supposition, as I understand it, is that it is impossible to maintain identity with Śiva while one is knowing particular objects of experience.

6. *paripūrṇa.* On the concept of "complete" (*pūrṇa*)/"completeness" (*pūrṇatva*), see VAP and VAPV 4.44, and p. 120, n. 7.

VERSE 37

The two categories of knowledge and the object of knowledge, when taken to be separate from the knower, are conceptual constructions. [Such conceptually constructed] knowledge and object of knowledge persist only for that limited duration that there is a lack of recognitive apprehension. Once recognitive apprehension is engendered, neither is any longer taken to be external to awareness. [Virūpākṣa] explains:

> **3.37. Objects of knowledge, such as the [fleshly] body and [other external] objects, enter knowledge. [Knowledge] is [thereby] penetrated by their sequence. By way of knowledge, the [object of knowledge] dissolves in the knower and takes on its character.**

"Objects of knowledge" are [illustrated in the phrase] "such as the [fleshly] body and [other external] objects." That is, they comprise the locus of experience, namely, the [fleshly] body; and objects of experience, such as yellow.[1]

[The words] ". . . Enter knowledge. [Knowledge] is [thereby] penetrated by their sequence" [may be explained as follows:] The object enters knowledge as its accidental qualification. [Knowledge] thereby assumes the form [of the object]. This accords with the principle "Knowledge is itself without form. Its particularity comes only from the object."

When there is no longer interest in cognizing, the operations of the sense organs cease. Then [the object] is realized to have the nature of knowledge, [as might be expressed] "The knowledge of yellow has occurred to me." Now [the statement] "By way of knowledge, the [object of knowledge] dissolves in the knower" [may be explained:] [The object of knowledge] follows the way of knowledge. On the occasion of the dissolution of knowledge, it dissolves in the knower. Having dissolved in this manner [in the knower, the object] "takes on its character." This is just like when foam dissolves in a wave. By way of the dissolution of the wave, [the foam dissolves] in the ocean. That is, it recurs to its actual identity with that [ocean].

According to this system, phenomenal multiplicity[2] is nothing but the bursting forth[3] of awareness. It consists in the differentiation of that [awareness] as the creation, preservation and [withdrawal] of all entities, beginning with [the emanated, lower] Śiva. Therefore nothing is experienced, demonstrable or even possible that is external to awareness.

The conceptual constructions of [a separate] knower, knowledge, and so on [object of knowledge] have their emergence from that [awareness], while remaining undifferentiated from it, just as waves and so on [have their emergence from the ocean while remaining undifferentiated from it]. That [emergence from awareness] is the being[4] of things [that are classified as] as the knower, and so on [knowledge and the object of knowledge]. The creation, and so on [preservation and withdrawal] of those [things] consist in the differentiation of that [awareness or being].

Identity with Śiva is nothing but the recognitive apprehension of this fact. Enlightenment is strong recognitive apprehension.[5] Bondage is the lack of recognitive apprehension. This is the essence of the teaching.

Notes

1. Although in the unenlightened state the fleshly body is the locus of experience, it also an object of experience like others.
2. *prapañca.* On this term, see below, VAPV 4.50, and p. 125, n. 2.
3. *sphuraṇa.*
4. *sattā.*
5. *amando vimarśaḥ.*

VERSE 38

[The verse] beginning [in the Sanskrit] "first, middle" [3.23] has already refuted the objection that there is a diversity of knowers which are the referents of the conceptions "He," "You," and ["I"]. Similarly, an objection might be made that there is a diversity of objects of knowledge, which are the referents of memory and [other modes of experience]. [Virūpākṣa] refutes that objection:

> **3.38. I, who am free,[1] manifest the universe as "That," "This," and "This is that" [respectively] due to the force of memory, direct experience, and recognitive synthesis.[2] And these are differentiated from each other through conceptual exclusion.**

From the force of memory, there is "That." From the force of direct experience, there is "This." Recognitive synthesis is recognition. From the force of that there is "This is that." "The universe" is that which begins with [the emanated, lower] Śiva.

"I, who am free, manifest" means that I, who am agentially self-determinative, create. How? [Virūpākṣa explains:] "And these are differentiated from each other through conceptual exclusion." That is, they are differentiated by their exclusion of each other. The word "And" indicates that they are also undifferentiated from each other. Such is the majesty of the one who is free. Exclusion of one another is reciprocal closure. Through that [exclusion], I create [the universe] as differentiated.

When the arguments that have been propounded bring about recognitive apprehension, and exclusion is eliminated, then [the universe is recognized] to be undifferentiated. Exclusion consists of numerous closures [between things]. Recognitive apprehension is solely of the nature of devouring [those closures]. Indeed, when recognitive apprehension diminishes, then [conceptions] arise that consist in exclusion, such as "That," "This," and ["This is that"]. However, when recognitive apprehension is brought about, particularities such as "That," and so on, dissolve.[3] Thus awareness has absolute sovereignty. That is the meaning.

Notes

1. *svairī.*

2. "This is that" is the typical expression of recognition (*pratyabhijñā*). It is significant that Virūpākṣa here chooses *anusaṁhiti,* an etymological and semantic equivalent of *anusaṁdhāna,* as a synonym for recognition.

3. The Śaiva philosophy discloses a subtle form of recognitive apprehension underlying the artificial distinctions of direct experience, memory and recognition. See the explanations of memory and recognitive synthesis below, VAP and VAPV 3.39, and pp. 113–114, nn. 1, 4.

VERSE 39

The proponent of differentiation does not accept that the differentiations "That," "This," and ["This is that"] have their origin, destruction, and [persistence] as undifferentiated from that [awareness]. Following the method already propounded, [Virūpākṣa] makes an argument that refutes [such a philosopher] by adverting to awareness as the background [of all differentiations]:

> **3.39. The wise know: Memory is the manifestation of a [past] direct experience [expressed] "That." [Direct experience is the manifestation] of an object. Recognitive synthesis [is the manifestation] of the two together. This triad [of manifestations]**

would not be possible without myself, who am unitary and devoid of sequence.

Knowledge refers to an object, [as might be expressed] "This is blue." "Memory is the manifestation of a [past] direct experience." That is, it is the manifestation [of the past experience that originally] referred to an object such as blue. From the reference to the object as "That," we recognitively apprehend the past experience which is the root of memory.[1]

[The word] "manifestation" [from the first statement] is carried down as applying to [the second statement, which has the terse expression] "of an object."[2] The meaning is that direct experience is the manifestation of an object.

"The two together" refers to both memory and direct experience. On the occasion of the synthesis of a [presently experienced] object with one formerly known, the two [memory and direct experience] become a single cognition. This synthesis is explained to be recognition.[3]

"This triad [of manifestations]," which is sequential, "would not be possible without myself, who am unitary and devoid of sequence." That is, it would be impossible without that unitary awareness which experiences and thus threads through all cognitions. One might not agree that awareness is the nonsequential recognitive synthesizer of everything. However, then [without that awareness, the triad of manifestations] that is understood [*abhimata*] to be sequential, referred to by "That," "This," and ["This is that"], would be [impossible]. It would be like a painting without a background surface.[4]

Notes

1. According to the Pratyabhijñā philosophy, memory, like all other cognitive processes, is actually constituted by a subtle form of recognition. The demonstrative "that" expresses that an item of previous experience is recognitively apprehended (or synthesized) *as having been previously experienced.* Besides this qualification, memory also involves the recognitive apprehension of the *similarity or correspondence between the memory and the original experience.* See Lawrence, *Rediscovering God,* 123–129. Just as what is in ordinary, ostensibly unenlightened parlance described as recognition identifies an object presently perceived with its past instance known in memory—the subtle form of recognition present in memory like all other experiences depends on a subtle form of memory. That is the "a priori" memory of Supreme Speech or semantic intuition (*pratibhā*). Subtle recognition is nothing other than the reexperience of that subtle memory. Ibid., 91–92.

2. This sort of implicit repetition of components of sentences is a common stylistic feature of Sanskrit texts.

3. To avoid redundancy in this passage, I have not included the usual "recognitive" with "synthesis" in translating *pratisaṁdhāna and anusaṁdhāna.*

4. The Self/Śiva is the recognitive synthesizer (*anusaṁdhātṛ*) of memory, direct perception, and ordinary recognitive synthesis (*anusaṁdhāna*). Vidyācakravartin now uses the same expression, *anu-saṁ-dhā,* employed in VAP and VAPV 3.38, to point to the subtle recognition constituting all experience. In the Śaiva idealism, such subtle recognition is ultimately God's reexperience or recognition of himself. For understanding this section, also see, the discussion in the Introduction, pp. 32–37, of the subsumption of difference and sequence.

VERSE 40

Since it is so, therefore:

> **3.40. Having shined[1] as if differentiated, the collection of objects reaches its sunset[2] in me, its manifestation having stopped. As one with my illumination,[3] it subsists [within me] like a river [subsists after merging] within the ocean.**

The collection of objects is said to shine as if differentiated because in actuality differentiation is impossible. When the knowledge "this blue" has ceased, the blue has reached its sunset. Thus its manifestation has stopped. It submerges into awareness. So it exists "as one with my illumination." In the end, therefore, the collection of objects comes to have the nature of awareness. That is the meaning.

NOTES

1. *bhātvā.*

2. I am glossing *astamitam* as "reaches its sunset" to give more force to the metaphor of setting. The significance of this metaphor is indicated by the linkage of the expression here with the description of *prakāśa,* "awareness," as *anastamita,* "unsetting," in the first verse of the book, VAP 3.22.

3. *madbhānaikātmyena.*

Thus ends the third book of the *Virūpākṣapañcāśikā* with the commentary, which is about recognitive apprehension.

Book 4

Now begins the fourth book, on powers.[1] The first section consists of four verses, beginning with [the verse that begins in the Sanskrit] "established within myself." It explains the modes of experience of the unenlightened and [other types of subject], with regard to the display of powers. In this connection, there are five types of subject: the unenlightened, the almost enlightened, the enlightened, the almost completely enlightened, and the completely enlightened.[2]

Notes

1. *Vibhūtiskandha.* The third chapter of the *Yoga Sūtra,* the *Vibhūtipāda,* likewise focuses on powers. YS, 3, 277–395. The recitation of the "Siddhi Skandha" of the VAP is enjoined in the *Kailāsasaṁhitā* of the *Śiva Purāṇa,* 19.42–45, 4:1756.

2. There are related lists of types of subjects in texts such as the *Svacchandra Tantra,* the *Mālinīvijaya Tantra,* and the *Tantrāloka.*

VERSE 41

[Virūpākṣa begins to] analyze these [various subjects' modes of] experience:

> **4.41. The collection of cosmic realms is established within myself. However, for those who have worldly existence, it appears as if external to me due to Māyā. Then, for those who have [only] a foot in worldly existence, it can, through Wisdom, be [experienced as both] internal and external.[1]**

[The assertion that the collection of worlds is] "established within myself" means that it is attached to the background that is myself. For, according to the arguments propounded, it has the nature of awareness. "The collection of cosmic realms" is the *maṇḍala* of cosmic realms, beginning with the unsupported and ending with the fire of time.[2] For those who have worldly existence, that [collection of worlds] appears as if external to me. Worldly existence is the experience of differentiation. Those who have that [experience of differentiation] are those who hold doctrines such as Sāṁkhya. The cause of that [experience of differentiation] is expressed [in the phrase] "due to Māyā." Māyā is the experience of the undifferentiated reality as if it were differentiated.

"Those who have [only] a foot in worldly existence" are those who do not have worldly existence, but who still have a foot in it, in the form of subliminal tendencies of that [worldly existence]. Those who have [only] a foot in worldly existence are Wisdom Subjects,[3] who have entered the lower level of *samādhi* with objective discernment.[4] For them [the collection of worlds] "can . . . be [experienced as both] internal and external." That is, it appears as internal, in forms such as intentionality;[5] and also as if differentiated [externally]. The cause of that [experience as both internal and external] is expressed [in the phrase] "through Wisdom," which means through Pure [Wisdom].[6]

Notes

1. Those who have worldly existence (*bhavin*) are mentioned in IPK and IPV 3.2.10, 2:253–254. On these terms also see Kṣemarāja's *Netratantrodyota,* in Vraj Vallabh Dwivedi, ed., *Netratantram [Mṛtyuñjaya Bhattārakah], With the Commentary Udyota of Kṣemarājācārya* (Delhi: Parimal Publications, 1985), chapter 16.

2. *kālāgni.* Vidyācakravartin is referring to this earth as the fire of time. On *kālāgni,* also see VAP and VAPV 4.51, and p. 127, n. 1.

3. *vidyāpramātṛ.* These are subjects who exist at the level of the cosmic principle of Pure Wisdom (*śuddhavidyā*).

4. *Samprajñāta samādhi* is described in YS, 1.17, 54. It is a lower stage of *samādhi* in which there is concentration on some kind of object. This is also interpreted as *savikalpa* ("with conceptual construction") and *sabīja* ("with a seed") *samādhi.*

5. *saṁkalpa.*

6. Pure Wisdom (*śuddhavidyā*) is the knowledge that one is the emanator and controller of the universe, disclosed by the revealing of Śakti (*śaktyāviṣkaraṇa*), including the Pratyabhijñā arguments for transcendental self-recognition/omnipotent agency. It has the typical expression, "I am this." See Lawrence, *Rediscovering God,* 62–65. Virūpākṣa and Vidyācakravartin advert to Pure Wisdom as inspiring the contemplative internalization of the universe.

VERSE 42

Now, of those two, the one who should be taught about consciousness is the bound creature for whom [the collection of worlds] appears as external.

> **4.42. [The first type] believes that the individual subject is sentient, and that the object of knowledge is insentient and other [than the subject]. Deluded by Māyā, he is a limited individual who has worldly existence. He should be enlightened by the wise.**

[The statement that] "the individual subject is sentient" means that [that subject] has the nature of consciousness. [The statement that] "the object of knowledge is insentient" means that it does not have the nature of consciousness. [According to this erroneous view, the object is] "other" [than the subject]. The one who believes [this view] "is deluded by Māyā." Māyā is the experience of something presumed to be [*abhimate*] an object as insentient and other [than oneself].[1] One who is deluded by that [Māyā] has not recognized his essential nature. Therefore such a one is a "limited individual who has worldly existence," that is, a bound creature.

[The statement that] "He should be enlightened by the wise" means that he should be instructed by gurus who have recognized their essential nature. As it has been said in the scriptural tradition:

> In other tantras are people who are liberated through the destruction of both *dharma* and *adharma*. In this system they are proclaimed to be Rudra-individuals,[2] and free from time and karma.[3]

Those such as Tārkikas[4] and Mīmāṁsakas distinguish consciousness from objects of consciousness. They have not recognized their essential nature as consciousness.[5] It has been taught that they are not eligible for instruction in the noble philosophy.[6] According to the Śruti, it is a sin to disclose[7] the Doctrine of Consciousness to them. [As the Śruti says]: "The one who explains without justification will obtain an untimely death." Therefore the meaning of the Doctrine of Consciousness should be hidden. This command of Śiva should not be violated in any way.[8]

Notes

1. It is important to understand the connection between this discussion and the original problem of the deluded egoistic identity (*abhimāna*) of Indra and all unenlightened individuals. It is Māyā that deludes one to presume an egoistic identity separate from objects, rather than correctly to perceive them as one's body.

2. *rudrāṇu.*

3. It is not clear to whom this quotation is referring.

4. Tārkikas are logicians, likely Naiyāyikas or others relying on the Nyāya methods.

5. This is obscure, and the text may be corrupt here. The most obvious interpretation of *apratyabhijñātacetyaviviktacitsvarūpānām* would appear to be "have not recognized their essential nature as consciousness that is distinguished from objects of consciousness." My translation is an attempt to maintain consistency with what was explained earlier in the verse and commentary.

6. *sacchāstra.*

7. *prakāśana.*

8. Evidently, some stubborn philosophers fall outside the purview of the program of universal redemption discussed in the Introduction.

VERSE 43

Thus the modes of experience that belong to the unenlightened and the almost enlightened have been explained distinctly. Now [Virūpākṣa] distinguishes that [mode of experience] that belongs to the enlightened:

> **4.43. This-ness is insentience. I-hood is sentience. The one who has feet in both knows them in the apposition "This is I."[1]**

"The one who has feet in both" is one who has subliminal tendencies of both worldly existence and the transcendence of worldly existence.[2] Due to the force [of those subliminal tendencies that person], abides in the conditions of both diversity and nondiversity.

"This-ness is insentience" means that the insentient entity is experienced as "This." "I-hood is sentience" means that the entity I is experienced as "noninsentient."

[The one who has feet in both] "knows them in the apposition. . . ." That is, he submerges the aspect of their differentiation through [contemplatively] superimposing[3] nondifferentiation. [Such knowledge is expressed]: "This is I." [In other words,] he perceives the two like his own body. This is the state of Īśvara.[4]

Notes

1. *Sāmānādhikaraṇya* is a technical term from Sanskrit grammar for apposition. It literally means "the condition of having the same locus." The apposition "This is I" or "I am this" is normally taken as characteristic of the realization of Pure Wisdom (*śuddhavidyā*). (There are various schemes for relating the experiences of "I" and "this" at the upper levels of the cosmic hierarchy.) We may question how this state contrasts with that described in VAP and VAPV 4.41 of the who has a foot in worldly existence (*bhavapadin*) and, through Pure Wisdom, understands the universe as both internal and external. It seems that Vidyācakravartin is here talking about a state in which internality and unity prevail more greatly over externality and differentiation.

2. Subliminal tendencies (*saṁskāra*) do not pertain only to what is unspiritual. Practice creates positive, spiritual subliminal tendencies. As is stated in the *Yoga Sūtra,* the subliminal tendency generated from wisdom (*prajñā*) prevents other subliminal tendencies. YS 1.50, 129.

3. *āropaṇa.*

4. The fourth of the thirty-six cosmic principles.

VERSE 44

[Virūpākṣa] now analyzes the modes of experience of the almost completely enlightened and the completely enlightened.

> **4.44. For those who have transcended worldly existence through abstract knowledge[1] [the object of knowledge] shines as submerged in the inner state. However, through the transmental[2] [the object of knowledge shines as] both submerged in, and emerged from me, who am complete.**

The transcendence of worldly existence is abstraction,[3] the character of which is the experience of nondifferentiation. For those who have [transcended worldly existence, the object of knowledge] shines as submerged in "the inner state," that is, in its essential nature, "I." This means that the object of knowledge, which is the referent of the conception "this," is experienced to be unmanifest.[4] Due to what cause? [He answers:] "Through . . . [abstract] knowledge," that is, Śakti, which is recognitive apprehension. This is the state of Sadāśiva,[5] in which this-ness is covered by I-hood and is indistinct.[6]

Next [Virūpākṣā describes] the one who is fully enlightened and, therefore, "complete."[7] For that one, the object of knowledge shines "as both submerged in, and emerged from me," that is, awareness. That is to say, [the object] is experienced in two ways, as both unmanifest and manifest. The waves in the ocean are both unmanifest and manifest, but in all conditions there is only the ocean. Similarly, the universe beginning with [the emanated, lower] Śiva appears, while remaining in essential nature only me. Though [apparently] separate from me, it disappears in me.

The cause of the recognition of reality in this manner is expressed [by the phrase] "through the transmental." The transmental is nothing but abiding in one's essential nature. As it has been said in the scriptural tradition: "The transmental should be known as that [condition] in which the mind is not known."[8]

Notes

1. *kevalayā dṛśā. Kevala dṛk* and the term used by Vidyācakravartin, *kaivalya,* refer to the salvific "isolation" of the self from matter in the Sāṁkhya and Yoga traditions. Though this is the background to the usage of the terms in the VAP and VAPV, the state described here is not exactly one of isolation. Rather, as Virūpākṣa explains, in it "worldly existence shines . . . as submerged in the inner state." This is an experience of only transcendence, whereas the highest realization is of the monistic Self/Śiva as pervading both transcendence and immanence.

2. *Unmanā,* the "transmental," is a Śaiva and Śākta term for a high state of spiritual consciousness. See the discussions of *unmanā* in Gopinath Kaviraj, *Bhāratīya Saṁskṛti aur Sādhanā,* 2 vols. (Patna: Bihar Rastrabhasa Parisad, 1977–1979), 1:148, 1:294. For Kaviraj, *unmanā* represents the highest stage of *jīvanmukti.*

3. *kaivalya.*

4. *nimiṣita.* See the explanation of *unmeṣa* and *nimeṣa* on p. 89, n. 13.

5. The third of the thirty-six cosmic principles.

6. *asphuṭa.*

7. "Complete" (*pūrṇa*)/"completeness" (*pūrṇatva*) is a basic epistemological, metaphysical and psychological concept in Pratyabhijñā thought—which overlaps with those of absolute egoity and the subsumption of difference and sequence. As illustrated below, VAP and VAPV 4.52, the Pratyabhijñā conceives the quest for enlightenment as a process of overcoming erroneous "incomplete" knowledge with the "complete knowledge" that is ultimately Śiva's self-recognition. On this epistemology of error and rectification, see my "The Plurality and Contingency of Knowledge, and its Rectification According to the Pratyabhijñā," and Navjivan Rastogi, "Theory of Error According to Abhinavagupta," *Journal of Indian Philosophy* 14 (1986): 1–33. Metaphysically, completeness describes the compact unity of ultimate reality. In philosophical psychology, including tantric understandings of aesthetics, completeness describes the self-sufficient bliss or enjoyment of the Self/Śiva, which is the telos of all limited and often misguided human desire. See IPVV 1.5.11, 2:174–179. For a general overview of the concept, also see Bettina Baumer and Debabrata Sensharma, "Pūrṇa," in *Kalātattvakośa,* vol. 2, *Concepts of Space and Time,* 429–447.

8. Chakravarty has suggested to me that this statement is from the *Yogavāsiṣṭha.*

VERSE 45

Thus the progression[1] of experiences has been taught. That yogin who contemplates[2] this realizes, through the transmental, the unwavering proficiency that is completeness. [Such a yogin] is said to be proficient, that is, completely enlightened. Through his mere intention, he displays whatever powers he desires [*abhimatānām*].[3] [Virūpākṣa] explains this with eight verses.

[With the first of these verses,] he expounds the manner in which one displays the lower proficiencies:

> **4.45. The yogin who firmly contemplates as being his Self—sun, moon, lightning, thunderbolt,[4] cloud, submarine fire, ocean, mountain, cave,[5] and forest—accomplishes their karmas.**

"Thunderbolt" means thunderstroke. [The expression that the yogin] "firmly contemplates as being his Self—sun," and so on, [means that he] firmly contemplates that they are his Self. The yogin who does this "accomplishes their karmas." The karmas that belong to the sun and the other entities, for example, illumining[6] the world, and so on, are established eternally. Through firmness of recognition, [the yogin] conducts [those karmas] to their completion, namely, the accomplishment of their purposeful actions.[7] That is the meaning.

This is the [deeper] purport: According to the stated position, [the yogin] himself exists in the forms of entities such as the sun. Due to weakness of recognitive apprehension, he is as if differentiated. Through strong recognitive apprehension, the subliminal tendencies for the delusion of differentition are removed. One then exists as identical with the universe. [One recognizes that] all proficiencies are eternally established as one's own. Through the firmness of one's recognition, they accomplish their purposeful actions.

Those who desire all-embracing proficiency [recognize that they] have the essential nature of perfectly complete, supreme awareness,[8] which is the essential nature of the universe. Thus their contemplation of identity with the sun, and so on, is undeviating. They bring [this contemplation of identity with the sun and other entities] to its completion, that is, the contemplation of their identity with the universe. This is what is the gurus explain.

Notes

1. *krama.*
2. *paryālocayato.*
3. See the discussion of the derivatives of *abhi-man* at the beginning of the text, pp. 62–63, n. 5. It is highly significant that Vidyācakrvartin here employs the

same term (in a surface sense of "desires") that he used to describe Indra's original false presumption that he was the Supreme Lord. Indra's conceit is not surrendered but rather transfigured into the genuine identity-conception of the Supreme Lord.

4. I have translated *taḍit* as "lightning," and *vajra* as "thunderbolt."

5. Cf. the identification of the Cave with Māyā in VAP and VAPV 4.49, and p. 124, n. 3. The interpretation of this verse as referring to an ordinary cave is uncertain, though it is supported by the references to the mountain, ocean, and so on.

6. *prakāśana.*

7. *arthakriyā.*

8. *paripūrṇaparaprakāśa.*

VERSE 46

4.46. A deity accomplishes a [particular] purpose. One who has that purpose firmly concentrates his I-concept on that [deity]. His purpose is instantly realized.[1]

"A deity," according to common usage, refers to one such as Heramba [a.k.a. Gaṇeśa], Bhāratī [a.k.a. Sarasvatī], Hari, Hara, and so on. That [a deity] "accomplishes a [particular] purpose," that is, produces an effect such as the destruction of obstacles, motivation for speech, preservation, destruction, and so on. "One who has that purpose" means one who has that objective, or who desires to accomplish that purpose. Such a yogin "firmly concentrates his I-concept on that [deity]." That is, he unwaveringly recognitively synthesizes his identity [with that deity]. "His purpose is instantly realized." That is, his purpose is accomplished without delay.

Note

1. VAP 4.46 is quoted in MMP, 47, 119.

VERSE 47

In this regard, [Virūpākṣa] now describes [several] proficiencies:[1]

4.47. The [five] elements have as their special characteristics [the actions of] bearing, accumulating, cooking, arranging, and being unobstructed. [Those elements] are possessed[2] **by the I-hood of the yogin. They thus bring about the action that he desires.**[3]

The earth element has the special characteristic of bearing. Water has the special characteristic of accumulating. Fire has the special characteristic of cooking. "Arranging" is the placing together of parts. Air has that special characteristic. "Being unobstructed" is expansion without restraint. Space has that special characteristic. These five elements are each firmly recognitively synthesized by the yogin as his Self. "They thus bring about the action that he desires." That is, they accomplish the karma, such as bearing, and so on, that he desires to accomplish.

Notes

1. VAP and VAPV 4.47–49 explain the possession by the I, and thereby the attainment of control over, all the thirty-six cosmic principles (*tattva*) emanated by and subordinate to the Supreme Śiva.

2. *niviṣṭa.*

3. Cf. VAP and VAPV 3.27, on correlations of the five elements with Śaktis and cosmic acts.

VERSE 48

4.48. Likewise, [the yogin] concentrates Śakti, which is consciousness, on the sense fields, the organs of action and knowledge, the mind, the I-am-ness, the intelligence, the unmanifest [i.e., matter], and the person.[1] He thus comes to possess their karmas.

I-am-ness is the I-concept. "[The yogin concentrates] Śakti, which is consciousness."[2] That is, following the method explained, [the yogin] concentrates the I-concept on the cosmic principles, beginning with the sense fields and ending with the person.[3] He "thus comes to posses their karmas," that is, he comes to possess the proficiencies [to perform] their various karmas.

Notes

1. *puṁsi,* that is, *puruṣa.*

2. I follow the reading *dhṛtacitiśaktiḥ* in T. Ganapati Śāstrī, 25, which corresponds to the verse, rather than *dhṛticitiśaktiḥ* in Kaviraj, 20. The expression *citiśakti,* usually translated as "power of consciousness," is used in YS 4.34, 463.

3. Vidyācakravartin has in effect equated Śakti and consciousness (*citi*) from the verse with I-am-ness (*asmitā*) and the I-concept (*ahaṁkāra*). The latter two terms are being used dialectically: At one level they refer to one of the three internal organs (like most of the *tattvas,* appropriated by the Śaivas from Sāṁkhya),

along with mind (*manas*) and intelligence (*dhī*, i.e., *buddhi*). However, they are transfigured as Śakti/divine egoity through deindividualization and identification with all the cosmic principles.

VERSE 49

> **4.49. [The yogin] similarly makes [that is, concentrates] his I-hood on attachment, causal necessity, time, [limited] knowledge, limited agency,[1] the Cave, Sarasvatī, Īśa, Sadāśiva, Śakti, and [the emanated, lower] Śiva.[2] [He thus comes to possess their respective karmas].**

The Cave is Māyā.[3] Sarasvatī is Pure Wisdom. This [action to obtain proficiencies is modified by the adverb] "similarly." [Thus the assertion that] "He thus comes to possess their karmas" is carried down [from 4.48].[4]

Notes

1. The first five items of the list, respectively, *rāga, niyati, kāla, vidyā,* and *kalā,* are the coverings (*kañcukas*) that obscure the true Self/Śiva in the limited individual.

2. Virūpākṣa has thus listed individually or in groups all the emanated cosmic principles from the lowest through that directly below the Supreme Śiva.

3. On the identification of the Cave (*guhā*) with Māyā, see TA and TAV 8.803, 9.138. On the symbolism of the cave, see Javier Ugaz Ortiz, "A Hermeneutics of the Symbolism of the Interior Domain (*Guhā* and *Hṛdguhā*)."

4. The same Sanskritic convention was noted earlier, at VAPV 3.39, and p. 113, n. 2.

VERSE 50

[Virūpākṣa] explains incidentally [the teachings] of those such as Śuka about the lesser proficiencies:

> **4.50. Indeed, in the writings of the sages Śuka, Vāmadeva, Kṛṣṇa, Dadhīci, and Vainya, identity with the universe is explained to be born of the yoga of identification with the elements.[1]**

"Born of the yoga of identification with the elements" means produced from contemplation on the five elements. "Identity with the universe" is possession of the form of phenomenal multiplicity, which consists of the five elements.[2] "In the writings of the sages" means in texts such as traditional histories,[3] and so on.

Among the proficiencies that have been explained, those that are not supreme are the [series of] proficiencies ending with [that resulting from concentration on identity with the] "cave" [4.49]. The other five that are supreme begin with [that which results from concentration on identity with] "Sārasvatī" [4.49].[4]

Notes

1. *bhūtātmayogaja.*

2. The word translated as "phenomenal multiplicity" is *prapañca.* This word is usually derived from the prefix *pra-* and the verb root *pac* or *pañc,* with the significance of expansion, multiplication, and manifestation. However, in some contexts such as the present, it has connotations of being fivefold. (Monier-Williams, *A Sanskrit-English Dictionary,* s.v., refers to the derivation of *pañcan,* "five," from *pac,* with the sense "to spread out the hand with its five fingers.") As has been indicated, the VAP and VAPV correlate the five elements with five Śaktis and the five cosmic acts. On the concept, also see Hemendra Nath Chakravarty, "The Pentadic Universe in the Shaivagamas," in *The Agamic Tradition and the Arts,* ed. Bettina Baumer (Delhi: Indira Gandhi National Center for the Arts, 1995) (online version at http://ignca.nic.in/ps_03005.htm, accessed on August 3, 2007).

3. *itihāsa.*

4. The break between the two groups is in the first Sanskrit line of VAP 4.49. It may be noted that the proficiencies that are not supreme come from concentration on identity with the cosmic principles at the impure and mixed levels of emanation, in the scheme presented at VAPV 2.21. The supreme proficiencies come from concentration on identity with the principles at the pure level.

VERSE 51

With two verses [Virūpākṣa] explains the two proficiencies that are preeminent among all proficiencies:

> **4.51. In burning the knots of [one's] bonds, strongly remember Śakti as blazing with crores of the fires of time.[1] In satiation, [strongly remember Śakti] as the embodiment of the shower of the stream of nectar.[2] Become [thereby] the guru of the universe.**

[The description] "blazing with crores of the fires of time" means: blazing as a net of unlimited brilliance that is capable of burning up all the courses, like the crores of the fires of time aroused[3] in the cosmic dissolution.

[The injunction] "In burning the knots of [one's] bonds, strongly remember Śakti" [may be interpreted as follows:] Purification may take the form of the burning of the bonds that are the six courses. In that [burning], you must uninhibitedly recognitively synthesize consciousness.

[The injunction] "In satiation, [strongly remember Śakti] as the embodiment of the shower of the stream of nectar" [may be interpreted as follows:] Purification may take the form of sprinkling. In that [sprinkling] strongly remember [Śakti] as consisting of the unbroken descent of thousands of oceans of nectar that are capable of traversing[4] all courses.[5]

By [the references to] burning and sprinkling, there is also implied[6] [the practice of] making whole.[7] This has been described by the excellent preceptor:

> O Mother! In the purification of the six courses your ladyship has the splendor of crores of the fires of time. In the sprinklings [you are] a shower of the stream of nectar. In making whole, [you are] dark, bending over from breasts that are firm masses. Those who meditate on you in this way become the gurus of the world.[8]

Thus making whole is defined as meditation on the universe as consisting of crores of desires,[9] and as the embodiment of one's chosen deity. This should be understood as the teaching.

[The exhortation] "Become the guru of the universe" [may be interpreted as follows:] You have performed the purification of the courses. Therefore, you should become the grace-bestowing guru, the eminent preceptor, of the entire universe.

This is the purport here: The purification is performed not only of the quantity of the six courses contracted as one's [fleshly] body, but rather of the entirety [of the six courses]. For, according to the stated position, every preceptor has the universe as his body. Indeed, preceptor-hood does not consist in having a body that is a particular body. Thus the purification of the universe must be performed by one who actually has the universe as his body.

Following the method of reasoning taught in [this] system,[10] one realizes the identity of the universe with awareness, and thus abides in one's essential nature. That [abiding in one's essential nature] is the burning of all the courses. Sprinkling is the relishing[11] of consciousness when one recognitively apprehends identity with awareness.

As the preceptor, glorious Yogīśvara has said:

> Recognition is a unitary compact mass[12] of recognitive apprehension. From the firmness [of that recognition] of awareness, there is making whole. [That making whole] is the revelation of supreme bliss.

Notes

1. *kālāgnikoṭi.* Here and below, this expression could also be translated with a more esoteric import as "in the point of the fire of time," referring to the location of the fire of time in the subtle physiology—characteristically the big toe of the right foot. On *kālāgni,* also see VAPV 4.41, and p. 116, n. 2.
2. *amṛtaughavṛṣṭimūrti.*
3. *prabuddha.*
4. *kramaṇa.*
5. As mentioned before, the contemplation of both burning and sprinkling is important to the purification of the elements (*bhūtaśuddhi*) preparatory for worship and generally of interiorized ritual practices. Virūpākṣa and Vidyācakravartin give a highly symbolic interpretation of these processes.
6. *Upalakṣyate* could also mean "characterized."
7. "Making whole" is one of a range of possible interpretations for the multivalent technical term of tantric ritual, *sakalīkaraṇa,* designating a process of divinization of the body related to *bhūtaśuddhi/nyāsa.* Other possible meanings are displaying the limbs of the deity, the realization of the deity with parts as opposed to without parts, empowerment, and the guru's imposition of mantric formulas on the body of the spiritual practitioner.
8. This is *Aṃbāstava,* in Vidvan N. S. Venkatanathacharya, ed., *Saundaryalaharī of Śrī Śaṅkarācārya with the Commentary of Lakṣmīdhara, Bhāvanopaniṣat with the Commentary of Bhāskararāya, and Devī Pañcastavī* (Mysore: Oriental Research Institute, 1969), 30, 308.
9. *saṁkalpa.*
10. *śāstra.*
11. *camatkāra.*
12. *ekaghana.* That is, it is an unbreakable state of realization.

VERSE 52

[Virūpākṣa] has thus taught the first of the supreme proficiencies, which is becoming a guru. Now he teaches the second:

4.52. Destroy incomplete knowledge by firmness of possession of complete knowledge.[1] According to your intention, create, preserve, withdraw, conceal, and illumine the worlds.

This is the essence, the crux of all your lessons. There are only two [types of knowledge: incomplete and complete. There is no other [sort of knowledge]. "Complete knowledge" is that which is authentic.[2] "Incomplete knowledge" is that which is inauthentic because it is contingent.[3] Having firmly established oneself in [complete knowledge], "destroy" [incomplete knowledge]. That is, eradicate [incomplete knowledge] every moment [that it may arise] through the firmness of recognitive synthesis.

When you are thus destroying [incomplete knowledge], "according to your intention, create, preserve, withdraw, conceal and illumine the worlds."[4] [This exhortation may be explained:] Conceptual constructions are the Śaktis that manifest entities. They are believed to conceal the respective essential natures [of entities]. However, for one who persists in this way [using complete knowledge to destroy incomplete knowledge], those [conceptual constructions] are recognized as creating, [preserving, withdrawing, concealing and illumining] the universe.[5] They reveal one's Supreme-Lordship, which comprises the totality of all the proficiencies. Thus, eternally abide in your essential nature. This is the sum of all the teachings.

With the verses beginning with ". . . accomplishes their karmas" [4.45], [Virūpākṣa] displays[6] indifference toward the powers, starting with those of "sun, moon" [4.45] and ending with that of "[the emanated, lower] Śiva" [4.49]. Then he reveals his preference by the approbation in his teaching [about the two highest powers, in the verses that contain the phrases] ". . . remember Śakti. . . . Become [thereby] the guru of the universe" [4.51]; and "Destroy incomplete knowledge . . . create . . . the worlds" [4.52]. Therefore, for one who has in this way recognized his essential nature, all other proficiencies are semblances.[7] One should not devote oneself [to realizing] them. [Virūpākṣa] teaches by implication that one should devote oneself [to realizing] the eternal recognitive apprehension that comprises the two preeminent proficiencies. Thus Śiva.

Notes

1. See VAP and VAPV 4.44, and p. 120, n. 7 on complete (*pūrṇa*) versus incomplete (*apūrṇa*) knowledge.
2. *vastubhūtām.*
3. *kādācitkatvād avastubhūtām.*

4. One becomes the Supreme Lord who performs the five cosmic acts.

5. That is, they are recognized to be Śaktis. The revealing of Śakti is here described in terms of the "purification of conceptual constructions" (*vikalpasaṁskāra*), which Abhinavagupta conceives as fundamental to the classification of spiritual practice called the *śākta upāya*. The Pratyabhijñā method can be understood as this sort of purification. See Lawrence, *Rediscovering God*, 60–65.

6. *prakāśanāt*.

7. *ābhāsa*.

VERSE 53

Now concluding the text, [Virūpākṣa] recounts:

> **4.53. Thus, having been enlightened, that Indra abandoned the impurity of his [presumed] sovereignty over the gods. Having possessed the Śakti principle, he perceived his own Self as Śiva.**

"Thus" [has the significance of drawing a conclusion from all the previous discussion, which may be summarized as follows]: Entities such as [the emanated, lower] Śiva had been presumed [*abhimate*] to be external to the body. The first book through arguments causes them to be recognized as the body.

The second book purifies [one's comprehension of the teaching that] the universe is the body. [This book] establishes through arguments that the universe is a compact mass of awareness. It thereby removes the delusion that there is a difference between possessor and possessed in one's relationship to the universe as one's body.

Thus it is established that one is the Self of the universe. There must be no mistakes [regarding this identity]. That is, there must be no errors such as a misunderstanding of it [or a doubt as to its possibility]. Therefore, the third book teaches the diverse modes of recognitively apprehending that one is the Self of the universe.[1]

The fourth book explains the display of the proficiencies. Two great proficiencies are being the guru of the universe and being Śiva. The unfaltering great proficiency is the recognition that both of those are eternally established.

"That Indra" has thus been "enlightened," that is, made completely to recognize such an identification with reality. He thus "abandoned the impurity of his [presumed] sovereignty over the gods." That is, he forsook the condition of a bound creature, defined by the contraction of one's supreme essential nature. [A contraction of Indra's essential nature was reflected in his original presumption that] "I am the king of heaven."

[The statement that] "He perceived his own Self as Śiva" may be interpreted as follows:] Śiva, who is the glorious and venerable preceptor, Lord Virūpākṣa, stood before him as the one who was enlightening him. Having thus been enlightened, [Indra] saw himself as him. This is because it is impossible that [Indra] could be other than Śiva, in the sense of being separate from his guru. There is not the slightest difference of degree between the knowledge of the enlightened and the enlightener. Rather, it has been established, without defects, that: I, perceptibly,[2] am none other than the Supreme Lord, who is the guru of this universe.[3] Thus Śiva.

Notes

1. See VAPV 1.intro., and p. 63, n. 10.
2. *sākṣāt.*
3. Cf. the translated excerpt from the *Akulavīratantra* on the state of *sahaja:* "He himself is the goddess, himself the God, himself the disciple, himself the preceptor; he is at once the meditation, the meditator and the divinity (meditated upon)." Dasgupta, *Obscure Religious Cults,* 196n.

Conclusion of the Commentary

Thus ends the fourth book on the powers, of the *Virūpākṣapañcāśikā,* with the commentary written by Vidyācakravartin, the great devotee of the Great Lord.

> Let this lucid commentary on the Fifty Verses be studied by those desiring easily to obtain the recognition of their essential nature.
>
> This light commentary was composed by the glorious Vidyācakravartin, and placed on the touchstone named the intelligence of Govindacandra.
>
> Homage to Śiva, the guru, the God, who is the embodiment of bliss, who is the essential nature of the supreme brahman, the God of gods, Śambhu.

Notes

Preface

1. "*Upodghata,*" to Vrajavallabha Dvivedi, ed. and Hindi trans., *Vijñāna Bhairava* (Delhi: Motilal Banarsidass, 2004), vii.

Chapter 1

1. The name Virūpākṣa has other referents, including one of Śiva's attendants, one of the multiple Rudras, and a demon.

2. VAP 1.2 is quoted in Maheśvarānanda, *Mahārthamañjarīparimala* (henceforth MMP) in *Mahārthamañjarī of Maheśvarānanda with the Auto-Commentary Parimala,* ed. Vrajavallabha Dvivedi (Varanasi: Varanaseya Sanskrit Vishvavidyalaya Press, 1972), 29, 73. VAP 2.18 is quoted, ibid., 27, 70. VAP 4.46 is quoted, ibid., 47, 119. The text is also cited in later literature. The *Kailāsa-saṁhitā,* in *Śiva Purāṇa,* 4 vols., trans. a board of scholars, Ancient Indian Tradition and Mythology Series (Delhi: Motilal Banarsidass, 1970), 19.42–45, 4:1756, enjoins in a ritual context the recitation of the "Siddhi Skandha" of the VAP. (I am grateful to David Dubois for pointing this out to me.) VAP 2.10 is quoted by the seventeenth to eighteenth century Śrīvidyā writer Bhāskararāya in his commentary on the *Yoginīhṛdayasetubandha,* in *Yoginīhṛdayam with the Commentaries Dīpikā of Amṛtānanda and Setubandha of Bhāskararāya,* ed., Gopinath Kaviraj (Varanasi: Sanskrit University, 1979), 21–22, 109. VAP 2.10 is likewise quoted by Naṭanāndanātha in his *Kāmakalāvilāsacidvallī,* in Puṇyānanda and Naṭanāndanātha, *Kāmakālavilāsa with Commentary Cidvallī,* ed. Svamiji Maharaja Vanakhandeshvara (Datia: Pitambarapith Sanskrit Parishad, 1979), 1.3, 17.

3. *The Virūpākṣapañcāśikā, with the Commentary of Vidyācakravartin,* ed. T. Ganapati Śāstrī, Trivandrum Sanskrit Series, vol. 9 (Trivandrum: Travancore Government Press, 1910).

4. E-mail of April 19, 2005.

5. The longest discussion of this ostensible individual and his life and thought (focusing on the poetics) is by S. S. Janaki, "Introduction," to *Alaṁkāra-sarvasva of Ruyyaka with Sañjivanī Commentary of Vidyācakravartin* (Delhi: Meharchand Lachhmandas, 1965), 6–127.

6. Ibid., 29–35.

7. E-mail of April 19, 2005. There was a Pāśupatācāryabhaṭṭāraka Śrividyācakravartin of North India, associated with the Paramāra King of Dhārā, Bhojadeva (1018–1060). However, as Sanderson observes, his dates are probably too early to support his identification with the author of the VAPV. Ibid.

8. Janaki, "Introduction," 10.

9. Ibid., 13.

10. I am using the term "medieval" as a rough indication of a historical period, and not as a characterization of a dead and irrelevant mentality. On the problematization of the notion of the medieval from the perspective of social and political history, see Ronald Inden, Jonathan Walters, and Daud Ali, *Querying the Medieval: Texts and the History of Practices in South Asia* (Oxford: Oxford University Press, 2000).

11. In the Sanskritic context, an important premodern usage identifies as tantras a group of scriptures of Hindu Śaivism, Hindu Śāktism, and Buddhist Vajrayāna. Tantra may likewise refer to the movements that adhere to those scriptures. However, other scriptures and movements with very similar characteristics have not been described as tantric. According to another traditional South Asian usage, "tantra" refers to a variety of folk traditions of "sorcery" to attain worldly ends. More recently, in both South Asia and the West, tantrism has been popularly conceived as methods for sexual pleasure. See Hugh B. Urban, *Tantra: Sex, Secrecy, Politics, and Power in the Study of Religion* (Berkeley: University of California Press, 2003), on how popular and academic understandings of tantra have developed, during colonial and postcolonial periods, in a complex dialectic of cultural exchange between Asia and the West.

12. Some scholars have endeavored to stipulate different meanings for the terms "tantra" and "tantrism." In this study, the terms will be treated as synonyms.

13. Sir John Woodroffe, who did not like the contemporary generalization, "tantra," thematized the importance of Śakti/Power to these traditions in his writings such as *The World as Power* (Madras: Ganesh & Company, 1981). On the disclosure of Śakti in tantric contemplations and philosophical arguments, see David Peter Lawrence, *Rediscovering God with Transcendental Argument: A Contemporary Interpretation of Monistic Kashmiri Śaiva Philosophy* (Albany: State University of New York Press, 1999), 53–65. The centrality of Śakti to both Śaiva and Śākta traditions is emphasized in Hemendra Nath Chakravarty, "Tantric Spirituality," in *Hindu Spirituality II: Postclassical and Modern,* ed. K. R. Sundararajan and Bithika Mukerji (New York: Crossroad, 1997), 209–231. For a recent general definition of tantra as the effort to ritually appropriate divine energy, see David Gordon White, "Introduction" to David Gordon White, ed., *Tantra in Practice* (Princeton:

Princeton University Press, 2000), 7–9. The conference of the Society for Tantric Studies in Flagstaff, Arizona, October 11–13, 2002, focused on Tantra: Constructions and Deployments of Power. Also see the discussion of monistic Śaiva "ascetic" power in Gavin Flood, "The Aceticism of Action: Tantra," in *The Ascetic Self: Subjectivity, Memory and Tradition* (Cambridge: Cambridge University Press, 2004), 95–103.

14. Although they are not our focus, it may be noted that most of the discussed characteristics of Hindu tantra have analogues in Buddhist tantra.

15. For enumerations of the characteristics of the scholarly category of tantra, see Senjukta Gupta, Teun Goudriaan, and Dirk Jan Hoens, *Hindu Tantrism* (Leiden: E. J. Brill, 1979), 7–9; Douglas Renfrew Brooks, *The Secret of the Three Cities: An Introduction to Hindu Śākta Tantrism* (Chicago: University of Chicago Press, 1990), 47–72; and Jeffrey J. Kripal, *Kālī's Child: The Mystical and the Erotic in the Life and Teachings of Ramakrishna,* 2nd ed. (Chicago: University of Chicago Press, 1998), 29–33. Also see the discussion of "polythetic" classifications in Urban, 6ff.

16. On the translation of this term, see p. 62, n. 2.

17. On the relation of medieval tantrism to political power, see Senjukta Gupta and Richard Gombrich, "Kings, Power and the Goddess," *South Asia Research* 6 (1986): 123–138; Ronald M. Davidson, *Indian Esoteric Buddhism: A Social History of the Tantric Movement* (New York: Columbia University Press, 2002); and David Gordon White, "The Power of the Yoginī: Tantric Actors in South Asia," chapter in *Kiss of the Yoginī: Tantric Sex in its South Asian Contexts* (Chicago: University of Chicago Press, 2003), 123–159. White emphasizes the role in tantric traditions of *maṇḍalas,* circular diagrams of the emanation of energy/power as the universe, and stresses their political sense as demonstrating the power of kings over their domains.

18. Alexis Sanderson's major articles include "Purity and Power Among the Brahmans of Kashmir," in *The Category of the Person: Anthropology, Philosophy, History,* ed. Michael Carrithers, Steven Collins, and Steven Lukes (Cambridge: Cambridge University Press, 1985), 190–216; "Maṇḍala and Āgamic Identity in the Trika of Kashmir," in *Mantras et diagrammes rituels dans L'Hindouisme,* ed. Andre Padoux (Paris: Centre National de la Recherche Scientifique, 1986), 169–214; "Śaivism and the Tantric Traditions," in *The World's Religions,* ed. Stewart Sutherland et al. (London: Routledge, 1988), 660–704; "The Visualization of the Deities of the Trika," in *L'Image divine: Culte et meditation dans L'Hindouisme,* ed. Andre Padoux (Paris: Centre National de la Recherche Scientifique, 1990), 31–88; "The Doctrine of the Mālinīvijayottaratantra," in *Ritual and Speculation in Early Tantrism: Studies in Honor of Andre Padoux,* ed. Teun Goudriaan, SUNY Series in Tantric Studies, ed. Paul Eduardo Muller-Ortega (Albany: State University of New York Press, 1992), 281–312; and "Meaning in Tantric Ritual," in *Essais sur le Rituel, III* (Colloque du Centenaire de la Section des Sciences Religieuses de l'Ecole Pratique des Hautes Etudes), ed. Anne-Marie Blondeau and Kristofer Schipper

(Louvain: Peeters, 1995), 15–95. Cf. the theory of "transgressive sacrality" of Sunthar Visuvalingam, "The Transgressive Sacrality of the Dīkṣita: Sacrifice, Criminality and *Bhakti* in the Hindu Tradition," in Alf Hiltebeitel, ed., *Criminal Gods and Demon Devotees: Essays on the Guardians of Popular Hinduism* (Albany: State University of New York Press, 1989), 427–462.

19. An important passage pertaining to the possibility of incest in the monistic Śaiva literature is *The Tantrāloka of Abhinavagupta with the Commentary of Jayaratha,* 8 vols., ed. Madhusudan Kaul Shastri and Mukunda Rama Shastri, Kashmir Series of Texts and Studies, republication, ed. R. C. Dwivedi and Navjivan Rastogi (Delhi: Motilal Banarsidass, 1987), 29.101–102. (Abhinavagupta's work will henceforth be referred to as TA, and Jayaratha's commentary, *Tantrālokaviveka,* will be referred to as TAV.) Sanderson, "Meaning in Tantric Ritual," 83, interprets this passage as a prescription by Abhinavagupta for incest between a man and his "mother, sister, daughter, granddaughter, grandmother, or sister's daughter." Cf. the alternative construal in Lilian Silburn, *Kuṇḍalinī: The Energy of the Depths; A Comprehensive Study Based on the Scriptures of Nondualistic Kashmir Śaivism,* trans. Jacques Gontier (Albany: State University of New York Press, 1988), 181. Scholars from Sigmund Freud to Claude Levi-Strauss have demonstrated that prohibitions against such forms of incest are among the most universal, strongest, and most ramified taboos in the world's cultures. Sudhir Kakar, *Shamans, Mystics and Doctors: A Psychological Inquiry into India and Its Healing Traditions* (Boston: Beacon Press, 1983), 159, who considers tantric "incest" practices largely a matter of a man imagining his wife to be an incestuous partner, proffers a psychoanalytic interpretation:

> As post-Freudians, we know that the child's unconscious incestuous fantasies, consequent to the momentous discovery of gender identity, provoke major anxieties which the child's immature ego copes with by building defensive structures in the psyche. Tantric practice, not unlike psychoanalysis, seeks to resurrect the elemental fantasies around incest, together with their associated anxiety, in order to find a new resolution for an old yet nagging dilemma of human development. The "power" acquired by the tantrik is then another name for the feeling of expansiveness which follows the reduction of the anxiety and which has its source in the release of psychic energy that was bound in maintaining inappropriate defensive structures.

20. This is the main argument of White, *Kiss of the Yoginī.*

21. A well-known later medieval formula summarizes transgressive practice in five "M's" (*makāras,* things whose designations start with the phoneme M): *madya* (wine), *matsya* (fish), *māṁsa* (meat), *mudrā* (many different things, from mystical or sexual postures to aphrodisiac beans and cereals), and *maithuna* (sexual intercourse). On the possible ingestion of human flesh in the contemporary Aghori movement, see Jonathan Parry, "Sacrificial Death and the Necrophagus

Ascetic," in *Death and the Regeneration of Life,* ed. Maurice Bloch and Jonathan Parry (Cambridge: Cambridge University Press, 1982), 75–110.

22. Ronald Inden develops R. G. Collingwood's concepts of a "scale of texts" or "scale of forms" to describe such an interpretive process by Kashmiri *Pāñcarātra* in the *Viṣṇudharmottara Purāṇa.* "Imperial Purāṇas: Kashmir as Vaiṣṇava Center of the World," in Inden, Walters, and Ali, *Querying the Medieval: Texts and the History of Practices in South Asia,* 29–98. Also see the study of the syncretism of schemes of yogic practice in Somadeva Vasudeva, *The Yoga of the Mālinīvijayottaratantra: Chapters 1–4, 7, 11–17* (Pondicherry: Institut Francais de Pondichery, 2004).

23. Brian K. Smith has described a similar process in the Vedic context as "encompassment" on the basis of presumed "hierarchical resemblances," in *Reflections on Resemblance, Ritual and Religion* (Oxford: Oxford University Press, 1989), 46–49, 186–189.

24. We may understand the hierarchization of alternative viewpoints in interreligious or intercultural interpretation to be entailed by the hermeneutic circle. For a comparative philosophical assessment of the described pattern of appropriation in monistic Śaiva philosophy, see David Peter Lawrence, "Zu Abhinavaguptas Offenbarungstheorie," *Polylog: Zeitschrift für interkulturelles Philosophieren* 5 (2000): 6–18; and "The Plurality and Contingency of Knowledge, and its Rectification According to the Pratyabhijñā," in *Perspectives on Abhinavagupta* (commemoration volume for K. C. Pandey), ed. Navjivan Rastogi and Meera Rastogi (forthcoming).

25. On the process of domesticization, see the articles by Sanderson, and White, *Kiss of the Yoginī,* particularly "The Sublimation of the Yoginī: The Subordination of the Feminine in High Hindu Tantra," ibid., 219–257.

26. According to a frequently quoted maxim, one should be "a Kaula inwardly, a Śaiva [that is, a nontransgressive one] outwardly, and a Vaidika in the affairs of the world." Quoted by Jayaratha in TAV 4.24b–25, 3:643. For any remaining Kashmiri and other high castes who practice concretely transgressive aspects of monistic Śaiva *sādhana,* this maxim may still describe their negotiation of esoteric praxis with what T. N. Madan, *Non-Renunciation: Themes and Interpretations of Hindu Culture* (Delhi: Oxford University Press, 1987), has described as social "personhood" defined by householder and caste duties.

27. Vasugupta is widely believed to have received the *Śiva Sūtra* as a revelation from Śiva.

28. The core text of this system is Utpaladeva's *Īśvarapratyabhijñākārikā, "Verses on the Recognition of the Lord."* This text, henceforth referred to as IPK, will be cited in the edition used for the *Īśvarapratyabhijñāvimarśinī* commentary on it by Abhinavagupta, referenced below. Utpaladeva wrote two commentaries on the IPK, the *Īśvarapratyabhijñākārikāvṛtti* (IPKV), in Raffaele Torella, ed. and trans., *The Īśvarapratyabhijñākārikā of Utpaladeva with the Author's Vṛtti,* corrected edition (Delhi: Motilal Banarsidass, 2002); and the *Īśvarapratyabhijñāvivṛti,*

which is presently available only in fragments. Other important works on the Pratyabhijñā by Utpaladeva are the trilogy of specialized philosophical studies, the *Siddhitrayī, "Three Proofs"—Īśvarasiddhi, "Proof of the Lord;" Ajaḍapramātṛsiddhi, "Proof of a Subject Who Is Not Insentient"*; and the *Sambandhasiddhi, "Proof of Relation."* Utpaladeva, *Siddhitrayī* and the *Īśvarapratyabhijñākārikāvṛtti,* ed. Madhusudan Kaul Shastri, Kashmir Series of Texts and Studies, no. 34 (Srinagar: Kashmir Pratap Steam Press, 1921). Utpaladeva also wrote a commentary on Somānanda's philosophical work. *The Śivadṛṣṭi of Srisomānandanātha with the Vritti by Utpaladeva,* ed. Madhusudan Kaul Shastri, Kashmir Series of Texts and Studies, no. 54 (Pune: Aryabhushan Press, 1934).

29. Abhinavagupta's commentary directly on the IPK is the *Īśvarapratyabhijñāvimarśinī of Abhinavagupta, Doctrine of Divine Recognition: Sanskrit text with Bhāskarī,* 2 vols., ed. K. A. Subramania Iyer and K. C. Pandey (Reprint, Delhi: Motilal Banarsidass, 1986). This commentary will henceforth be referred to as IPV. As mentioned, I will refer to the verses of the IPK in this edition. Abhinava's commentary on the missing *Īśvarapratyabhijñāvivṛti* is *The Īśvarapratyabhijñāvivṛtivimarśinī by Abhinavagupta,* 3 vols., ed. Madhusudan Kaul Shastri, Kashmir Series of Texts and Studies (Reprint, Delhi: Akay Book Corporation, 1987). Henceforth IPVV.

30. I have taken my gloss of the title of Abhinava's magnum opus from Sanderson, "Meaning in Tantric Ritual," 18.

31. See Mark S. G. Dyczkowski, "The Doctrine of Vibration and Recognition," in Vasugupta, Kṣemarāja, Kallaṭabhaṭṭa, Rājānaka Rāma and Bhagavadutpala, *The Stanzas on Vibration: The Spanda Kārikā with Four Commentaries,* trans. with introduction and exposition by Mark S. G. Dyczkowski, SUNY Series in the Shaiva Traditions of Kashmir, ed. Harvey Alper (Albany: State University of New York Press, 1992), 33–48, on the legacy of the application of the Pratyabhijñā to tantric exegesis. Cf. David Tracy, *The Analogical Imagination: Christian Theology and the Culture of Pluralism* (New York: Crossroad, 1975), 183 n. 26, on the role of philosophical theology (which Tracy calls "fundamental theology") in critically structuring systematic theology and practical theology in Christianity.

32. White, *Kiss of the Yoginī,* 14.

33. Ibid., 16.

34. Ibid., xiii.

35. See the defense of the method of dialogue using comparative philosophy in Lawrence, *Rediscovering God,* 1–16.

36. *Vijñānabhairava or Divine Consciousness: A Treasury of 112 Types of Yoga,* ed. and trans. Jaideva Singh (Delhi: Motilal Banarsidass, 1979), 20, 17.

37. On tantric traditions that provide greater roles and opportunities for women, see Loriliai Biernacki, *Renowned Goddess of Desire: Women, Sex, and Speech in Tantra* (New York: Oxford University Press, 2007).

38. The purposes and methods of the Pratyabhijñā system are discussed in Lawrence, *Rediscovering God,* 35–65. The philosophers explain the soteriological realization epistemologically as the *recognition* (*pratyabhijñā*) "I am Śiva" in order

to address and refute arguments of the Buddhist logic school of Dharmakīrti. That school had denied the validity of the reference to reality of conceptual and linguistic interpretation (*vikalpa*); they viewed such reference as epitomized in the experience of recognition. Ibid., 67–106. Somānanda had already begun cursorily to address these debates. Ibid., 29.

39. *Śuddhavidyā* or *sadvidyā* is intermediate in the Trika cosmic triads, and the fifth principle of emanation from the Supreme Lord in the thirty-six-fold scheme of *tattvas.* The roots of this concept may be found in the Upaniṣads.

40. *aham idam.*

41. In his *Tantrāloka,* Abhinavagupta synthesizes the themes of the revealing of Śakti, the purification of conceptualization, and other discursive-gnoseological modes of spiritual praxis as typifying one of the principal spiritual means-types (*upāya*), that is, the means-type of Śakti (*śākta upāya*). Lawrence, *Rediscovering God,* 57–65.

42. The monistic Śaivas articulate their innovative theory of recognition with three sets of terms. The first, the word *pratyabhijñā* along with cognates such as *abhijñā,* may usually be translated as just "recognition." The second set comprises various derivatives from the root *mṛś,* such as *vimarśa, parāmarśa, pratyavamarśa, āmarśa,* and so on. These words convey notions of linguistic apprehension or judgment with a *recognitive structure,* and may be translated as "recognitive apprehension" or "recognitive judgment." *Ahampratyavamarśa* is thus the "recognitive apprehension of I." (Recently, Kerry Skora has been endeavoring to retrieve the original significance of *mṛś* as "touch," in order to emphasize that recognition is understood in tantric traditions as an embodied epistemic process.) A third set of terms is derived from attaching various initial prefixes to the second prefix *sam* and the root *dhā,* for example, *anusaṁdhāna, pratisaṁdhāna,* and *abhisaṁdhi,* and may be translated as "recognitive synthesis"; this set of terms is used to emphasize how God in his self-recognition unites moments of experience extending through time. See "Basic Vocabulary of the Śaiva Theory of Recognition," ibid., 86–87, 208–209 n. *Pratisaṁdhāna* is also translated as "recognitive synthesis" in Kisor Kumar Chakrabarti, *Classical Indian Philosophy of Mind: The Nyāya Dualist Tradition* (New York: State University of New York Press, 1999), 60–61.

43. *vimarśa,* as the essential nature of *prakāśa,* "awareness."

44. The Pratyabhijñā system is compared with Western idealism in Lawrence, *Rediscovering God.*

45. The paradox of the Pratyabhijñā inference for the sake of others is that the recognition "I am Śiva" is in effect both the conclusion as well as the reason, that is, Śakti. However, a destructive circularity is obviated by the system's explanations of various technical philosophical subjects, which provide further ostensible justification—reasons for the reason—that is the revealing of Śakti as self-recognition. Ibid., 95–102.

46. Michel Hulin, "La notion de *pūrṇāhaṁtā* dans le Śivaisme du Kaśmīr," in *Le principe de l'ego dans la pensee Indienne classique* (Paris: Institut de Civilisation

Indienne, 1978), 279–358; Dyczkowski, "Self Awareness, Own Being, Egoity," in *The Stanzas on Vibration,* 37–48. Also see Flood, "The Asceticism of Action: Tantra."

47. Dyczkowski, "The Doctrine of Vibration and Recognition," 39.

48. Thus see the section translated from the *Mālinīvijayottara* on the introspection of egoism or pride (*garva*), in Somadeva Vasudeva, 351–352. The correlation of this practice with the expansion of the sense of the body is clearly precursory to the contemplations of the VAP and VAPV. See Gavin Flood, *The Tantric Body: The Secret Tradition of Hindu Religion* (London: I. B. Tauris, 2006), 115, on the divinization of the I-concept (*ahaṁkāra*) in the Vaiṣṇava *Jayākhya Saṁhitā.* Similar notions are also found in Vajrayāna Buddhism.

49. In Advaita Vedānta, by contrast, the realization conveyed by the *mahāvākyas* such as "I am *brahman*" negates the *ahaṁkāra.*

50. As accessed through concrete instances of semantic intuition (*pratibhā*), manifestation (*sphoṭa*), and recognition (*pratyavamarśa, pratyabhijñā*).

51. See the discussion of these schemes in VAP and VAPV 2.9 and 2.18, and chapter 3, pp. 30–31.

52. *Āgama* includes in its significance religious scriptures as well as religious tradition more generally.

53. Abhinavagupta nevertheless affirms that competing traditions are eternal (*anādi*) and of superhuman origin (*apauruṣeya*). According to Abhinavagupta, the Self as Śiva includes the fruits of ostensibly lower traditions—such as wealth, duty, and various forms of liberation—but not vice versa. He compares the followers of other traditions to those who disparage the enjoyment of a king in favor of lesser enjoyments. See Lawrence, "Zu Abhinavaguptas Offenbarungstheorie."

54. David Peter Lawrence, "The Mythico-Ritual Syntax of Omnipotence," *Philosophy East and West* 48 (1998): 592–622; *Rediscovering God,* 133–154.

55. These correspond to the Indo-European cases designated in English as the nominative, accusative, instrumental, locative, dative, and ablative. However, the same *kāraka* can be declined with different case endings; for example, the agent is declined as nominative in active syntax and as instrumental in passive syntax. Because they unite considerations pertaining to the referenced action with those of grammar, the Sanskrit *kārakas* are sometimes described as "syntactico-semantic categories." Sanskritic grammatical concerns about the relation of verbs and declined nouns seem to have originated in priestly interpretations of the Veda as expressing injunctions for the action of sacrifice. They articulate a kind of narrative syntax of myths and rituals that I have compared with Kenneth Burke's *Grammar of Motives.*

56. Edwin Gerow, "What Is Karma (Kiṁ Karmeti): An Exercise in Philosophical Semantics," *Indologica Taurinensia* 10 (1982): 87–116; Lawrence, "Mythico-Ritual Syntax." It should be understood that the following discussion pertains to religious and philosophical conceptions of agency, which have a complex relationship to the historical agency of South Asian persons.

57. Gerow claims that it is a tendency of the Sanskrit language itself toward denigrating agency that underlies the doctrine of karma in rebirth and is secondarily articulated in traditional theories of Sanskrit grammar.

58. In this vein, the Pratyabhijñā thinkers reduce the "action" of existence itself to agency. As Utpaladeva states, "Being is the condition of one who becomes, that is, the agency of the act of becoming" (*sattā bhavattā bhavanakartṛtā*). IPKV 1.5.14, 23. Lawrence, *Rediscovering God,* interprets the Pratyabhijñā theory of syntax as an ontology corresponding to the epistemology of self-recognition/Speech.

59. The aspirant cultivates this understanding through *nyāsa* and various other preparations. TA 15.147–151, 6:2516–2518; TA 15.157–158, 6:2520. Also see TS 13, 135ff.

60. Abhinavagupta correlates the hierarchy of grammatical persons with a similar ranking of single, dual, and plural numbers. Abhinavagupta, *Parātrīśikāvivaraṇa,* in *A Trident of Wisdom,* ed. and trans. Jaideva Singh (Albany: State University of New York Press, 1989), 1, 25–28. (This text will henceforth be referred to as PTV.) Cf. ibid., 1, 19. These theories are further investigated in David Peter Lawrence, "Abhinavagupta's Philosophical Hermeneutics of Grammatical Persons," in *Journal of Hindu Studies,* forthcoming. Flood, *Tantric Body,* 181–184 (which I read after having completed the interpretation provided in the article just mentioned as well as the present discussion), pursuing a social constructionist methodology, describes tantric traditions as perpetuated through the identification of the reader's indexical I with the third person, anaphoric I of the texts. For general studies of the grammatical persons, see Emile Benveniste, "Man and Language," in *Problems in General Linguistics,* trans. Mary Elizabeth Meek (Coral Gables, FL: University of Miami Press, 1971), 194–246; Milton Singer, "Pronouns, Persons, and the Semiotic Self," in *Semiotics, Self, and Society,* ed. Benjamin Lee and Greg Urban (New York: Mouton de Gruyter, 1989), 229–296; and the psychoanalytic theory of Ana-Maria Rizutto, "First Person Personal Pronouns and their Psychic Referents," *International Journal of Psychoanalysis* 74 (1993): 535–546.

61. For an overview of conceptions of the body in Hindu Sanskrit traditions, see Prem Lata Sharma, "*Śarīra,*" in *Kalātattvakośa,* general editor, Kapila Vatsyayan, vol. 1, *Eight Selected Terms,* ed. Bettina Baumer (Delhi: Indira Gandhi National Centre for the Arts, 1992), 71–96. With regard to the Hindu tantric interpretation of the universal body, Sanderson, "Śaivism and the Tantric Traditions," 679, explains how Kaula tantric traditions gave a new meaning to the concept of the clan (*kula*) of Yoginīs emanating from higher Mother (*mātṛ*) Śaktis:

> Kaulism developed from within these Yoginī cults. It preserved the original meaning of the term *kula* and its derivatives but it introduced a new level of esotericism based on a homonym. For *kula* was also taken to mean the body and, by further extension, the totality (of phenomena), the "body" of power (*śakti*). This last meaning neatly encompassed the original, for this cosmic "body" was said to consist of the powers of the eight families of the Mothers.

Buddhist tantric traditions similarly identify the cosmos as the highest body of their favored Buddha, for example, Mahā Vairocana. Tantric notions of the body are also related to South Asian conceptions of the universal body of the king. See the discussion of medieval conceptions and their implicit continuity in programs of modernist emancipation in Ronald Inden, "Embodying God: From Imperial Progresses to National Progress in India," *Economy and Society* 24 (1995): 245–278.

62. *The Shiva Sūtra Vimarshinī: Being the Sūtras of Vasu Gupta with the Commentary Called Vimarshinī by Kṣhemarāja,* ed., J. C. Chatterji (Srinagar: Nirnaya-Sagar Press, 1911), 1.14, 32. Vasugupta's text will henceforth be abbreviated SS.

63. Gavin Flood, *Body and Cosmology in Kashmir Śaivism* (San Francisco: Mellen Research University Press, 1993), 4.

64. Ibid., 5–6. Flood's more recent work, *Tantric Body,* is a rich and sophisticated study of how the varieties of tantric transformation of the body are mediated by texts. This mediation, which Flood calls the "entextualization" of the body, is illustrated in the translation of the *Dehasthadevatācakrastotra,* "Hymn to the Circle of Deities Situated in the Body," which some have attributed to Abhinavagupta, ibid., 155–156. Whereas Flood explains the entextualization of the body in terms of social construction, I would prefer to interpret it as a *disclosure of possibilities* that may be engaged dialogically through comparative philosophy. (See the synthesis of the triad of dialogical criteria possibility-coherence-practice from William James and philosophical hermeneutics, with disclosure assimilated to possibility, in David Tracy, "The Question of Criteria for Inter-Religious Dialogue: On Revisiting William James," in *Dialogue with the Other: The Inter-Religious Dialogue* [Louvain: Peeters Press, 1990], 27–47; and the engagement of the same with the Pratyabhijñā in Lawrence, "The Plurality and Contingency of Knowledge, and its Rectification According to the Pratyabhijñā.")

65. Marcel Mauss, "Techniques of the Body," *Economy and Society* 2, 1 (1973): 70–87. Mauss also emphasized the bodily aspects of all techniques for spiritual realization. Ibid., 86–87.

66. For examples of these practices in various traditions, see Richard H. Davis, "Becoming a Śiva and Acting as One in Śaiva Worship," in Teun Goudriaan, ed., *Ritual and Speculation in Early Tantrism: Studies in Honor of Andre Padoux* (Albany: State University of New York Press, 1992), 107–119; Vrajavallabha Dwivedi, "Having Become a God, He Should Sacrifice to the Gods," in Goudriaan, ed., *Ritual and Speculation in Early Tantrism,* 121–138; Sir John Woodroffe, "Purification of the Elements" and "Nyāsa" in *Principles of Tantra,* 2 vols. (Madras: Ganesh & Company, 1986), vol. 2., 476–490; Gavin Flood, "The Purification of the Body," in White, ed., *Tantra in Practice,* 509–520; "The Purification of the Body (Bhūtaśuddhi)," "Bhūtaśuddhi and Aṅganyāsa," and "A Yogin's Vision of His Inner Body," in Senjukta Gupta, trans., *Lakṣmī Tantra: A Pāñcarātra Text* (Leiden: E. J. Brill, 1972), 202–211, 363–367.

67. On Kuṇḍalinī in Abhinavagupta and the monistic Kashmiri Śaiva traditions, see Silburn, along with White's speculative but provocative interpretation in *Kiss of the Yoginī*, 229–234. Sir John Woodroffe, trans., *The Serpent Power: The Secrets of Tantric and Shaktic Yoga* (New York: Dover, 1974), though dated, remains an invaluable resource.

68. Sometimes the essences of the divinized couple—semen and menstrual fluid—are mixed to form the *kuṇḍagolaka* and ingested. On the sexual ritual, see John R. Dupuche, trans. with introduction, *Abhinavagupta: The Kula Ritual, as Elaborated in Chapter 29 of the Tantrāloka* (Delhi: Motilal Banarsidass, 2003); White, *Kiss of the Yoginī;* Silburn, "*Kulayāga,* Esoteric Sacrifice," in *Kuṇḍalinī*, 177–205; Elizabeth Chalier-Visuvalingam, Elizabeth, "Union and Unity in Hindu Tantrism," online, www.infinityfoundation.com/mandala/i_es/i_es_visuv_e_unity.htm [accessed August 3, 2007]. Abhinavagupta praises the body as the supreme *liṅga* and *maṇḍala* within which there is the worship of both the God and the Goddess. TA, 29.170–176, 7:3406–3408.

69. Tantric alchemical traditions bring to the fore the pursuit of physical immortality. In tantric alchemy the divine male and female sexual essences are often conceived to be embodied, respectively, in mercury and sulfur, which are chemically compounded and ingested like the *kuṇḍagolaka.* In the "internal" alchemy of the Nāth Siddhas, the chemical procedure is understood as symbolic of subtle spiritual-physical processes. See David Gordon White, *The Alchemical Body: Siddha Traditions in Medieval India* (Chicago: University of Chicago Press, 1996); and Shashibhusan Dasgupta, "The Nāth Cult," in *Obscure Religious Cults* (Calcutta: Firma K. L. Mukhopadhyay, 1969), 191–255. Kukai, the founder of Shingon Buddhism is believed still to be alive in his temple in Japan, although immobile in the meditation posture. On Kukai and his techniques for realizing the body of Mahā Vairocana, see Yoshito S. Hakeda, trans., *Kukai: Major Works* (New York: Columbia University Press, 1972); and Thomas Kasulis, "Reality as Embodiment: An Analysis of Kukai's *Sokushinjobutsu* and *Hosshin Seppo,*" in Jane Marie Law, ed., Religious *Reflections on the Human Body* (Bloomington: Indiana University Press, 1995), 166–185. I mention that, according to a popular Kashmiri legend, Abhinavagupta along with twelve hundred disciples disappeared into a cave called Bhairava. What happened to their physical bodies is a mystery.

70. Phyllis Granoff, "Portraits, Likenesses and Looking Glasses: Some Literary and Philosophical Reflections on Representation and Art in Medieval India," in Jan Assmann and Albert L. Baumgarten, eds., *Representation in Religion: Studies in Honor of Moshe Barasch* (Leiden: E. J. Brill, 2001), 101–102; and "Maitreya's Jewelled World: Some Remarks on Gems and Visions in Buddhist Texts," *Journal of Indian Philosophy* 26 (1998): 360–361. Cf. the remarks on reflections and shadows in Wendy Doniger, *Splitting the Difference: Gender and Myth in Ancient Greece and India* (Chicago: University of Chicago Press, 1999), 70–74; and the earlier study of Alex Wayman, "The Mirror as a Pan-Buddhist Metaphor-Simile," *History of Religions* 13 (1974): 251–269.

71. David Peter Lawrence, "Remarks on Abhinavagupta's Use of the Analogy of Reflection," *Journal of Indian Philosophy* 33 (2005): 583–599.

72. There is the reflection of the mantra *aham,* "I," as *mahā,* "great."

Chapter 2

1. VAPV, 1.intro. and 1.1.

2. On the history of the Indra religion and Indra myths, see Usha Choudhuri, *Indra and Varuṇa in Indian Mythology* (Delhi: Nag Publishers, 1981); Uma Chakravarty, *Indra and Other Vedic Deities: A Euhemeristic Study* (Delhi: D. K. Printworld, 1997); Klaus K. Klostermaier, "Salvation in Vedic Religion," in *Mythologies and Philosophies of Salvation in the Theistic Traditions of India* (Waterloo, Ontario: Wilfred Laurier University Press, 1984), 6–55; idem, *Hinduism: A Short History* (Oxford: Oneworld Publications, 2000), 52–68; idem, *Hindu Writings: A Short Introduction to the Major Sources* (Oxford: Oneworld Publications, 2000), 12–22; and Renate Sohnen, "Rise and Decline of the Indra Religion in the Veda," in Michael Witzel, ed., *Inside the Texts . . . Beyond the Texts: New Approaches to the Study of the Vedas,* Department of Sanskrit and Indian Studies, Harvard University (Columbia, MO: South Asia Books, 1997), 235–243.

3. An alternative approach to validating Vedāntin innovations was the identification of Indra with the Ultimate (*ātman-brahman*) in the *Bāṣkalamantra Upaniṣad,* in Jagadīśa Śāstrī, ed., *Upaniṣatsaṅgraha* (Delhi: Motilal Banarsidass, 1970), 2:37–39. I am grateful to Mislav Jezic of the University of Zagreb for pointing this text out to me. Similar interpretations are scattered throughout other early Upaniṣads, for example, *Kauṣītakibrāhmaṇa Upaniṣad,* ibid., 3, 1:201–204. On the basis of such metaphysical and spiritual interpretations of Indra, there developed conceptions of the organs of sense and action as his capacities (*indriyas*). See Kapila Vatsyayana, "Indriya," in *Kalātattvakośa,* vol. 4, *Manifestation of Nature: Sṛṣṭi Vistāra,* ed. Advaitavadini Kaul and Sukumar Chattopadhyay (Delhi: Indira Gandhi National Centre for the Arts, 1999), 1–68.

4. I think that it is also possible that some of the subordinations of Indra reflect delimitations of royal power in relation to Brahmanic, yogic, or tantric authority.

5. *Chāndogya Upaniṣad,* in Śāstrī, *Upaniṣatsaṅgraha,* 8.7–12, 1:80–83.

6. *Chāndogya Upaniṣad,* in Robert Ernest Hume, trans., *The Thirteen Principal Upanishads,* 2nd. ed. (Oxford: Oxford University Press, 1977), 8.7.1, 268.

7. Ibid., 8.7.4, 268.

8. Śaṅkarācarya, *Chandogya Upanishad Bhasya,* in *Complete Works of Sri Shankacharya, in the Original Sanskrit,* 10 vols. (Madras: Samata Books, 1983), 8.7.4, 9:510–511. There are Brāhmaṇas and Upaniṣads that identify Indra as the person residing in the eye, usually the right eye. See Choudhuri, 70, 79, 81, 211. It is interesting that many of the languages of the world use the same term to refer to the pupil of the eye and a human being, small human being, or humanlike

object. Cecil H. Brown and Stanley R. Witkowski, "Figurative Language in a Universalist Perspective," *American Ethnology* 8 (1981): 596–615.

9. *Chāndogya Upaniṣad,* in Hume, 8.7.4, 268.

10. Ibid.

11. Ibid., 269.

12. *Chāndogya Upaniṣad,* in Śāstrī, 8.8.5, 1:81.

13. Ibid., 8.9–11, 1:81–82.

14. *Chāndogya Upaniṣad,* in Hume, 8.12.1, 272.

15. *Chāndogya Upaniṣad,* in Śāstrī, 8.12.4–5, 83.

16. *Chāndogya Upaniṣad,* in Hume, 8.12.2, 272.

17. Sigmund Freud, "The Libido Theory and Narcissism," in *Introductory Lectures on Psychoanalysis,* Standard Edition, ed. and trans. James Strachey (New York: Norton, 1966), 518–519, explains:

> As regards the state of sleep, we assumed that it was based on turning-away from the external world and adopting a wish to sleep [p. 107]. The mental activity during the night which is manifested in dreams takes place, we found, in obedience to a wish to sleep and is moreover dominated by purely egoistic motives [p. 174]. We may now add, on the lines of the libido theory, that sleep is a state in which all object-cathexes, libidinal as well as egoistic, are given up and withdrawn into the ego. May not this throw a fresh light on the recuperating effect of sleep and on the nature of fatigue in general? The picture of the blissful isolation of intra-uterine life which a sleeper conjures up once more before us every night is in this way completed on its psychical side as well. In a sleeper the primal state of distribution of the libido is restored—total narcissism, in which libido and ego-interest, still united and indistinguishable, dwell in the self-sufficing ego.

Jacques Lacan likewise affirms the constitutive role of the mirror reflection of the body in the imaginary of dreams and hallucinations. Jacques Lacan, "The Mirror Stage as Formative of the Function of the I as revealed in psychoanalytic experience," in *Ecrits: A Selection,* trans. Alan Sheridan (London: Routledge, 1997), 3. Lacan's notion of mirroring will also be further discussed in chapter 4.

18. For an alternative interpretation of this narrative, see Matthew T. Kapstein, "Indra's Search for the Self and the Beginnings of Philosophical Perplexity in India," in *Reason's Traces: Identity and Interpretation in Indian and Tibetan Buddhist Thought* (Delhi: Oxford University Press, 2001), 53–76.

19. C. L. Goswami, ed. and trans., *Śrīmad Bhāgavata Mahāpurāṇa,* 2 vols. (Gorakhpur, India: Gita Press, 1982), 10.24–27, 2:1158–1171.

20. *kālātmanā bhagavatā śakradarpam jighāṁsatā.* Ibid., 10.24.31, 2:1161.

21. R. C. Zaehner, ed. and trans., *The Bhagavad-Gīta* (Oxford: Oxford University Press, 1973), 11.32, 311.

22. *Śrīmad Bhāgavata,* 10.27.6–7, 2:1169.

23. Indra has associations with mountains in myths since the *Rig Veda.* Other humiliations of Indra also feature the elephant Airāvata. For example, Śiva beheads Airāvata to provide a new head for his son Ganeśa. I also mention that in South Asian traditions elephants are associated with pride and other physical, psychological, and spiritual tendencies that need to be controlled. Basavaṇṇa, in A. K. Ramanujan, trans., *Speaking of Śiva* (Harmondsworth: Penguin Books, 1979), 639, 86, refers to "rutting elephants of pride." In alchemical and Nāth traditions, the fixing of mercury (equated with Śiva's seed) is described as the subduing of a wild elephant. David Gordon White, "Why Gurus Are Heavy," *Numen* 31 (1984): 49, 63, 70–71. On controlling the elephant of the mind in the Nāth traditions, also see Dasgupta, *Obscure Religious Cults,* 105.

24. Heinrich Zimmer, *Myths and Symbols in Indian Art and Civilization,* ed. Joseph Campbell (Princeton: Princeton University Press, 1974), 3–11. This is part of the chapter on "Shattering the Pride of Indra," in Shanti Lal Nagar, trans., and Acharya Ramesh Chaturvedi, ed., *Brahmavaivarta Purāṇa,* 2 vols. (Delhi: Parimal Publications, 2001), *Krisna-Janma-Khanda* 47, 2:372–383. That section in turn is part of a longer narrative on the shattering of the pride of various deities. I note that Zimmer's account is rather embellished.

25. I mention that, in the tantric context, the ninth to twelfth century Pāṇcarātra scripture, the *Lakṣmī Tantra,* is also framed as Lakṣmī's instruction of Indra. This occurs after she and Viṣṇu rescue him from a powerful sage's curse, in the broader mythic context of the churning of the milky ocean. Senjukta Gupta, trans., *Lakṣmī Tantra,* 1.27–61, 4–7. It is also of interest that the classic text of South Asian medicine (Āyurveda), the *Caraka Saṁhitā*—in treating correspondences between the person and the cosmos—homologizes the ego (*ahaṁkāra*) with Indra. Kakar, *Shamans, Mystics and Doctors,* 293n.

Chapter 3

1. VAP and VAPV 4.51–52, VAPV 4.53.
2. See VAPV 1.2, 2.18–19; pp. 65–67, nn. 1, 7, 8; and p. 88, nn. 1, 2, 7.
3. VAP 1.2.
4. The category *śūnyapada* synthesizes a variety of concepts. The Śaivas conceive it to encompass the apophatic witness Selves of Sāṁkhya-Yoga and Advaita Vedānta, and, as the reference to a void suggests, the incomprehensible ultimate of Mādhyamika Buddhism (thus taking a metaphysical rather than semantic approach to the latter).
5. SS 1.14–15, 15. For the qualification of sleep as "deep and void of contents" I follow Kṣemarāja's gloss: *svāpasya etadabhāvarūpasya.* I likewise follow his clarification *svāṅgakalpatayā* "as one's own body or limbs." Ibid. Whether or not Kṣemarāja provides the best interpretation of the text, it seems that the author of the VAP had his commentary in mind.

6. VAPV 1.51.
7. VAP 1.5.
8. VAP 1.6. Cf. IPK 3.2.3, 246:

> The subject who regards entities as one's own limbs is called Lord. [However, the subject who] due to Māyā, regards them as differentiated is the creature, who has the defilements of afflictions, karma, and so on.

9. On this term, also see pp. 62–63, n. 5.
10. Patañjali, *Yoga Sūtra,* in Patañjali et al., *Pātañjalayogadarśanam,* ed., Srinarayan Mishra (Varanasi: Bharatiya Vidya Prakashan, 1971), 2.3, 141. This text will henceforth be referred to as YS.
11. YS 2.6, 151. *Puruṣa* and *prakṛti* are here respectively referred to as *dṛkśakti* and *darśanaśakti,* that is, *buddhi.*
12. YS 1.17–18, 54–58.
13. See VAP and VAPV 1.8–2.9.
14. *antaḥkaraṇa.*
15. VAP and VAPV 1.3–4.
16. The Supreme (Parama) Śiva is distinguished from an emanated, lower form of himself who is artificially distinguished from Śakti. See p. 69, n. 4.
17. VAPV 1.4. Rājanaka Rāma, a direct disciple of Utpaladeva, likewise explains that the body is that which the ego conceives as itself. See the discussion in Dyczkowski, "The Doctrine of Vibration and Recognition," in *The Stanzas on Vibration,* 41–42; and the translation of Rājanaka Rāma's *Spandavivṛti,* ibid., 116.
18. VAP 2.14.
19. See VAP and VAPV 2.15. The most detailed account in English of Krama contemplations is found in Navjivan Rastogi, "The Philosophy of Krama Monism of Kashmir: An Analytical Study," 2 vols. (Ph.D. thesis, Lucknow University, 1967).
20. Bhāsvatī, Parispandā, Hlādā, Dhūmāvatī, and Vibhvī. Dhūmavatī, "Smokey," is well known as one of the ten tantric Mahāvidyās. See David Kinsley, "Dhūmavatī: The Widow Goddess," in *Tantric Visions of the Divine Feminine: The Ten Mahāvidyās* (Delhi: Motilal Banarsidass, 1997), 176–192. Kinsley observes: "Dhūmavatī is barely known outside the Mahāvidyās. If she had an independent cult prior to her inclusion in the group, we know nothing about it." Ibid., 176. In Gauḍiya and Sahajīya Vaiṣṇavism, Kṛṣṇa's consorts and lovers, especially Rādhā, are identified as expressions of his Hlādinī Śakti. See Edward C. Dimock, Jr., *The Place of the Hidden Moon: Erotic Mysticism in the Vaiṣṇava Sahajīya Cult of Bengal* (Chicago: University of Chicago Press, 1966), 133–134, 203–204; idem, "Doctrine and Practice among the Vaiṣṇavas of Bengal," in *Krishna: Myths, Rites, and Attitudes,* ed. Milton Singer (Chicago: University of Chicago Press, 1968), 48; and Barbara Stoler Miller, ed. and trans., *Love Song of the Dark Lord: Jayadeva's Gita Govinda* (New York: Columbia University Press, 1977), 59n.

21. VAP and VAPV 3.26–27. My order of listing the Śaktis differs from that of Virūpākṣa and Vidyācakravartin. I have arranged them according to the standard order for enumerating Śiva's cosmic acts.

22. VAP 3.28.

23. The sixfold "course" was mentioned in VAP 1.4, previously quoted, as a designation of the universe.

24. See the excellent discussion in Andre Padoux, "The Sixfold Course," in *Vāc: The Concept of the Word in Selected Hindu Tantras,* trans. Jacques Gontier (Albany: State University of New York Press, 1990), 330–371.

25. VAP and VAPV 1.4, 2.18–19.

26. VAP and VAPV 2.9–10. See PTV, 1, 18–19. Abhinavagupta's discussions also address a number of other symbolic and metaphysical issues.

27. VAPV 2.10.

28. For an overview, see Hemendra Nath Chakravarty, "Bindu," in *Kalātattvakośa,* general editor, Kapila Vatsyayan, vol. 2, *Concepts of Space and Time,* ed. Bettina Baumer (Delhi: Indira Gandhi National Centre for the Arts, 1992), 1–24.

29. See VAP and VAPV 1.7, along with note p. 73, n. 2; and VAP and VAPV 2.15–16 and 2.18–19.

30. White, *Kiss of the Yoginī,* passim.

31. VAP and VAPV 1.8. Also see VAPV 2.20, VAPV 3.38. VAPV 3.30 seems to allude to the Pratyabhijñā syntax of the Krama contemplation of the epistemic triad of knower (agent of knowing), knowledge, and the object of knowledge. That is discussed in Lawrence, *Rediscovering God,* 150–152.

32. VAPV, 1.intro.; VAP and VAPV 1.6; VAPV 1.7; VAP and VAPV 1.20; VAPV 4.45; VAP and VAPV 4.52. The monistic Śaivas also identify intention as a modality of Śakti, that is, the Īcchā Śakti.

33. VAP and VAPV 3.23–24.

34. VAPV 3.23.

35. VAPV 3.24.

36. The specific terms *anuvṛtta* and *vyāvṛtta* also have roots in Pāṇinian grammar. See pp. 79–80, n. 3.

37. See the interesting thematization of a "henological" argument for the existence of God in John Macquarrie, *In Search of Deity: An Essay in Dialectical Theism* (New York: Crossroad, 1987), 203–206. For a reading of the entire philosophical quest along these lines, see Frederick Copleston, *Religion and the One: Philosophies East and West* (New York: Crossroad, 1982).

38. The Pratyabhijñā system follows Bhartṛhari in positing the Time (*kāla*) Śakti as one of the primary capacities of the Ultimate for emanating into multiplicity. See Peri Sarveswara Sharma, trans., *The Kālasamuddeśa of Bhartṛhari's Vākyapadīya* (Delhi: Motilal Banarsidass, 1972); and Lawrence, *Rediscovering God,* 136–138. For Bhartṛhari, the "suppression" of sequence is a primary feature of *śabdapūrvayoga.* See Harold G. Coward, "The Reflective Word: Spirituality in

the Grammarian Tradition of India," in *Hindu Spirituality I: Vedas through Vedanta,* ed. Krishna Sivaraman (New York: Crossroad, 1989), 222–223. Another important background to the approaches to time in Bhartṛhari and the monistic Śaivas is theorization on both Vedic and tantric ritual sequence. These reflections have particular importance in the meditations of Krama tantrism on cycles of Śaktis. Besides those theories already mentioned, the Pratyabhijñā also notably pursues progressively inclusive categories in its treatments of semantic exclusion (*apoha*), relations (*sambandha*), and universals (*sāmānya*). Lawrence, *Rediscovering God,* 119–120, 129–130, 137–138.

39. VAPV 2.11.

40. Ibid. IPK and IPV 1.6.4–5, 1.312–323, distinguish the pure from the impure recognitive apprehensions of "I" on the grounds that the former includes all within itself, and the latter excludes things.

41. VAPV 2.12.

42. VAPV 1.2. (Vidyācakravartin explains this in the course of interpreting the meaning of a word, *dṛśyatvāt,* in the verse.) Also see VAPV 2.12.

43. VAP and VAPV 3.38–39.

44. See the notes to the translation of this section for further discussion of the interpretive issues.

45. Also commonly referred to as *prameya, pramāṇa,* and *pramātṛ.*

46. VAP and VAPV 3.32; VAP and VAPV 3.36–37. Consciousness (*citi*) is identified with recognitive apprehension in VAPV 3.32. It is in effect identified with Śakti by the alternation between the terms in VAP and VAPV 3.33. The I is identified with awareness (*prakāśa*) in VAPV 3.32 and VAPV 3.35.

47. VAPV 3.32.

48. VAP and VAPV 3.33.

49. VAP and VAPV 3.33, and VAPV 3.34 describe similarities using terms such as *iva.* VAP and VAPV 3.35 prescribe the contemplation of the identities of the items.

50. VAP 3.33.

51. VAPV 3.33.

52. See Wendy Doniger O'Flaherty, *Dreams, Illusion and Other Realities* (Chicago: University of Chicago Press, 1984), for a comparison of the cosmology of the *Yogavāsiṣṭha* with a Möbius strip. Vidyācakravartin goes into further detail, describing the degrees of sequence in the relations between the terms. VAPV 3.33–34.

53. VAP and VAPV 3.35–37. Vidyācakravartin observes in VAPV 3.35 that Virūpākṣa has stated the identities between the terms without a verb, that is, by apposition—in order to emphasize that their identities are eternally established. Abhinavagupta is fond of the maxim that "Everything has the nature of everything" (*sarvaṁ sarvātmakam*). Cf. the discussion in PTV, 26–28, of how the hierarchical triad of grammatical persons can be converted into each other on the basis of this principle.

54. YS 3.4, 281.

55. YS 3, 277–395. See Patañjali, "Perfect Discipline and Extraordinary Powers," in *Yoga: Discipline of Freedom,* trans. Barbara Stoler Miller (New York: Bantam, 1998), 60–73.

56. VAP and VAPV 4.45–4.49. VAP and VAPV 4.47–49 explain the possession by the I and thereby the attainment of control over all the thirty-six cosmic principles (*tattva*) emanated by the Supreme Śiva.

57. YS 3.50, 379.

58. VAPV 4.52.

59. VAPV 4.45.

60. VAP and VAPV 4.53.

61. VAPV 4.53.

Chapter 4

1. Antihierarchism subordinates hierarchism. The Śaiva approach to the hierarchization of alternative viewpoints also implements the broader explanatory and contemplative subsumption of difference within their emanationist metaphysics.

2. The reader is directed to the defense of the method of dialogue using comparative philosophy, as an alternative to interpretive dogmatism and cultural relativism, in Lawrence, *Rediscovering God,* 1–16.

3. Ibid., particularly 85–132, 155–170. The Pratyabhijñā articulates this idealism in the "*prakāśa* arguments," which complement the "*vimarśa* arguments" that epistemic processes are intrinsically recognitive. In supporting Śaiva monism-emanationism over monotheistic dualism, I have also adverted to recent efforts to reconstruct religious metaphysics that emphasize the simultaneous transcendence and immanence of Ultimate Reality. These are discussed further below.

4. Martin Buber, *I and Thou,* trans. Walter Kaufmann (New York: Scribner's, 1970), 131ff.; Emmanuel Levinas, *Collected Philosophical Papers,* trans. Alphonso Lingis (Dordrecht: Martinus Nijhoff, 1987); idem, *Totality and Infinity: An Essay on Exteriority,* trans. Alphonso Lingis (Pittsburgh: Duquesne University Press, 1969). Levinas views all metaphysics as obstructing the proper respect for others. For another comparative philosophical approach to the problem, see J. N. Mohanty, *The Self and Its Other: Philosophical Essays* (Delhi: Oxford University Press, 2000).

5. See R. C. Zaehner, *Mysticism, Sacred and Profane: An Inquiry into Some Varieties of Praeternatural Experience* (Oxford: Oxford University Press, 1975); Arthur C. Danto, *Mysticism and Morality: Oriental Thought and Moral Philosophy* (New York: Columbia University Press, 1987); and the dialogue between Danto, Wayne Proudfoot, and William J. Wainwright on the general category of mysticism in "Focus on Ethics and Mysticism," *Journal of Religious Ethics* 4 (1976):

3–46. Cf. the criticism, from a postmodern-deconstructive perspective, of programs of human divinization in Nicholas F. Gier, *Spiritual Titanism: Indian, Chinese and Western Perspectives* (Albany: State University of New York Press, 2000).

6. Jeffrey J. Kripal, "Debating the Mystical as the Ethical: An Indological Map," *Crossing Boundaries: Essays on the Ethical Status of Mysticism,* ed. G. William Barnard and Jeffrey J. Kripal (New York: Seven Bridges, 2002), 15–69. Kripal is more affirmative of tantric and some other Asian traditions in their stances toward embodiment and nature, while still maintaining their nonethical character. He follows James R. Horne in advocating a "mixed mysticism" that combines monistic mysticism with ethics. For an opposing argument, see G. William Barnard, "Debating the Mystical as the Ethical: A Response," ibid., 70–99. Urban, *Tantra,* 203–263, likewise discusses the scandals surrounding gurus promoting tantrism in the West.

7. The most complete ancient account is Ovid, "The Story of Echo and Narcissus," in *Metamorphoses,* trans. Rolfe Humphries (Bloomington: Indiana University Press, 1955), 67–73.

8. However, not all interpretations of the Narcissus story throughout history have focused on his pride. Other important themes have been the general "disease" of infatuation and Narcissus's attainment of self-knowledge. Two important studies of the history of these interpretations are Louise Vinge, *The Narcissus Theme in Western European Literature up to the Early 19th Century,* trans. Robert Dewsnap et al. (Lund: Gleerups, 1967); and Paul Zweig, *The Heresy of Self-Love: A Study of Subversive Individualism* (Princeton: Princeton University Press, 1980).

9. Psychoanalytic theories of narcissism will be considered later. Classic social critiques are Christopher Lasch, *The Culture of Narcissism: American Life in an Age of Diminishing Expectations* (New York: Warner, 1979); and Richard Sennett, *The Fall of Public Man* (New York: Knopf, 1977). For an alternative feminist perspective, see Gayatri Chakravorty Spivak, "Echo," in *The Spivak Reader: Selected Works of Gayatri Chakavorty Spivak,* ed. Donna Landry and Gerald MacLean (New York: Routledge, 1996), 175–202.

10. Zweig, 12–21. On God's self-recognition through the logos, see Lawrence, *Rediscovering God,* 21–23, 89–90, 163–164.

11. Plotinus, *The Enneads,* trans. Stephen Mackenna (New York: Larson Publications, 1992), 6.8.15, 690.

12. Ibid., 6.8.16, 691.

13. St. Thomas Aquinas, *Summa Contra Gentiles, Book One: God,* trans. Anton C. Pegis (South Bend, IN: University of Notre Dame Press, 1955), 246.

14. Meister Eckhart, "Creatures Seek God Through Me," in *Meister Eckhart: A Modern Translation,* trans. Raymond B. Blakney (New York: Harper & Row, 1941), 224–225.

15. Zweig, 12–21.

16. Ibid., 31.

17. Ibid., 19.

18. Ibid., 21.

19. Ibid., 243–244.

20. Plotinus, 1.6.8, 71.

21. Julia Kristeva, "Narcissus: The New Insanity," in *Tales of Love,* trans. Leon S. Roudiez (New York: Columbia University Press, 1987), 103–121. Also see the rich study of A. H. Armstrong, "Platonic Mirrors," in *Hellenic and Christian Studies* (Hampshire, Great Britain: Variorum, 1990), 147–181.

22. Bernard of Clairvaux, "On Loving God," in *Bernard of Clairvaux: Selected Works,* trans. G. R. Evans, *Classics of Western Spirituality* (New York: Paulist Press, 1987), 195–196.

23. William of Saint Thierry, *Exposition on the Song of Songs,* trans. Columba Hart (Kalamazoo: Cistercian Publications, 1968), 26.

24. Ibid., 81. Also see 102. For an excellent discussion, see Bernard McGinn, "William of St. Thierry: Spirit-Centered Mysticism," in *The Growth of Mysticism* (New York: Crossroad, 1994), 225–274.

25. John Ruusbroec, *The Spiritual Espousals, in The Spiritual Espousals and Other Works,* trans. James A. Wiseman, Classics of Western Spirituality (New York: Paulist Press, 1985), 151–152.

26. Ruusbroec, *A Mirror of Eternal Blessedness,* ibid., 247. He also describes this as a grace-inspired realization of the sense of "contentment" typifying the eternal, loving embrace between the three members of the Trinity, in *The Little Book of Clarification,* ibid., 262–263. I mention that in Hindu bhakti traditions there are analogous examples of intimate participation in God's self-love. In *Śrīmad Bhāgavata,* 10.33.17, 2:1192, Kṛṣṇa is said to sport with the *gopīs,* his exemplary devotees, like a child plays with reflections in a mirror. As mentioned before, in Gauḍīya Vaiṣṇavism, Kṛṣṇa is said to enjoy himself in Rādhā and the other *gopīs* through his Hlādinī Śakti. The twelfth century South Indian Vīraśaiva poet-saint, Basavaṇṇa, likewise describes the devotee as a mirror back for Śiva. Ramanujan, trans., *Speaking of Śiva,* 860, 90.

27. Thus, for Marsilio Ficino, the human soul may, as in medieval Neoplatonism, ascend to God through love and dialectic and redescend to observe the reflection of his ideas in nature. However, Ficino also advocated the Godlike production of artistic and intellectual artifacts, the manipulation of nature through magical images, and a cult of intimate, self-reflective love in friendships (by Platonizing courtly traditions). In his medical theories, Ficino likewise endeavored to balance Christian Neoplatonic asceticism with the needs of the body. I have discussed these subjects in "The Doctrine of Love of Marsilio Ficino and its Relations to His Conceptions of Dialectic and Magic" (unpublished).

28. Facile generalizations about the absence of individuality in South Asia are refuted by Mattison Mines, *Public Faces, Private Voices: Community and Individuality in South India* (Berkeley: University of California Press, 1994).

29. Meister Eckhart likewise speaks of the mystic unified with the Godhead as cocreating the universe with him.

30. Some of the controversy is reviewed in Kripal, "Preface to the Second Edition: 'Pale Plausibilities,'" in *Kālī's Child,* xi–xxiv. For a useful overview of psychoanalytic studies of Hinduism, see T. G. Vaidyanathan and Jeffrey J. Kripal, eds., *Vishnu on Freud's Desk: A Reader in Psychoanalysis and Hinduism* (New Delhi: Oxford University Press, 1999).

31. My approach to such dialogue is less committed to psychoanalysis than those of Kripal or Sudhir Kakar.

32. His foundational statement for psychoanalytic theorization on mysticism is Sigmund Freud, *Civilization and Its Discontents,* standard edition, ed. and trans. James Strachey (New York: Norton, 1961), 5–21. For an illuminating and provocative study of the Freud-Rolland correspondence, see William B. Parsons, *The Enigma of the Oceanic Feeling: Revisioning the Psychoanalytic Theory of Mysticism* (Oxford: Oxford University Press, 1999). Freud's most detailed treatment of narcissism is "On Narcissism," in *Standard Edition of the Complete Psychological Works of Sigmund Freud,* ed. and trans. James Strachey (London: Hogarth Press, 1953), 14:67–102. Also see Freud, "The Libido Theory and Narcissism."

33. Freud, *Civilization and Its Discontents,* 15.

34. VAP and VAPV 2.13, 2.20, 3.40; VAPV 3.28.

35. Freud, "On Narcissism," 14:75. Freud further discusses the role of narcissism in magical thinking, drawing analogies with neurosis and art, in "Animism, Magic and the Omnipotence of Thoughts," in *Totem and Taboo: Some Points of Agreement between the Mental Lives of Savages and Neurotics,* Standard Edition, trans. James Strachey (New York: Norton, 1950), 75–99.

36. Sudhir Kakar, whose theories are generally close to those of Heinz Kohut (discussed later), attempts to demonstrate that South Asian religions cultivate narcissistic experiences in a manner that is psychologically appropriate to their distinctive social and familial contexts. He lays the theoretical groundwork by arguing for the greater importance of narcissism in South Asian mother–son relationships, due to the traditional expectation for women to have sons to gain status in their husband's families. Sudhir Kakar, *The Inner World: A Psycho-Analytic Study of Childhood and Society in India,* 2nd ed. (Delhi: Oxford University Press, 1982). He further applies psychoanalytic theories of narcissism, sexuality, and aggression in *Shamans, Mystics and Doctors.* See his discussions of narcissistic fantasies of omnipotence and issues of sexuality in "Shiva and Narcissus," in *The Inner World,* 154–160; and "Tantra and Tantric Healing," in *Shamans, Mystics and Doctors,* 151–190. Kakar provides general methodological reflections in *The Analyst and the Mystic: Psychoanalytic Reflections on Religion and Mysticism* (Chicago: University of Chicago Press, 1991). Jeffrey Moussaieff Masson, *The Oceanic Feeling: The Origins of Religious Sentiment in Ancient India* (Dordrecht: D. Reidel, 1980) is more idiosyncratic in emphasizing the character of narcissism as an escape from

traumatic events. See his discussion of "Yogic Powers and Symptom Formation," ibid., 125–141.

37. Lacan, "The Mirror Stage as Formative of the Function of the I as revealed in psychoanalytic experience," 1–7.

38. For psychoanalysis, the body remains a basic referent of the ego-sense and a preoccupation of narcissistic libido throughout life. See Paul Schilder, "Narcissism and the Love of One's Own Body," in *The Image and Appearance of the Human Body* (New York: International Universities Press, 1978), 119–124. According to Sigmund Freud, *The Ego and the Id,* standard edition, trans. Joan Riviere, revised and ed. James Strachey (New York: Norton, 1960), 20, "the ego is first and foremost a bodily ego." Kakar, *Inner World,* 156, describes the Hindu male youth after the rupture of primal narcissism: "In the young boy's inner life, the compensatory restitution of self-assurance and control is expressed primarily in a fantasied over-valuation of his body, its strength, intactness, invincibility, and especially of his penis." He compares Indian and Western body images in *Shamans, Mystics and Doctors,* 232–238.

39. At several points, Lacan follows Hegel in describing the dialectics of mirroring. However, aligning himself with Heidegger, he repudiates the Kantian and Hegelian transcendental subject. Some resources are Jacques Lacan, "Some Reflections on the Ego," *International Journal of Psychoanalysis* 34 (1953): 11–17; *The Ego in Freud's Theory and in the Technique of Psychoanalysis 1954–1955: The Seminar of Jacques Lacan, Book II,* ed. Jacques Alain-Miller, trans. Sylvana Tomaselli (New York: Norton, 1991); idem, "Aggressivity in Psychoanalysis," in *Ecrits,* 8–9; William J. Richardson, "The Mirror Inside: The Problem of the Self," *Review of Existential Psychology and Psychiatry* 16 (1978–1979): 95–112; John P. Muller, *Beyond the Psychoanalytic Dyad: Developmental Semiotics in Freud, Peirce, and Lacan* (New York: Routledge, 1996); idem., "Ego and Subject in Lacan," *Psychoanalytic Review* 69 (1982): 234–240; idem, "Cognitive Psychology and the Ego: Lacanian Theory and Empirical Research," *Psychoanalysis and Contemporary Thought* 5 (1982): 257–291; Joseph H. Smith and William Kerrigan, eds., *Interpreting Lacan* (New Haven: Yale University Press, 1983); and Bruce Fink, *The Lacanian Subject: Between Language and Jouissance* (Princeton: Princeton University Press, 1995). The Slovenian cultural theorist, Slavoj Žižek, has attempted in a complex and sometimes ironic manner to reconstruct features of German idealism within Lacanian theory. Representative of his works on this theme are *Tarrying with the Negative* (Durham: Duke University Press, 1993), *The Indivisible Remainder* (London: Verso, 1996), and *The Ticklish Subject* (London: Verso, 2000).

40. As a well-known Lacan scholar suggested to me, Lacan would likely view Virūpākṣa's project as a refusal of the necessary "symbolic castration" by denying limits and otherness. How the Pratyabhijñā may challenge the Lacanian critique of the subject is a difficult question that I am unable to pursue presently. Whereas the Pratyabhijñā along with Western idealism treats the recognition

of identity as primordial—Lacan's psychodynamic structuralism resonates with contemporary ethical concerns in privileging difference and otherness.

41. Donald W. Winnicot, "Mirror-role of Mother and Family in Child Development," in *Playing and Reality* (New York: Tavistock, 1982), 111–118. Malcolm Pines describes the crucial difference between Lacan and Winnicott's theories of mirroring:

> Lacan's thesis that mirroring is essentially an alienating experience of aloneness with the self contrasts with Winnicott's that the child first *finds* himself in the mirror of the mother's face.

Malcolm Pines, "Mirroring and Child Development," in "The Mirror: Psychoanalytic Perspectives," ed. Melvin Bornstein, Donald Silver, and Warren Poland, *Psychoanalytic Inquiry: A Topical Journal for Mental Health Professionals* 5, 2 (1985): 220. This dedicated issue of *Psychoanalytic Inquiry* provides a useful overview of psychoanalytic discussions of mirroring until the mid-1980s.

42. Despite this basic difference between Kohut and Lacan, Muller, *Beyond the Psychoanalytic Dyad,* 135–136n, observes a variety of similarities between them.

43. Heinz Kohut, "Forms and Transformations of Narcissism," in *The Search for the Self: Selected Writings of Heinz Kohut,* 4 vols., ed. Paul H. Ornstein (Madison: International Universities Press, 1978–1991), 1:430.

44. Heinz Kohut, "The Psychoanalytic Treatment of Narcissistic Personality Disorders: Outline of a Systematic Approach," in *The Search for the Self: Selected Writings of Heinz Kohut,* ed. Paul H. Ornstein, 1:489–490.

45. Ibid., 1:479.

46. Kakar, *Shamans, Mystics and Doctors,* 145. Also see Kakar, "The Guru as Healer," in *The Analyst and the Mystic,* 35–54.

47. Kohut, "Forms and Transformations of Narcissism," 1:440; and "Psychoanalytic Treatment," 1:477–478.

48. Kohut, "Forms and Transformations," 1:454-455.

49. Ibid., 1:455–456. Actually, Rolland himself believed that the oceanic feeling was enduring rather than fleeting. Parsons, *The Enigma of the Oceanic Feeling,* attempts to document the antecedents to Kohut's more positive "transformational" approach to mysticism in Freud's understanding of empathy as well as his correspondence with Rolland. Cf. the discussions of empathic identification with others in Hinduism, in Kakar, *Inner World,* 19–20; and tantric "focused receptivity" in Kakar, *Shamans, Mystics and Doctors,* 177–178.

50. In describing the experience, Kohut, "Forms and Transformations of Narcissism," 1:455, quotes St. Paul and Goethe. Kohut is known to have had special admiration for the activist mysticism of Dag Hammarskjöld. See Heinz Kohut, *Self Psychology and the Humanities: Reflections on a New Psychoanalytic Approach,* ed. Charles B. Strozier (New York: Norton, 1985), 70–71. Kohut says that in cosmic narcissism, as in higher forms of humor, "in contrast to states of extreme

object cathexis," such as patriotic fervor, "the ego remains active and deliberate." Kohut, "Forms and Transformations of Narcissism," 1:457. I note that critical assessments of cosmic narcissism and identification with the universe are elaborated in two recent studies of "cult" leaders. Len Oakes, *Prophetic Charisma: The Psychology of Revolutionary Religious Personalities* (Syracuse: Syracuse University Press, 1997); and Robert Jay Lifton, *Destroying the World to Save It: Aum Shinrikyo, Apocalyptic Violence, and the New Global Terrorism* (New York: Henry Holt, 2000).

51. This deindividualization likewise precludes the classification of monistic Śaivism as a species of "manic mysticism," as evinced by figures such as Arthur Rimbaud and John Custance. See G. William Barnard, "Manic Mysticism," in "Debating the Mystical as the Ethical," 90—typifying the sort of monistic mysticism correlated with mania by Zaehner, *Mysticism: Sacred and Profane.*

52. For a reading that emphasizes Kohut's ambiguity about whether God is real or merely an answer to needs of psychological development, see Charles B. Strozier, "God and Religion," in *Heinz Kohut: The Making of a Psychoanalyst* (New York: Farrar, Straus and Giroux, 2001), 327–333.

53. Parsons, *The Enigma of the Oceanic Feeling,* 160–161.

54. Ibid., 159, 219n. Parson's treatment of these backgrounds is justified by Kohut's own remarks in "Forms and Transformations of Narcissism," 1:453–454. See Sigmund Freud, "Dreams and Occultism," in *New Introductory Lectures on Psychoanalysis,* standard edition, ed. and trans. by James Strachey (New York: Norton, 1965), 28–50. Parsons observes the close historical relations between Freud's views on such matters and Rolland's conception of "unmitigated" mystical intuition. Parsons, 68–71, 159.

55. Arthur J. Deikman, "Deautomatization and the Mystic Experience," in *Understanding Mysticism,* ed. Richard Woods (Garden City, NY: Image Books, 1980), 240–260; Parsons, 160–161. Also see Parsons, 220 n. 85. There may be some support for Deikman's theory of deautomatization in the argument of Robert K. C. Forman, *Mysticism, Mind, Consciousness* (Albany: State University of New York Press, 1999) that mystical practices overcome cognitive intentionality and social construction in leading aspirants to pure consciousness. Forman does not, however, relate this process to childhood cognitive or psychological development.

56. I am formulating it along the lines of religious pluralisms as have been espoused by scholars such as John Hick and Diana Eck. That is, while my claim is situated and contestable, it does not appeal to allegiance to a particular religious tradition. The Pratyabhijñā thinkers' own approaches to the problem of religious plurality are engaged in my "Zu Abhinavaguptas Offenbarungstheorie," and "The Plurality and Contingency of Knowledge, and its Rectification According to the Pratyabhijñā."

57. Cf. the rather analogous defense of a synthesis of absolute idealism and Leibnizian monism as a "transpersonal" explanation of "extrovertive" mysticism in Paul Marshall, *Mystical Encounters with the Natural World: Experiences and Expla-*

nations (Oxford: Oxford University Press, 2005). Whereas the Pratyabhijñā system, and my interpretation in *Rediscovering God,* are concerned with the grounds of the intelligibility of all experience, Marshall focuses particularly on formulating a metaphysics that accounts for the phenomenological data of mysticism as well as the findings of mind-brain research.

58. Forman, 109–127.

59. See Paul Ricoeur, "Dialectic: Archeology and Teleology," in *Freud and Philosophy: An Essay on Interpretation,* trans. Denis Savage (New Haven: Yale University Press, 1970), 459–493; idem, "A Philosophical Interpretation of Freud," trans. Willis Domingo, in *The Conflict of Interpretations,* ed. Don Ihde (London: Continuum, 2004), 157–172. According to Ricoeur, Freud's archaeological orientation prevented him from satisfactorily explaining the implicit teleological significance of processes such as identification and sublimation. The teleological aspects of psychoanalytic conceptions of development seem to me to be incontrovertible. See Lawrence, *Rediscovering God,* 99–102, on teleology in the Pratyabhijñā system as a recapitulation of cosmogony.

60. To adapt Collingwood and Inden's "scale of forms."

61. Arindam Chakrabarti, "Logic, Morals and Meditation: *Tarka, Dharma,* Yoga," *Evam* 3 (2004): 190–200, discusses morality in Hindu and Buddhist monistic traditions, including monistic Kashmiri Śaivism. T. S. Rukmani has recently written "Value Ethics in the Early Upaniṣads: A Hermeneutic Approach," in Rita Sherma and Arvind Sharma, eds., *Hermeneutics and Hindu Thought: Toward a Fusion of Horizons* (New York: Springer, forthcoming). As she indicates, texts such as the *Taittirīya Upaniṣad* evince a clear attention to social morality, even independent of eschatological concerns. Cf. Zweig, 244, 256–257 on the subversive egoist's need to send something back to society.

62. Barnard, "Debating the Mystical as the Ethical: A Response," 76. Barnard prefers the term "nondualism" to "monism."

63. Geoffrey Samuel, *Civilized Shamans: Buddhism in Tibetan Societies* (Washington, DC: Smithsonian Institution Press, 1993), 242–243, argues that the ethical parameter expressed in the bodhisattva ideal is "on the whole absent from Hindu Tantra." White concurs in "Introduction," *Tantra in Practice,* 13.

64. VAPV 4.51.

65. VAP and VAPV 4.51–52.

66. Abhinavagupta, however, suggests that the acts are ethical, in indicating his agreement with the view of the "doctrine of difference" (Nyāya) that "the purpose of creation, and so on, by the Lord is nothing but the good of others." IPV 1.1 benedictory verse, 1:32. In including delusion and consequent suffering under the purview of the divine will, the Śaivas share some problems of theodicy with other theistic traditions.

67. Cf. *Gorakh Sabadi,* trans. in White, "Why Gurus Are Heavy," 64, on how the perfection of the body leads to universal guru-hood:

> By seating the primal Brahman between the two (*nāḍīs*), the siddhi of *Guṭika bandha* (= the fixing of a pill of mercury, in *Rasārṇavam*) is obtained, and one's body lives as long as the earth. Transmute the diamond with the proper sounds, using the tongue as a stamp. Good qualities are produced from lesser qualities. In this way all of existence becomes one's disciple.

The motivation articulated in this expression of a goal of yogic practice is worthy of further investigation.

68. IPK 1.1 benedictory verse, 1:18. See the discussion of this verse, including different interpretations of the last clause, in Lawrence, *Rediscovering God,* 35–57, passim.

69. IPV 1.1 on IPK benedictory verse, 1:17.

70. IPKV 1.1.1, 1–2.

71. *Nyāya Sūtra* 1.1.24, quoted in IPV 1.1 benedictory verse, 1:32.

72. IPV 1.1 benedictory verse, 1:32.

73. IPV 1.1 benedictory verse, 1:32.

74. IPV 1.1 benedictory verse, 1:29–30; 4.1.18, 2:316.

75. *Śrīmad Bhagavad Gītā with Commentary by Mahāmāheshvara Rājānaka Abhinava Gupta,* ed. Lakshman Raina Brahamachārī (Srinagar: Kashmir Pratap Steam Press, 1933), 9.33–34, 108.

76. TA 15.576, 6:2714. All this is not to deny that there must be some receptivity to salvation. Note VAPV 4.42 on the de facto limit to universal redemption.

77. TA and TAV 2.39, 2:342–343. Also see TAV 2.46, 2:348.

78. TA 15.521–611.

79. On the influence of the Nyāya categories in South Asian traditions of philosophical discourse, see Bimal Krishna Matilal, "The Nature of Philosophical Argument," in *Perception: An Essay on Classical Indian Theories of Knowledge* (Oxford: Clarendon Press, 1986), 69–93. On their application in the Pratyabhijñā system, see Lawrence, *Rediscovering God,* 48–57. For an attempt to derive a global ethics from ostensibly transcendental norms of intellectual discourse, see Karl Otto Apel, "A Planetary Macroethics for Humankind: The Need, the Apparent Difficulty, and the Eventual Possibility," in *Culture and Modernity: East-West Philosophic Perspectives,* ed. Eliot Deutsch (Honolulu: University of Hawaii Press, 1991), 261–278.

80. David Peter Lawrence, "The Dialectic of Transcendence and Immanence in Contemporary Western and Indian Theories of God," in *Transcendence and Immanence: Comparative and Multi-Dimensional Perspectives,* ed. Liu Shuhsien et al. (Hong Kong: New Asia College, Chinese University of Hong Kong, 2001), 347–363; and *Rediscovering God,* 169. For further historical perspective, see the situation of nineteenth to twentieth century interpretations of extrovertive mysticism in Marshall, as well as the argument that a conception of a "vaguely panentheistic ultimate" is characteristic of popular and syncretic "grassroots spiritu-

ality," in Robert Forman, *Grassroots Spirituality: What It Is, Why It Is Here, Where It Is Going* (Charlottesville, VA: Imprint Academic, 2004), 52–60.

81. Rita Dasgupta Sherma, "Sacred Immanence: Reflections of Ecofeminism in Hindu Tantra," in *Purifying the Earthly Body of God: Religion and Ecology in Hindu India,* ed. Lance E. Nelson (Albany: State University of New York Press, 1998), 89–131.

82. As the ethical orientation was there from the beginning, the "mixing," as Kripal would describe it, consists in extending the orientation to address contemporary problematics.

CHAPTER 5

1. "The *Virūpākṣa-Pañcāśikā,*" ed. L. D. Barnett, *Le Museon* 9 (1908): 299–309.

2. *The Virūpākṣapañcāśikā, with the Commentary of Vidyācakravartin,* ed. T. Ganapati Śāstrī, Trivandrum Sanskrit Series, vol. 9 (Trivandrum: Travancore Government Press, 1910).

3. *Virūpākṣapañcāśikā Vidyācakravartikṛtavivṛtisametā,* ed. Gopinath Kaviraj, in *Tantrasaṁgraha (Part 1)* (Varanasi: Sansar Press, 1970), 1–22. Pt. Hemendra Nath Chakravarty, Kaviraj's student and secretary, has informed me of Kaviraj's use of T. Ganapati Śāstrī's edition. This edition has recently been republished as *Virūpākṣapañcāśikā, with the Commentary of Śrī Vidyācakravartin,* ed. Gopinath Kaviraj, with introduction by Sitaram Kaviraj (Varanasi: Sampurnanand Sanskrit University, 1992).

4. Henri Lenaerts, "A Study of the Pratyabhijñā Philosophy of Kashmir, with an Original Translation from the Sanskrit of the Virūpākṣapañcāśikā with Commentary, Followed by an Analysis of the Īśvara Pratyabhijñā Vimarśinī" (Ph.D. thesis, Banaras Hindu University, 1971).

5. VAPV, 1.intro.

6. As already mentioned, the recitation of the "Siddhi Skandha" of the VAP is enjoined in *Kailāsasaṁhitā,* in *Śiva Purāṇa,* 19.42–45, 4:1756. However, the age of various sections of the *Śiva Purāṇa* is not easily determined.

Glossary

abhimāna Pride, conception, or presumption pertaining to personal identity; desire related to such a conception.

abhisaṁdhi See *anusaṁdhāna.*

ādhāra Contemplative support.

adhikāra Eligibility for studying a religious or philosophical tradition.

adhvan Course of emanation. This refers either (1) collectively or individually to the six courses of emanating Speech; these are grouped in two triads, that is, phoneme (*varṇa*), empowered speech formula (mantra) and word (*pada*) as the triad of expressive speech (*vācaka*); and cosmic segment (*kalā*), cosmic principle (*tattva*), and cosmic realm (*bhuvana*) as the triad of speech referents (*vācya*); or (2) the three levels of the emanation of cosmic principles: the pure course (*śuddhādhvan*), the mixed course (*miśrādhvan*), and the impure course (*aśuddhādhvan*).

adhyavasāya Determinate ascertainment.

āgama Scriptural tradition, including in its significance oral and written scriptures as well as religious tradition more generally.

aham I.

ahambhāva See *ahaṁtā.*

ahaṁkāra I-concept.

ahampratyavamarśa Recognitive apprehension of I; self-recognition.

ahaṁtā, ahambhāva I-hood.

antaḥkaraṇa Inner organ, mind.

anusaṁdhāna, anusaṁhiti, abhisaṁdhi, pratisaṁdhāna Recognitive synthesis; synthesis having the structure of recognition between items of experience, extending from ordinary epistemic experience to Śiva's self-recognition.

anusaṁdhātṛ Recognitive synthesizer, Śiva/the highest Self as the agent of recognitive synthesis (*anusaṁdhāna*).

anusaṁhiti See *anusaṁdhāna.*

anuvṛtta Inclusive, subsuming difference and sequence. This qualification is applied increasingly to items at progressively higher cosmic levels, culminating in the all-inclusive Śiva.

anuvṛtti Inclusiveness, subsumption of difference and sequence. This quality is found increasingly in items at progressively higher cosmic levels, culminating in the all-inclusive Śiva.

anvaya Inferential concomitance, determined between items through induction.

apoha Semantic or conceptual exclusion.

apūrṇa Incomplete or imperfect; antonym of complete or perfect (*pūrṇa*).

arthakriyā Purposeful action.

asamprajñāta samādhi Contemplative enstasy (*samādhi*) without objective discernment or objective support.

asmitā I-am-ness.

aśuddhādhvan, śuddhetarādhvan Impure course (*adhvan*), lowest of the three levels of the emanation of cosmic principles (*adhvan*).

ātman The highest Self, identified by the monistic Śaivas with Śiva.

Bhāsvatī Illuminator, a Śakti.

bhava Worldly existence.

bhūtaśuddhi Purification of the elements, a practice of divinization of the body.

bhuvana, pada Cosmic realm, one of the set of six courses (*adhvan*).

bindu Germinal essence, often understood as equivalent to I-hood as Supreme Speech and self-recognition.

brahman Term for the absolute, particularly favored in the Upaniṣads and later Vedānta philosophy.

buddhi, dhī Intelligence.

cakra (1) Circle or wheel of modalities of Śakti that the practitioner endeavors to possess (cf. *maṇḍala*). (2) Energy centers in subtle physiology, activated as Kuṇḍalinī ascends in divinizing the body.

citi Consciousness. Other important terms for consciousness are *cit, caitanya,* and *saṁvid.*

dāsya Servitude, term for high spiritual realization, understood by the Pratyabhijñā as the recognition of identity with Śiva.

Dhūmāvatī Smokey, a Śakti.

dṛśya That which is perceptible or observable; object of cognition.

dṛśyatva Perceptibility.

dhī See *buddhi.*

guhā Cave, symbol of inner domain, identified by the VAPV with Māyā.

hetu Reason, in inference identifies a property in the subject that is invariably concomitant with that which is to be established regarding it.

Hlādā Happiness, a Śakti.

icchā Intention.

jīvanmukti Liberation while living.

jñāna Knowledge.
jñātṛ Knower, agent of knowing.
jñeya Object of knowledge.
kaivalya Abstraction, isolation; the experience of the Self as only transcendent by disregarding its immanent aspect.
kalā (1) Cosmic segment, one of the set of six courses (*adhvan*). (2) Limited agency, one of the five coverings (*kañcuka*).
kāla Time, limited time as one of the five coverings (*kañcuka*).
kālāgni Fire of time.
kañcuka Five coverings that obscure Śiva/the highest Self in the limited individual, namely, limited agency (*kalā*), limited knowledge (*vidyā*), attachment (*rāga*), causal necessity (*niyati*), and limited time (*kāla*).
kāraka In Sanskrit grammar, declined nouns referring to the concomitants of action, paralleling in certain respects conceptions of Indo-European cases.
kartṛtā Agency, conceived both grammatically and metaphysically as a quality of Śiva/the highest Self.
Kaula Movement of tantrism now known particularly for its sexual practices.
kevala dṛk Abstract, isolative knowledge; the experience of the Self as only transcendent by disregarding its immanent aspect.
kleśa Affliction that obstructs spiritual progress.
krama Sequence.
Krama Tradition of tantrism the practices of which typically involve the contemplation of sequences of Śaktis associated with phases of cognition.
kriyā Action, expressed by verbs in sentences, all forms of which are subsumed within Śiva's cosmic acts.
Kuṇḍalinī Śakti conceived in the form of a serpent, ordinarily dormant at the base of the spine but awakened through religious practice and thereby divinizing embodied experience.
madhyamā Intermediate, stage of emanating Speech second below Supreme Speech (*parāvāk*) in the Śaiva scheme.
mahāvākya Great sentence or utterance, referring to Upaniṣadic statements such as "I am brahman" and "You are that."
maṇḍala Circular diagrams of cosmogenesis and cosmocracy through Śakti, employed in external or internal ritual. Cf. *cakra.*
mantra Empowered speech formula employed in external or internal ritual, one of the set of six courses (*adhvan*).
miśrādhvan Mixed course, intermediate of the three levels of the emanation of cosmic principles (*adhvan*).
mokṣa: Liberation from cycle of suffering in reincarnation (*saṁsāra*).
nimeṣa Literally "eye-shutting," referring to Śiva's nonmanifestation of the cosmos, and also the nonmanifestation or "closure" between mutually exclusive things.
nirodha Mental arrest, correlated with the experience of the void (*śūnya*).

niyati Causal necessity, one of the five coverings (*kañcuka*).

nyāsa Projection of mantric syllables on the body and ritual implements, a practice of divinization of the body.

pada (1) Word, one of the set of six courses (*adhvan*). (2) See *bhuvanā.*

Paramaśiva Supreme Śiva; the highest, essential nature of Śiva before he bifurcates himself from Śakti.

parārthānumāna Inference for the sake of others, publicly assessible form of argument developed by the Nyāya tradition and applied in the Pratyabhijñā philosophy.

parāvāk Supreme Speech.

Parispandā Cosmic Pulsation personalized as a Śakti.

paśyantī Seeing, stage of emanating Speech first below Supreme Speech (*parāvāk*) in the Śaiva scheme.

prabuddha One who is enlightened.

prabuddhatā Enlightenment.

prakāśa Awareness.

pramāṇa Means of knowledge.

pramātṛ Knower, agent of knowledge.

prameya Object of knowledge.

prāṇa Breath, life-breath.

prapañca Phenomenal multiplicity.

pratibhā Semantic intuition, extending from the ordinary cognition of the meanings of words and their references to Śiva's Supreme Word (*parāvāk*).

pratibimba Reflection. Some monistic Śaiva practices contemplate the emanated universe as the reflection of Śiva/the highest Self.

pratisaṁdhāna See *anusaṁdhāna.*

pratyabhijñā Recognition, extending from ordinary epistemic experience to Śiva's self-recognition.

Pratyabhijñā Tradition of monistic Śaiva philosophical apologetics originated out of the Trika tradition, aims to lead students to participation in Śiva's self-recognition, further developed by Abhinavagupta and his successors for the exegesis of tantric symbolism and practice.

pratyāhara Abbreviation, in Sanskrit grammar. According to this procedure, a set of phonemes is designated by the combination of its first and last members.

pratyavamarśa See *vimarśa.*

pūrṇa Complete or perfect, describes the integral quality of the divine.

pūrṇāhaṁtā Complete or perfect I-hood.

pūrṇatva Completeness or perfection, the integral quality of the divine.

rāga Attachment, one of the five coverings (*kañcuka*).

śabdapūrvayoga Religious practice according to the tradition of the linguistic philosopher Bhartṛhari, involving the mastery of proper speech and the contemplation of its essential nature.

sādhana General term for spiritual practice.

sadvidyā See *śuddhavidyā.*

Śaiva A devotee of Śiva as the ultimate deity. Monistic Śaivas believe Śiva to comprehend the universe and all its individuals in identity with himself, as emanated through his integral power and consort, Śakti.

sakalīkarāṇa Making whole, a practice of divinization of the body.

Śākta A devotee of Śakti as the ultimate deity.

Śakti Literally Power or Energy; refers to the Goddess or her modalities.

śaktiman The possessor of Śakti, that is, Śiva as understood by the monistic Śaivas.

śaktipāta Gracious descent of Śakti.

śaktyāviṣkaraṇa The revealing of Śakti, Pratyabhijñā description of the basic modus operandi of monistic Śaiva religious practices. One realizes identity with Śiva by contemplating oneself as the possessor of Śakti (*śaktiman*).

samādhi Contemplative enstasy.

sāmānya Universal, distinguished from particular (*viśeṣa*), ontological counterpart to the epistemological category of recognition.

samāveśa Possession of the practitioner by the divine and its powers or of the divine and its powers.

samaya Rules of behavior for monistic Śaiva practitioners.

saṁkalpa Focusing attention on; intentionality; desire.

samprajñāta samādhi Contemplative enstasy (*samādhi*) with objective discernment or objective support.

saṁsāra Cycle of reincarnation in which unenlightened creatures suffer from life's contingencies and temporal finitude.

saṁskāra (1) Subliminal tendency. (2) Purification.

santāna Phenomenal series; patterned succession of moments of experience.

śarīra Body.

sattā Being.

sattarka Good reasoning, embodying the insight of Pure Wisdom (*śuddhavidyā*), employed to lead students to the realization of identity with Śiva.

siddhi Proficiency or power realized through yogic practices.

śivatattva Śiva principle, the "emanated, lower Śiva" as first emanation from the "Supreme Śiva" (*paramaśiva*) when he bifurcates himself from Śakti.

spanda Cosmic, creative pulsation.

Spanda Monistic Śaiva tradition the doctrines and practices of which emphasize the nature of Śakti as creative vibration (*spanda*).

śuddhādhvan Pure course, highest of the three levels of the emanation of cosmic principles (*adhvan*).

śuddhavidyā, sadvidyā Pure Wisdom, a cosmic principle intermediate in the Trika triads and fifth from the Supreme Lord in the thirty-six-fold scheme, consisting in the awareness of oneself as the emanator of the universe, expressed "I am this."

śuddhetarādhvan See *aśuddhādhvan.*

śuddhi Purity; purification.

śūnya, śūnyapada Void, a mode of subjectivity without any cognitive contents.
śūnyapada See *śūnya.*
suprabuddha One who is completely enlightened.
svatantratā See *svātantrya.*
svātantrya, svatantratā Agential self-determination, conceived both grammatically and metaphysically as a quality of Śiva/the highest Self.
svātmāsvāda Self-relishing of Śiva/the highest Self.
svātmaviśrānti Self-repose, rest in Śiva/the highest Self.
svātmopabhoga Self-enjoyment of Śiva/the highest Self.
tattva Cosmic principle, one of the set of six courses (*adhvan*).
Trika Literally "Triadism," a tradition of monistic Śaivism named for its explanatory and practical emphasis on various triads of modalities of Śakti and cosmic levels.
unmanā Transmental, a state of high spiritual realization.
unmeṣa Literally "eye-opening," referring to Śiva's manifestation of the cosmos.
vācaka Expressive speech, one of the two triads of courses (*adhvan*).
vācya Referent of speech, one of the two triads of courses (*adhvan*).
vaikharī Gross, lowest stage of emanating Speech, third below Supreme Speech (*parāvāk*) in the Śaiva scheme.
Vaiṣṇava A devotee of Viṣṇu as the ultimate deity.
varṇa Phoneme, one of the set of six courses (*adhvan*).
vibhūti (1) Power or proficiency realized through yogic practices. (2) Ashes with which Śiva and his devotees smear their bodies.
Vibhvī Omnipresent, a Śakti.
vidyā (1) Wisdom, shortened expression for Pure Wisdom (*śuddhavidyā*). (2) Limited knowledge, one of the five coverings (*kañcuka*).
vikalpa Conceptual construction.
vikalpasaṁskāra Purification of conceptual constructions (*vikalpa*) through good reasoning (*sattarka*)/Pure wisdom (*śuddhavidyā*), leading to the realization of identity with Śiva.
vimarśa, pratyavamarśa Recognitive apprehension or judgment; apprehension or judgment having the structure of the recognition of the application of subtle or gross speech to experience, extending from ordinary epistemic experience to Śiva's self-recognition.
viśeṣa Particular, distinguished from universal (*sāmānya*).
vyatireka Inferential exclusion; nonconcomitance between items determined through induction.
vyāvṛtta Exclusive, affected by difference and sequence. This qualification is applied increasingly to items at progressively lower cosmic levels.
vyāvṛtti Exclusiveness, correlated with difference and sequence. This quality is found increasingly in items at progressively lower cosmic levels.

Bibliography

Abhinavagupta. *The Īśvarapratyabhijñāvivṛtivimarśinī by Abhinavagupta.* 3 vols. Edited by Madhusudan Kaul Shastri. Kashmir Series of Texts and Studies. Reprint, Delhi: Akay Book Corporation, 1987.

———. *The Paramārtha-Sāra of Abhinavagupta with the Commentary of Yogarāja.* Edited by J. C. Chatterji. Srinagar: Kashmir Pratap Steam Press, 1916.

———. *Parātrīśikā Laghuvṛtti.* Edited by Jagaddhara Zadoo Shastri. Kashmir Series of Texts and Studies, no. 68. Srinagar: Mercantile Press, 1947.

———. *Śrīmad Bhagavad Gītā with Commentary by Mahāmāheshvara Rājānaka Abhinava Gupta.* Edited by Lakshman Raina Brahamachārī. Srinagar: Kashmir Pratap Steam Press, 1933.

———. *The Tantrasāra of Abhinavagupta.* Edited by Mukunda Ram Sastri. Kashmir Series of Texts and Studies, no. 17. Reprint, Delhi: Bani Prakashan, 1982.

———. *A Trident of Wisdom: Translation of Parātrīśikā-Vivaraṇa.* Edited and translated by Jaideva Singh. SUNY Series in Tantric Studies, Paul Muller-Ortega, ed. Albany: State University of New York Press, 1989.

Abhinavagupta and Bhāskara. *Īśvarapratyabhijñāvimarśinī of Abhinavagupta, Doctrine of Divine Recognition.* 3 vols. Vols. 1–2 are Sanskrit text with *Bhāskarī,* edited by K. A. Subramania Iyer and K. C. Pandey. Vol. 3 is translation of Abhinavagupta's text by K. C. Pandey. Reprint, Delhi: Motilal Banarsidass, 1986.

Abhinavagupta and Jayaratha. *The Tantrāloka of Abhinavagupta with the Commentary of Jayaratha.* 8 vols. Edited by Madhusudan Kaul Shastri and Mukunda Rama Shastri. Kashmir Series of Texts and Studies. Republication, edited by R. C. Dwivedi and Navjivan Rastogi. Delhi: Motilal Banarsidass, 1987.

———. *Abhinavagupta: The Kula Ritual, As Elaborated in Chapter 29 of the Tantrāloka.* Translated with introduction by John R. Dupuche. Delhi: Motilal Banarsidass, 2003.

Amrtanandanatha. *Sattrimsattattvasandoha: A Text of Trika Philosophy of Kashmir and the Commentary of Rajanaka Ananda Kavi.* Translated by Debabrata Sen Sharma. B. N. Chakravarty University Sanskrit series, no. 3. Kurukshetra: B. N. Chakravarty University, 1977.

Apel, Karl Otto. "A Planetary Macroethics for Humankind: The Need, the Apparent Difficulty, and the Eventual Possibility." In *Culture and Modernity: East-West Philosophic Perspectives,* ed. Eliot Deutsch, 261–278. Honolulu: University of Hawaii Press, 1991.

Armstrong, A. H. "Platonic Mirrors." In *Hellenic and Christian Studies,* 147–181. Hampshire, Great Britain: Variorum, 1990.

Banerjea, Akshaya Kumar. *Philosophy of Gorakhnath, with Goraksha-Vacana-Sangraha.* Delhi: Motilal Banarsidass, 1988.

Barnard, G. William. "Debating the Mystical as the Ethical: A Response." In *Crossing Boundaries: Essays on the Ethical Status of Mysticism.* Edited by G. William Barnard and Jeffrey J. Kripal, 70–99. New York: Seven Bridges, 2002.

Barnard, G. William, and Jeffrey J. Kripal, eds. *Crossing Boundaries: Essays on the Ethical Status of Mysticism.* New York: Seven Bridges, 2002.

Baumer, Bettina, and Debabrata Sensharma. "Pūrṇa," In *Kalātattvakośa,* general editor, Kapila Vatsyayan, vol. 2, *Concepts of Space and Time,* ed. Bettina Baumer, 429–447. Delhi: Indira Gandhi National Centre for the Arts, 1992.

Benjamin, Jessica. "An Outline of Intersubjectivity: The Development of Recognition." *Psychoanalytic Psychology* 7 (1990), supplement, 33–46.

Benveniste, Emile. *Problems in General Linguistics.* Translated by Mary Elizabeth Meek. Coral Gables, FL: University of Miami Press, 1971.

Bernard of Clairvaux. *Bernard of Clairvaux: Selected Works.* Translated by G. R. Evans. Classics of Western Spirituality. New York: Paulist Press, 1987.

Bhartṛhari. *The Kālasamuddeśa of Bhartṛhari's Vākyapadīya* (together with Helārāja's Commentary). Translated by Peri Sarveswara Sharma. Delhi: Motilal Banarsidass, 1972.

———. *Vākyapadīya of Bhartṛhari* (with commentaries). 4 vols. Edited by K. A. Subramania Iyer. *kāṇḍa* 1, Pune: Deccan College, 1966. *kāṇḍa* 2, Delhi: Motilal Banarsidass, 1983. *kāṇḍa* 3, part 1, Pune: Deccan College, 1963. *kāṇḍa* 3, part 2, Pune: Deccan College, 1973.

Biernacki, Loriliai. *Renowned Goddess of Desire: Women, Sex, and Speech in Tantra.* New York: Oxford University Press, 2007.

———. "Taboo and Orthodoxy: Making Tantra Respectable in 11th Century Kashmir." Ph.D. diss., University of Pennsylvania, 1999.

Bion, Wilfred. *Attention and Interpretation: A Scientific Approach to Insight in Psycho-Analysis and Groups.* London: Tavistock, 1970.

Bleandonu, Gerard. *Wilfred Bion: His Life and Works 1897–1979.* Translated by Claire Pajaczkowska. New York: Other Press, 2000.

Bornstein, Melvin, Donald Silver, and Warren Poland, eds. "The Mirror: Psychoanalytic Perspectives." *Psychoanalytic Inquiry: A Topical Journal for Mental Health Professionals* 5, 2 (1985).

Bozovic, Miran. *An Utterly Dark Spot: Gaze and Body in Early Modern Philosophy.* Ann Arbor: University of Michigan Press, 2000.

Braverman, Marcy Alison. "Totally Soaked: Immersion (*samāveśa*) and Intoxication of Devotion (*bhaktyunmāda*) in the Nondual Śaiva Yoga Traditions of Kashmir." Ph.D. diss., University of California, Santa Barbara, 2002.

Briggs, George Weston. *Gorakhnāth and the Kānphaṭa Yogīs.* Delhi: Motilal Banarsidass, 1982.

Brooks, Douglas Renfrew. *The Secret of the Three Cities: An Introduction to Hindu Śākta Tantrism.* Chicago: University of Chicago Press, 1990.

Brown, Cecil H., and Stanley R. Witkowski. "Figurative Language in a Universalist Perspective." *American Ethnology* 8 (1981): 596–615.

Buber, Martin. *I and Thou.* Translated by Walter Kaufmann. New York: Scribner's, 1970.

Burke, Kenneth. *A Grammar of Motives.* Berkeley: University of California Press, 1962.

Butler, Judith. *Bodies that Matter: On the Discursive Limits of "Sex."* New York: Routledge, 1993.

Carrithers, Michael, Steven Collins, and Steven Lukes, eds. *The Category of the Person: Anthropology, Philosophy, History.* Cambridge: Cambridge University Press, 1985.

Cash, Thomas F., and Thomas Pruzinsky. *Body Images: Development, Deviance, and Change.* New York: Guilford Press, 1990.

Chakrabarti, Arindam. "Logic, Morals and Meditation: *Tarka, Dharma,* Yoga." *Evam* 3 (2004): 190–200.

Chakrabarti, Kisor Kumar. *Classical Indian Philosophy of Mind: The Nyāya Dualist Tradition.* Albany: State University of New York Press, 1999.

Chakravarty, Hemendra Nath. "Bīja." In *Kalātattvakośa,* general editor, Kapila Vatsyayan, vol. 1, *Eight Selected Terms,* ed. Bettina Baumer, 117–133. Delhi: Indira Gandhi National Centre for the Arts, 1992.

———. "Bindu." In *Kalātattvakośa,* general editor, Kapila Vatsyayan, vol. 2, *Concepts of Space and Time,* ed. Bettina Baumer, 1–24. Delhi: Indira Gandhi National Centre for the Arts, 1992.

———. "The Pentadic Universe in the Shaivagamas." In *The Agamic Tradition and the Arts,* ed. Bettina Baumer. Delhi: Indira Gandhi National Center for the Arts, 1995. Online, http://ignca.nic.in/ps_03005.htm [accessed August 3, 2007].

———. "Sthūla-Sūkṣma-Para." In *Kalātattvakośa,* general editor, Kapila Vatsyayan, vol. 4, *Manifestation of Nature: Sṛṣṭi Vistāra,* ed. Advaitavadini Kaul and Sukumar Chattopadhyay, 275–316. Delhi: Indira Gandhi National Centre for the Arts, 1999.

———. "Tantric Spirituality." In *Hindu Spirituality II: Postclassical and Modern.* Edited by K. R. Sundararajan and Bithika Mukerji, 209–231. New York: Crossroad, 1997.

Chakravarty, Uma. *Indra and Other Vedic Deities: A Euhemeristic Study.* New Delhi: Printworld, 1997.

Chalier-Visuvalingam, Elizabeth. "Union and Unity in Hindu Tantrism." Online, www.infinityfoundation.com/mandala/i_es/i_es_visuv_e_unity.htm [accessed August 3, 2007].

Choudhuri, Usha. *Indra and Varuna in Indian Mythology.* Delhi: Nag Publishers, 1981.

Coakley, Sarah, ed. *Religion and the Body.* Cambridge: Cambridge University Press, 1997.

Copleston, Frederick. *Religion and the One: Philosophies East and West.* New York: Crossroad, 1982.

Coward, Harold G. "The Reflective Word: Spirituality in the Grammarian Tradition of India." In *Hindu Spirituality I: Vedas through Vedanta.* Edited by Krishna Sivaraman, 209–228. New York: Crossroad, 1989.

Danto, Arthur C. *Mysticism and Morality: Oriental Thought and Moral Philosophy.* New York: Columbia University Press, 1987.

Dasgupta, Shashibhusan. *An Introduction to Tantric Buddhism.* Calcutta: University of Calcutta, 1974.

———. *Obscure Religious Cults.* Calcutta: Firma K. L. Mukhopadhyay, 1969.

Davidson, Ronald M. *Indian Esoteric Buddhism: A Social History of the Tantric Movement.* New York: Columbia University Press, 2002.

Davis, Richard H. "Becoming a Śiva and Acting as One in Śaiva Worship." In *Ritual and Speculation in Early Tantrism: Studies in Honor of Andre Padoux.* Edited by Teun Goudriaan, 107–119. Albany: State University of New York Press, 1992.

Deikman, Arthur J. "Deautomatization and the Mystic Experience." In *Understanding Mysticism.* Edited by Richard Woods, 240–260. Garden City, NY: Image Books, 1980.

Deussen, Paul. *The Philosophy of the Upanishads.* Reprint, New York: Dover, 1966.

Dimock, Edward, Jr. "Doctrine and Practice among the Vaiṣṇavas of Bengal." In *Krishna: Myths, Rites, and Attitudes.* Edited by Milton Singer, 41–63. Chicago: University of Chicago Press, 1968.

———. *The Place of the Hidden Moon: Erotic Mysticism in the Vaiṣṇava Sahajīya Cult of Bengal.* Chicago: University of Chicago Press, 1966.

Doniger, Wendy [Wendy Doniger O'Flaherty]. *Dreams, Illusion and Other Realities.* Chicago: University of Chicago Press, 1984.

———. *Splitting the Difference: Gender and Myth in Ancient Greece and India.* Chicago: University of Chicago Press, 1999.

Dupuche, John R. "Person to Person: *Vivaraṇa* of Abhinavagupta on *Parātriṁśikā* Verses 3–4." *Indo-Iranian Journal* 44 (2001): 1–16.

Dvivedi, Vrajavallabha. "Having Become a God, He Should Sacrifice to the Gods In *Ritual and Speculation in Early Tantrism: Studies in Honor of Andre Padoux.* Edited by Teun Goudriaan, 121–138. Albany: State University of New York Press, 1992.

———, ed. *Netratantram [Mṛtyuñjaya Bhaṭṭārakaḥ], with the Commentary Udyota of Kṣemarājācārya.* Delhi: Parimal Publications, 1985.

———, ed. *The Svacchanda Tantra with Commentary-'Udyota' by Kṣemarājācārya.* 2 vols. Delhi: Parimal Publications, 1985.

———, ed. and Hindi trans. *Vijñāna Bhairava.* Delhi: Motilal Banarsidass, 2004.

Dyczkowski, Mark S. G. *The Canon of the Śaivāgama and the Kubjikā Tantras of the Western Kaula Tradition.* SUNY Series in the Shaiva Traditions of Kashmir, ed. Harvey Alper. Albany: State University of New York Press, 1988.

———. *The Doctrine of Vibration: An Analysis of the Doctrines and Practices of Kashmir Shaivism.* SUNY Series in the Shaiva Traditions of Kashmir, ed. Harvey Alper. Albany: State University of New York Press, 1987.

Eckhart, Meister. *Meister Eckhart: The Essential Sermons, Commentaries, Treatises, and Defense.* Translated by Edmund Colledge and Bernard McGinn. New York: Paulist Press, 1981.

———. *Meister Eckhart: A Modern Translation.* Translated by Raymond B. Blakney. New York: Harper & Row, 1941.

Epstein, Mark. "Meditation and the Dilemma of Narcissism." *Journal of Contemplative Psychotherapy* 7 (1990): 3–19.

Faure, Bernard. *The Red Thread: Buddhist Approaches to Sexuality.* Princeton: Princeton University Press, 1998.

———. *Visions of Power: Imagining Medieval Japanese Buddhism.* Princeton: Princeton University Press, 1996.

Faviez, Michel. *L'Orient et Lacan.* Paris: Accarias-L'Originel, 2002.

Fink, Bruce. *The Lacanian Subject: Between Language and Jouissance.* Princeton: Princeton University Press, 1995.

Flood, Gavin. *The Ascetic Self: Subjectivity, Memory and Tradition.* Cambridge: Cambridge University Press, 2004.

———. *Body and Cosmology in Kashmir Śaivism.* San Francisco: Mellen Research University Press, 1993.

———. "The Purification of the Body." In *Tantra in Practice.* Edited by David Gordon White, 509–520. Princeton: Princeton University Press, 2000.

———. *The Tantric Body: The Secret Tradition of Hindu Religion.* London: I. B. Tauris, 2006.

"Focus on Ethics and Mysticism." *Journal of Religious Ethics* (1976): 3–46.

Forman, Robert K. C. *Grassroots Spirituality: What It Is, Why It Is Here, Where It Is Going.* Charlottesville, VA: Imprint Academic, 2004.

———. *Mysticism, Mind, Consciousness.* Albany: State University of New York Press, 1999.

Freud, Sigmund. *Civilization and Its Discontents.* Standard Edition. Edited and translated by James Strachey. New York: Norton, 1961.

———. "A Disturbance of Memory on the Acropolis: An Open Letter to Romain Rolland on the Occasion of His Seventieth Birthday." In *Standard Edition of the Complete Psychological Works of Sigmund Freud.* Edited and translated by James Strachey. London: Hogarth Press, 1953, 22:237–248.

———. *The Ego and the Id.* Standard Edition. Translated by Joan Riviere. Revised and edited by James Strachey. New York: Norton, 1960.

———. *Introductory Lectures on Psychoanalysis.* Standard Edition. Edited and translated by James Strachey. New York: Norton, 1966.

———. "On Narcissism." In *Standard Edition of the Complete Psychological Works of Sigmund Freud.* Edited and translated by James Strachey. London: Hogarth Press, 1953, 14:67–102.

———. *New Introductory Lectures on Psychoanalysis.* Standard Edition. Edited and translated by James Strachey. New York: Norton, 1965.

———. *Totem and Taboo: Some Points of Agreement between the Mental Lives of Savages and Neurotics.* Standard Edition. Translated by James Strachey. New York: Norton, 1950.

Friedman, Lenore, and Susan Moon, eds. *Being Bodies: Buddhist Women on the Paradox of Embodiment.* Boston: Shambhala, 1997.

Gerow, Edwin. "What Is Karma (Kiṁ Karmeti): An Exercise in Philosophical Semantics." *Indologica Taurinensia* 10 (1982): 87–116.

Gier, Nicholas F. *Spiritual Titanism: Indian, Chinese and Western Perspectives.* Albany: State University of New York Press, 2000.

Goldberg, Arnold. *A Fresh Look at Psychoanalysis: The View from Self Psychology.* Hillsdale, NJ: Analytic Press, 1988.

Goswami, C. L., ed. and trans. *Śrīmad Bhāgavata Mahāpurāṇa.* 2 vols. Gorakhpur, India: Gita Press, 1982.

Goudriaan, Teun. *Māyā Divine and Human.* Delhi: Motilal Banarsidass, 1978.

———, ed. *Ritual and Speculation in Early Tantrism: Studies in Honor of Andre Padoux.* Albany: State University of New York Press, 1992.

———. "Some Beliefs and Rituals Concerning Time and Death in the Kubjikāmata." In *Selected Studies on Ritual in Indian Religions: Essays to D. J. Hoens,* ed. Ria Kloppenborg, 92–117. Leiden: Brill, 1983.

Granoff, Phyllis. "Maitreya's Jewelled World: Some Remarks on Gems and Visions in Buddhist Texts." *Journal of Indian Philosophy* 26 (1998): 347–371.

———. "Portraits, Likenesses and Looking Glasses: Some Literary and Philosophical Reflections on Representation and Art in Medieval India." In *Representation in Religion: Studies in Honor of Moshe Barasch,* ed., Jan Assmann and Albert L. Baumgarten, 63–103. Leiden: Brill, 2001.

Gupta, Senjukta, trans. *Lakṣmī Tantra: A Pāñcarātra Text.* Leiden: Brill, 1972.

Gupta, Senjukta, and Richard Gombrich. "Kings, Power and the Goddess." *South Asia Research* 6 (1986): 123–138.

Gupta, Senjukta, Teun Goudriaan, and Dirk Jan Hoens. *Hindu Tantrism.* Leiden: Brill, 1979.

Homans, Peter. *The Ability to Mourn: Disillusionment and the Social Origins of Psychoanalysis.* Chicago: University of Chicago Press, 1989.

———. "Introducing the Psychology of the Self and Narcissism into the Study of Religion." *Religious Studies Review* 7 (1981): 193–199.

Hulin, Michael. *Le Principe de l'Ego dans le Pensee Indienne Classique: La Notion d'Ahamkara.* Paris: de Boccard, 1978.

Hume, Robert Earnest, trans. *The Thirteen Principal Upanishads.* Oxford: Oxford University Press, 1977.

Inden, Ronald. "Embodying God: From Imperial Progresses to National Progress in India." *Economy and Society* 24 (1995): 245–278.

Inden, Ronald, Jonathan Walters, and Daud Ali. *Querying the Medieval: Texts and the History of Practices in South Asia.* Oxford: Oxford University Press, 2000.

Jakobson, Roman, and Grette Lubbe-Grothues. "The Language of Schizophrenia: Holderlin's Spech and Poetry." In *Verbal Art, Verbal Sign, Verbal Time,* ed. K. Pomorska and S. Rudy, 133–140. Minneapolis: University of Minnesota Press, 1985.

Jayadeva. *Love Song of the Dark Lord: Jayadeva's Gita Govinda.* Edited and translated by Barbara Stoler Miller. New York: Columbia University Press, 1977.

Jee, Swami Lakshman. *Kashmir Śaivism: The Secret Supreme.* Srinagar: Universal Shaiva Trust, 1985.

Jonas, Hans. *The Gnostic Religion: The Message of the Alien God and the Beginnings of Christianity.* 2nd ed. Boston: Beacon Press, 1963.

Kakar, Sudhir. *The Analyst and the Mystic: Psychoanalytic Reflections on Religion and Mysticism.* Chicago: University of Chicago Press, 1991.

———. "The Body Image." In *The Essential Writings of Sudhir Kakar,* 161–166. New Delhi: Oxford University Press, 2001.

———. *The Essential Writings of Sudhir Kakar.* With Introduction by T. G. Vaidyanathan. New Delhi: Oxford University Press, 2001.

———, ed. *Identity and Adulthood.* Delhi: Oxford University Press, 1982.

———. *The Inner World: A Psycho-Analytic Study of Childhood and Society in India.* 2nd ed. Delhi: Oxford University Press, 1982.

———. *Shamans, Mystics and Doctors: A Psychological Inquiry into India and its Healing Traditions.* Boston: Beacon Press, 1983.

Kapstein, Matthew. *Reason's Traces: Identity and Interpretation in Indian and Tibetan Buddhist Thought.* Delhi: Oxford University Press, 2001.

Kasulis, Thomas. "Reality as Embodiment: An Analysis of Kukai's *Sokushinjobutsu* and *Hosshin Seppo.* In *Religious Reflections on the Human Body.* Edited by Jane Marie Law, 166–185. Bloomington: Indiana University Press, 1995.

Kaviraj, Gopinath. *Bhāratīya Saṁskṛti aur Sādhanā.* 2 vols. Patna: Bihar Rastrabhasa Parisad, 1977–1979.

———, ed. *Yoginīhṛdayam with the Commentaries Dīpikā of Amṛtānanda and Setubandha of Bhāskararāya.* Varanasi: Sanskrit University, 1979.

Kelley, C. F. *Meister Eckhart on Divine Knowledge.* New Haven: Yale University Press, 1977.

Kinsley, David. "'Through the Looking Glass': Divine Madness in the Hindu Religious Traditions." *History of Religions* 13 (1974): 270–305.

———. *Tantric Visions of the Divine Feminine: The Ten Mahāvidyās.* Delhi: Motilal Banarsidass, 1997.

Klein, Anne Carolyn. *Meeting the Great Bliss Queen: Buddhists, Feminists, and the Art of the Self.* Boston: Beacon Press, 1995.

Klostermaier, Klaus K. *Hindu Writings: A Short Introduction to the Major Sources.* Oxford: Oneworld Publications, 2000.

———. *Hinduism: A Short History.* Oxford: Oneworld Publications, 2000.

———. *Mythologies and Philosophies of Salvation in the Theistic Traditions of India.* Waterloo, Ontario: Wilfred Laurier University Press, 1984.

Kochhar-Lindgren, Gray. *Narcissus Transformed: The Textual Subject in Psychoanalysis and Literature.* University Park: Pennsylvania State University Press, 1993.

Kohut, Heinz. "Forms and Transformations of Narcissism." In *The Search for the Self: Selected Writings of Heinz Kohut.* 4 vols. Edited by Paul H. Ornstein. Madison: International Universities Press, 1978–1991, 1:427–460.

———. "Introspection, Empathy, and Psychoanalysis: An Examination of the Relationship Between Mode of Observation and Theory." In *The Search for the Self: Selected Writings of Heinz Kohut.* 4 vols. Edited by Paul H. Ornstein. Madison: International Universities Press, 1978–1991, 1:205–232.

———. "The Psychoanalytic Treatment of Narcissistic Personality Disorders: Outline of a Systematic Approach." In *The Search for the Self: Selected Writings of Heinz Kohut.* 4 vols. Edited by Paul H. Ornstein. Madison: International Universities Press, 1978–1991, 1:477–509.

———. *The Search for the Self: Selected Writings of Heinz Kohut.* 4 vols. Edited by Paul H. Ornstein. Madison: International Universities Press, 1978–1991.

———. *Self Psychology and the Humanities: Reflections on a New Psychoanalytic Approach.* Edited by Charles B. Strozier. New York: Norton, 1985.

Kripal, Jeffrey J. "Debating the Mystical as the Ethical: An Indological Map." In *Crossing Boundaries: Essays on the Ethical Status of Mysticism.* Edited by G. William Barnard and Jeffrey J. Kripal, 15–69. New York: Seven Bridges, 2002.

———. *Kālī's Child: The Mystical and the Erotic in the Life and Teachings of Ramakrishna.* 2nd ed. Chicago: University of Chicago Press, 1998.

———. *Roads of Excess: Palaces of Wisdom: Eroticism and Reflexivity in the Study of Mysticism.* Chicago: University of Chicago Press, 2001.

Kristeva, Julia. *Tales of Love.* Translated by Leon S. Roudiez. New York: Columbia University Press, 1987.

Kṣemarāja. *Pratyabhijñāhṛdayam: The Secrect of Self-Recognition.* Edited, translated, and with introduction by Jaideva Singh. Delhi: Motilal Banarsidass, 1980.

———. *Spanda Sandoha.* Edited by Mukunda Rama Shastri. Kashmir Series of Texts and Studies, no. 16. Bombay: Shri Venkateshwar Steam Press, 1917.

Kūkai. *Kūkai: Major Works.* Translated by Yoshito S. Hakeda. New York: Columbia University Press, 1972.

Lacan, Jacques. *Ecrits: A Selection.* Translated by Alan Sheridan. London: Routledge, 1997.

———. *The Ego in Freud's Theory and in the Technique of Psychoanalysis 1954–1955: The Seminar of Jacques Lacan, Book II.* Edited by Jacques-Alain Miller and translated by Sylvana Tomaselli. New York: Norton, 1991.

———. *The Ethics of Psychoanalysis 1959–1960: The Seminar of Jacques Lacan, Book VII.* Edited by Jacques-Alain Miller and translated by Dennis Porter. London: Routledge, 1999.

———. *Feminine Sexuality: Jacques Lacan and the Ecole Freudienne.* Edited by Juliet Mitchell and Jacqueline Rose. Translated by Jacqueline Rose. New York: Norton, 1982.

———. *The Four Fundamental Concepts of Psychoanalysis.* Edited by Jacques-Alain Miller. Translated by Alan Sheridan. London: Vintage, 1998.

———. "Some Reflections on the Ego." *International Journal of Psychoanalysis* 34 (1953): 11–17.

Lasch, Christopher. *The Culture of Narcissism: American Life in an Age of Diminishing Expectations.* New York: Warner, 1979.

Lavelle, Louis. *The Dilemma of Narcissus.* Translated by William T. Gairdner. Burdett, NY: Larson Publications, 1993.

Law, Jane Marie, ed. *Religious Reflections on the Human Body.* Bloomington: Indiana University Press, 1995.

Lawrence, David Peter. "Zu Abhinavaguptas Offenbarungstheorie." *Polylog* 5 (2000): 6–18.

———. "Abhinavagupta's Philosophical Hermeneutics of Grammatical Persons." In *Journal of Hindu Studies,* forthcoming.

———. "The Dialectic of Transcendence and Immanence in Contemporary Western and Indian Theories of God." In *Transcendence and Immanence: Comparative and Multi-Dimensional Perspectives,* ed. Liu Shu-hsien et al. 347–363. Hong Kong: New Asia College, Chinese University of Hong Kong, 2001.

———. "The Doctrine of Love of Marsilio Ficino and its Relations to his Conceptions of Dialectic and Magic." Unpublished manuscript.

———. "The Mythico-Ritual Syntax of Omnipotence." *Philosophy East and West* 48 (1998): 592–622.

———. "The Plurality and Contingency of Knowledge, and its Rectification According to the Pratyabhijñā," in *Perspectives on Abhinavagupta* (commemoration volume for K. C. Pandey. Edited by Navjivan Rastogi and Meera Rastogi, forthcoming.

———. *Rediscovering God with Transcendental Argument: A Contemporary Interpretation of Monistic Kashmiri Śaiva Philosophy.* Albany: State University of New York Press, 1999.

———. "Remarks on Abhinavagupta's Use of the Analogy of Reflection." *Journal of Indian Philosophy* 33 (2005): 583–599.

———. "Śiva's Self-Recognition and the Problem of Interpretation," *Philosophy East and West* 48 (1998): 197–231.

———. "Tantric Argument: The Transfiguration of Philosophical Discourse in the Pratyabhijñā System of Utpaladeva and Abhinavagupta," *Philosophy East and West* 46 (1996): 165–204.

Lee, Benjamin, and Greg Urban, eds. *Semiotics, Self, and Society.* New York: Mouton de Gruyter, 1989.

Lenaerts, Henri. "A Study of the Pratyabhijñā Philosophy of Kashmir, with an Original Translation from the Sanskrit of the Virūpākṣapañcāśikā with Commentary, Followed by an Analysis of the Īśvara Pratyabhijñā Vimarśinī." Ph.D. thesis, Banaras Hindu University, 1971.

Levinas, Emmanuel. *Collected Philosophical Papers.* Translated by Alphonso Lingis. Dordrecht: Martinus Nijhoff, 1987.

———. *Totality and Infinity: An Essay on Exteriority.* Translated by Alphonso Lingis. Pittsburgh: Duquesne University Press, 1969.

Lichtenberg, Joseph D. "Mirrors and Mirroring: Developmental Experiences." In "The Mirror: Psychoanalytic Perspectives." Edited by Melvin Bornstein, Donald Silver, and Warren Poland. *Psychaonalytic Inquiry: A Topical Journal for Mental Health Professionals* 5, 2 (1985): 199–210.

Lifton, Robert Jay. *Destroying the World to Save It: Aum Shinrikyo, Apocalyptic Violence and the New Global Terrorism.* New York: Henry Holt, 2000.

Macquarrie, John. *In Search of Deity: An Essay in Dialectical Theism.* New York: Crossroad, 1987.

Madan, T. N. *Non-Renunciation: Themes and Interpretations of Hindu Culture.* Delhi: Oxford University Press, 1987.

Maheśvarānanda. *Mahārthamañjarī of Maheśvarānanda with the Auto-Commentary Parimala.* Edited by Vrajavallabha Dvivedi. Varanasi: Varanaseya Sanskrit Vishvavidyalaya Press, 1972.

Marglin, Frederique Apffel. *Wives of the God-King: The Rituals of the Devadasis of Puri.* Delhi: Oxford University Press, 1985.

Marriot, McKim. "Hindu Transactions; Diversity without Dualism." In *Transaction and Meaning: Directions in the Anthropology of Exchange and Symbolic Behavior.* Edited by Bruce Kapferer. Philadelphia: Institute for the Study of Human Issues, 1976, 109–142.

Marshall, Paul. *Mystical Encounters with the Natural World: Experiences and Explanations.* Oxford: Oxford University Press, 2005.

Masson, Jeffrey Moussaieff. *The Oceanic Feeling: The Origins of Religious Sentiment in Ancient India.* Dordrecht: D. Reidel, 1980.

Matilal, Bimal Krishna. *Perception: An Essay on Classical Indian Theories of Knowledge.* Oxford: Clarendon Press, 1986.

Mauss, M. "Techniques of the Body." *Economy and Society* 2, 1 (1973): 70–87.

McGinn, Bernard. *The Growth of Mysticism.* New York: Crossroad, 1994.

Merleau-Ponty, Maurice. *The Primacy of Perception, and Other Essays on Phenomenological Psychology, the Philosophy of Art, History and Politics.* Evanston: Northwestern University Press, 1964.

Mines, Mattison. *Public Faces, Private Voices: Community and Individuality in South India.* Berkeley: University of California Press, 1994.

Mohanty, J. N. *The Self and Its Other: Philosophical Essays.* Delhi: Oxford University Press, 2000.

Morley, James. "Inspiration and Expiration: Yoga Practice Through Merleau-Ponty's Phenomenology of the Body." *Philosophy East and West* 51 (2001): 73-82.

Muller, John P. *Beyond the Psychoanalytic Dyad: Developmental Semiotics in Freud, Peirce, and Lacan.* New York: Routledge, 1996.

———. "Cognitive Psychology and the Ego: Lacanian Theory and Empirical Research." *Psychoanalysis and Contemporary Thought* 5 (1982): 257–291.

———. "Ego and Subject in Lacan." *The Psychoanalytic Review* 69 (1982): 234–240.

———. "Lacan's Mirror Stage." In "The Mirror: Psychoanalytic Perspectives." Edited by Melvin Bornstein, Donald Silver and Warren Poland. *Psychaonalytic Inquiry: A Topical Journal for Mental Health Professionals* 5, 2 (1985): 233–252.

———. "Langauge, Psychosis and the Spirit." In *Attachment and the Therapeutic Process,* ed. J. Sacksteder, D. Schwartz, and Y. Akabane, 99–116. New York: International Universities Press, 1987.

———. "Langauge, Psychosis, and the Subject in Lacan." In *Interpreting Lacan,* ed. Josheph H. Smith and William Kerrigan, 21–32. New Haven: Yale University Press, 1983.

———. "The Psychoanalytic Ego in Lacan: Its Origins and Self-Serving Functions." In *Psychological Perspectives on the Self,* vol. 3, ed. Jerry Suls and Anthony G. Greenwald, 79–106. Hillsdale, NJ: Lawrence Erlbaum, 1986.

Muller, John P., and William J. Richardson. *Lacan and Language: A Reader's Guide to the Ecrits.* New York: International Universities Press, 1982.

Muller, John P., and Joseph Brent, eds. *Peirce, Semiotics, and Psychoanalysis.* Baltimore: Johns Hopkins University Press, 2000.

Muller-Ortega, Paul Eduardo. *The Triadic Heart of Śiva: Kaula Tantricism of Abhinavagupta in the Non-Dual Shaivism of Kashmir.* SUNY Series in the Shaiva Traditions of Kashmir, ed. Harvey Alper. Albany: State University of New York Press, 1989.

Nagar, Shanti Lal, trans., and Acharya Ramesh Chaturvedi, ed. *Brahmavaivarta Purāṇa,* 2 vols. Delhi: Parimal, 2001.

Oakes, Len. *Prophetic Charisma: The Psychology of Revolutionary Religious Personalities.* Syracuse: Syracuse University Press, 1997.

Obeyesekere, Gananath. *The Work of Culture: Symbolic Transformation in Psychoanalysis and Anthropology.* Chicago: University of Chicago Press, 1990.

O'Donovan-Anderson, Michael. *The Incorporated Self: Interdisciplinary Perspectives on Embodiment.* Lanham, MD: Rowman & Littlefield, 1996.

Ovid. *Metamorphoses.* Translated by Rolfe Humphries. Bloomington: Indiana University Press, 1955.

Padoux, Andre. *Vāc: The Concept of the Word in Selected Hindu Tantras.* Translated by Jacques Gontier. SUNY Series in the Shaiva Traditions of Kashmir, ed. Harvey Alper. Albany: State University of New York Press, 1990.

Pagels, Elaine. *The Gnostic Gospels.* New York: Vintage Books, 1979.

Palihawadana, Mahinda. "Ideological Religion: An Example from Early India." *Kalyani: Journal of Humanities & Social Social Science* 1 (1982): 1–23.

———. "The Indra Cult as Ideology: A Clue to Power Struggle in an Ancient Society (including a discussion of the semantics of Rgvedic ari and its sociopolitical background)." *Vidyodaya Journal of Arts, Sciences and Letters* 9 (1981): 37–112; and 10 (1982): 1–59.

———. "A New Approach to the Interpretation of Rgvedic Ari." In *OH de A Wijesekera Felicitation Volume,* 88–98. Peradeniya, Sri Lanka, 1970.

Paranjpe, Anand C. *Self and Identity in Modern Indian Thought.* New York: Plenum Press, 1998.

Parry, Jonathan. "Sacrificial Death and the Necrophagus Ascetic." In *Death and the Regeneration of Life,* ed. Maurice Bloch and Jonathan Parry, 75–110. Cambridge: Cambridge University Press, 1982.

Parsons, William B. *The Enigma of the Oceanic Feeling: Revisioning the Psychoanalytic Theory of Mysticism.* Oxford: Oxford University Press, 1999.

Pāśupata-Sūtram with Pañcārtha-bhāṣya of Kauṇḍinya. Translated by H. Chakraborti. Calcutta: Academic Publishers, 1970.

Patañjali. *Yoga: Discipline of Freedom.* Translated by Barbara Stoler Miller. New York: Bantam Books, 1998.

Patañjali et al. *Pātañjalayogadarśanam.* Edited by Srinarayan Mishra. Varanasi: Bharatiya Vidya Prakashan, 1971.

Pines, Malcolm. "Mirroring and Child Development." In "The Mirror: Psychoanalytic Perspectives." Edited by Melvin Bornstein, Donald Silver, and Warren Poland. *Psychaonalytic Inquiry: A Topical Journal for Mental Health Professionals* 5, 2 (1985): 211–231.

Pirrucello, Ann. "Making the World My Body: Simone Weil and Somatic Practice." *Philosophy East and West* 52 (2002): 479–497.

Plakun, Eric M, ed. *New Perspectives on Narcissism.* Washington, DC: American Psychiatric Press, 1990.

Plato. *The Collected Dialogues of Plato, Including the Letters.* Edited by Edith Hamilton and Huntington Cairns. Bollingen Series 57. Princeton: Princeton University Press, 1989.

Plotinus, *The Enneads: A New, Definitive Edition with Comparisons to other Translations on Hundreds of Key Passages.* Translated by Stephen MacKenna. New York: Larson Publications, 1992.

Potter, Karl H. ed. *Encyclopedia of Indian Philosophies.* Vol. 4, *Sāṁkhya,* edited by Gerald James Larson and Ram Shankar Bhattacharya. Delhi: Motilal Banarsidass, 1987.

Puṇyānanda and Naṭanāndanātha. *Kāmakalāvilāsa with Commentary Cidvallī.* Edited by Svamiji Maharaja Vanakhandeshvara. Datia: Pitambarapith Sanskrit Parishad, 1979.

Ramanujan, A. K., trans. *Speaking of Śiva.* Harmondsworth: Penguin Books, 1979.

Rastogi, Navjivan. *The Krama Tantricism of Kashmir: Historical and General Sources.* Volume 1. Delhi: Motilal Banarsidass, 1979.

———. "The Philosophy of Krama Monism of Kashmir: An Analytical Study." 2 vols. Ph.D. thesis, Lucknow University, Lucknow, India, 1967.

———. "Some More Nyāyas as Employed by Abhinavagupta." *Annals of the Bhandarkar Oriental Research Institute* 65 (1984): 27–42.

———. "Theory of Error According to Abhinavagupta." *Journal of Indian Philosophy* 14 (1986): 1–33.

Richardson, William J. "Lacan and the Subject of Psychoanalysis." In *Interpreting Lacan,* ed. Josheph H. Smith and William Kerrigan, 51–74. New Haven: Yale University Press, 1983.

———. "The Mirror Inside: The Problem of the Self." *Review of Existential Psychology and Psychiatry* 16 (1978–1979): 95–112.

———. "Psychoanalysis and the Being-question." In *Interpreting Lacan,* ed. Josheph H. Smith and William Kerrigan, 51–74. New Haven: Yale University Press, 1983.

Ricoeur, Paul. "Approaching the Human Person." *Ethical Perspectives* 6 (1999): 45–54.

———. *The Conflict of Interpretations.* Edited by Don Ihde. London: Continuum, 2004.

———. *Freud and Philosophy: An Essay on Interpretation.* Translated by Denis Savage. New Haven: Yale University Press, 1970.

Rizzutto, Ana-Maria. "First Person Personal Pronouns and Their Psychic Referents." *International Journal of Psychoanalysis* 74 (1993): 535–546.

Robinson, James M, ed. *The Nag Hammadi Library in English.* Revised ed. San Francisco: Harper, 1990.

Roland, Alan. *Cultural Pluralism and Psychoanalysis: The Asian and North American Experience.* New York: Routledge, 1996.

———. *In Search of Self in India and Japan: Toward a Cross-Cultural Psychoanalysis.* Princeton: Princeton University Press, 1988.

Rorty, Amelie Oksenberg, ed. *The Identities of Persons.* Berkeley: University of California Press, 1976.

Rucaka [Ruyyaka] and Vidyācakravartin. *Alaṁkāra-sarvasva of Ruyyaka with Sañjivanī Commentary of Vidyācakravartin.* Edited by S. S. Janaki. Delhi: Meharchand Lachhmandas, 1965.

Rukmani, T. S. "Value Ethics in the Early Upaniṣads: A Hermeneutic Approach." In *Hermeneutics and Hindu Thought: Toward a Fusion of Horizons,* ed. Rita Sherma and Arvind Sharma. New York: Springer, forthcoming.

Ruusbroec, John. *The Spiritual Espousals and Other Works.* Translated by James A. Wiseman. Classics of Western Spirituality. New York: Paulist Press, 1985.

Samuel, Geoffrey. "The Body in Buddhist and Hindu Tantra: Some Notes." *Religion* 19 (1989): 197–210.

———. *Civilized Shamans: Buddhism in Tibetan Societies.* Washington, DC: Smithsonian Institution Press, 1993.

Sanderson, Alexis. "The Doctrine of the Mālinīvijayottaratantra." In *Ritual and Speculation in Early Tantrism: Studies in Honor of Andre Padoux,* 281–312, ed. Teun Goudriaan. SUNY Series in Tantric Studies, ed. Paul Eduardo Muller-Ortega. Albany: State University of New York Press, 1992.

———. "Maṇḍala and Āgamic Identity in the Trika of Kashmir." In *Mantras et diagrammes rituels dans L'Hindouisme,* ed. Andre Padoux, 169–214. Paris: Centre National de la Recherche Scientifique, 1986.

———. "Meaning in Tantric Ritual." In *Essais sur le Rituel, III* (Colloque du Centenaire de la Section des Sciences Religieuses de l'Ecole Pratique des Hautes Etudes), ed. Anne-Marie Blondeau and Kristofer Schipper, 15–95. Louvain: Peeters, 1995.

———. "Purity and Power Among the Brahmans of Kashmir." In *The Category of the Person: Anthropology, Philosophy, History,* ed. Michael Carrithers, Steven Collins, and Steven Lukes, 190–216. Cambridge: Cambridge University Press, 1985.

———. "Śaivism and the Tantric Traditions." In *The World's Religions,* ed. Stewart Sutherland et al., 660–704. London: Routledge, 1988.

———. "The Visualization of the Deities of the Trika." In *L'Image divine: Culte et meditation dans L'Hindouisme,* ed. Andre Padoux, 31–88. Paris: Centre National de la Recherche Scientifique, 1990.

Śaṅkarācarya. *Complete Works of Sri Shankacharya, in the Original Sanskrit.* 10 vols. Madras: Samata Books, 1983.

Sarukkai, Sundar. "Inside/Outside: Merleau Ponty/Yoga." *Philosophy East and West* 52 (2002): 459–478.

Śāstrī, Jagadīśa, ed. *Upaniṣatsaṅgraha.* Delhi: Motilal Banarsidass, 1970.

Scarry, Elaine. *The Body in Pain: The Making and Unmaking of the World.* Oxford: Oxford University Press, 1985.

Schilder, Paul. *The Image and Appearance of the Human Body.* New York: International Universities Press, 1950.

Schneider, Laurie. "Mirrors in Art." In "The Mirror: Psychoanalytic Perspectives." Edited by Melvin Bornstein, Donald Silver, and Warren Poland. *Psychaonalytic Inquiry: A Topical Journal for Mental Health Professionals* 5, 2 (1985): 283–324.

Sennett, Richard. *The Fall of Public Man.* New York: Knopf, 1977.

Shaner, David Edward. *The Bodymind Experience in Japanese Buddhism: A Phenomenological Study of Kukai and Dogen.* Albany: State University of New York Press, 1985.

Sharma, Prem Lata. "*Śarīra.*" In *Kalātattvakośa,* general editor, Kapila Vatsyayan, vol. 1, *Eight Selected Terms,* ed. Bettina Baumer, 71–96. Delhi: Indira Gandhi National Centre for the Arts, 1992.

Shastri, Gaurinath. *The Philosophy of Word and Meaning: Some Indian Approaches with Special Reference to the Philosophy of Bhartṛhari.* Calcutta Sanskrit College Research Series, no. 5. Calcutta: Sanskrit College, 1959.

Shastri, Madhusudan Kaul, ed. *Śrī Mālinīvijayottara Tantram.* Kashmir Series of Texts and Studies. Reprint, Delhi: Butala & Company, 1984.

Sheets-Johnstone, Maxine, ed. *Giving the Body Its Due.* Albany: State University of New York Press, 1992.

Sherma, Rita Dasgupta. "Sacred Immanence: Reflections of Ecofeminism in Hindu Tantra." In *Purifying the Earthly Body of God: Religion and Ecology in Hindu India,* ed. Lance E. Nelson, 89–131. Albany: State University of New York Press, 1998.

Shipper, Kristofer. *The Taoist Body.* Tanslated by Karen C. Duval. Berkeley: University of California Press, 1994.

Shweder, Richard. *Thinking Through Cultures: Expeditions in Cultural Psychology.* Cambridge: Harvard University Press, 1991.

Siegel, Allen M. *Heinz Kohut and the Psychology of the Self.* London: Routledge, 1996.

Silburn, Lilian. *Kuṇḍalinī: The Energy of the Depths; A Comprehensive Study Based on the Scriptures of Nondualistic Kashmir Śaivism.* Translated by Jacques Gontier. Albany: State University of New York Press, 1988.

Singer, Milton. "Pronouns, Persons, and the Semiotic Self." In *Semiotics, Self, and Society,* ed. Benjamin Lee and Greg Urban, 229–296. New York: Mouton de Gruyter, 1989.

Singh, Jaideva, ed. and trans. *Vijñānabhairava or Divine Consciousness: A Treasury of 112 Types of Yoga.* Delhi: Motilal Banarsidass, 1979.

Śiva Purāṇa. 4 vols. Translated by a board of scholars. Ancient Indian Tradition and Mythology Series. Delhi: Motilal Banarsidass, 1970.

Skora, Kerry Martin. "Consciousness of Consciousness: Reflexive Awareness in the Trika Śaivism of Abhinavagupta." Ph.D. diss., University of Virginia, 2001.

Smith, Brian K. *Reflections on Resemblence, Ritual and Religion.* Oxford: Oxford University Press, 1989.

Smith, David. "Aspects of the Interrelationship of Divine and Human Bodies in Hinduism." *Religion* 19 (1989): 211–219.

Smith, Frederick M. *The Self Possessed: Deity and Spirit Possession in South Asian Literature and Civilization.* New York: Columbia University Press, 2006.

Smith, Joseph H., and William Kerrigan, eds. *Interpreting Lacan.* New Haven: Yale University Press, 1983.

Snellgrove, David, ed. and trans. *The Hevajra Tantra.* London: Oxford University Press, 1959.

Sohnen, Renate. "Rise and Decline of the Indra Religion in the Veda." In *Inside the Texts . . . Beyond the Texts: New Approaches to the Study of the Vedas,* ed. Michael Witzel, 235–243. Department of Sanskrit and Indian Studies, Harvard University. Columbia, MO: South Asia Books, 1997.

Somānānda and Utpaladeva. *The Śivadṛṣṭi of Srisomānandanātha with the Vritti by Utpaladeva.* Edited by Madhusudan Kaul Shastri. Kashmir Series of Texts and Studies, no. 54. Pune: Aryabhushan Press, 1934.

Spivak, Gayatri Chakravorty. "Echo." In *The Spivak Reader: Selected Works of Gayatri Chakavorty Spivak,* ed. Donna Landry and Gerald MacLean, 175–202. New York: Routledge, 1996.

Stott, David. "Offering the Body: The Practice of GCod in Tibetan Buddhism." *Religion* 19 (1989): 221–226.

Strozier, Charles B. *Heinz Kohut: The Making of a Psychoanalyst.* New York: Farrar, Straus and Giroux, 2001.

Suls, Jerry, and Anthony G. Greenwald, eds. *Psychological Perspectives on the Self.* Volume 3. Hillsdale, NJ: Lawrence Erlbaum, 1986.

Thomas Aquinas, St. *Summa Contra Gentiles, Book One: God.* Translated by Anton C. Pegis. South Bend: University of Notre Dame Press, 1955.

Thomas, David Emil. "Mirror Images." *Scientific American* 243 (December 1980): 206–228.

Tiemersma, Douwe. *Body Schema and Body Image: An Interdisciplinary and Philosophical Study.* Amsterdam: Swets and Zeitlinger, 1989.

Todes, Samuel. *Body and World.* Cambridge: MIT Press, 2001.

Tracy, David. *The Analogical Imagination: Christian Theology and the Culture of Pluralism.* New York: Crossroad, 1975.

———. "The Question of Criteria for Inter-Religious Dialogue: On Revisiting William James." In *Dialogue with the Other: The Inter-Religious Dialogue,* 27–47. Louvain: Peeters Press, 1990.

Ugaz-Ortiz, Javier. "A Hermeneutics of the Symbolism of the Interior Domain (*Guhā* and *Hṛdguhā*) in Abhinavagupta's Śivaism and Vedānta." *Orientalia Lovaniensia Periodica* 19 (1988): 157–188.

———. "The Symbolic Meaning of Light and Its Relation to Heart in the Śivaism of Kāśmīr and Vedānta." *Orientalia Lovaniensia Periodica* 14 (1983): 275–292.

———. "Triangle and Triad, and Their Relation to 'Heart' in the Śivaism of Kāśmīr and Śaktism." *Orientalia Lovaniensia Periodica* 17 (1986): 209–231.

Urban, Hugh B. *Tantra: Sex, Secrecy, Politics, and Power in the Study of Religion.* Berkeley: University of California Press, 2003.

Utpaladeva. *The Īśvarapratyabhijñākārikā of Utpaladeva with the Author's Vṛtti.* Corrected Edition. Edited and translated by Raffaele Torella. Delhi: Motilal Banarsidass, 2002.

———. *Īśvara Pratyabhijñā Kārikā: Verses on the Recognition of the Lord.* Translated by B. N. Pandit. Delhi: Motilal Banarsidass, 2004.

———. *The Siddhitrayī and the Īśvarapratyabhijñākārikāvṛtti.* Edited by Madhusudan Kaul Shastri. Kashmir Series of Texts and Studies, no. 34. Srinagar: Kashmir Pratap Steam Press, 1921.

Vaidyanathan, T. G., and Jeffrey J. Kripal, eds. *Vishnu on Freud's Desk: A Reader in Psychoanalysis and Hinduism.* New Delhi: Oxford University Press, 1999.

Vasudeva, Somadeva. *The Yoga of the Mālinīvijayottaratantra: Chapters 1–4, 7, 11–17.* Pondicherry: Institut Francais de Pondichery, 2004.

Vasugupta and Kṣemarāja. *The Shiva Sūtra Vimarshinī: Being the Sūtras of Vasu Gupta with the Commentary Called Vimarshinī by Kṣhemarāja.* Edited by J. C. Chatterji. Srinagar: Nirnaya-Sagar Press, 1911.

Vasugupta and Kṣemarāja. *Spanda-Kārikās: The Divine Creative Pulsation* (with Kṣemarāja's *Nirṇaya*). Edited and translated by Jaideva Singh. Delhi: Motilal Banarsidass, 1980.

Vasugupta, Kṣemarāja, Kallaṭabhaṭṭa, Rājānaka Rāma, and Bhagavadutpala. *The Stanzas of Vibration: The Spandakārikā with Four Commentaries.* Translated with introduction and exposition by Mark S. G. Dyczkowski. SUNY Series in the Shaiva Traditions of Kashmir, ed. Harvey P. Alper. Albany: State University of New York Press, 1992.

Vatsyayan, Kapila. "Indriya." In *Kalātattvakośa,* general editor, Kapila Vatsyayan, vol. 4, *Manifestation of Nature: Sṛṣṭi Vistāra,* ed. Advaitavadini Kaul and Sukumar Chattopadhyay, 1–68. Delhi: Indira Gandhi National Centre for the Arts, 1999.

Venkatanathacharya, Vidvan N. S., ed. *Saundaryalaharī of Śrī Śaṅkarācārya with the Commentary of Lakṣmīdhara, Bhāvanopaniṣat with the Commentary of Bhāskararāya, and Devī Pañcastavī.* Mysore: Oriental Research Institute, 1969.

Ver Eecke, Wilfried. "Hegel as Lacan's Source for Necessity in Psychoanalytic Theory." In *Interpreting Lacan,* ed. Joseph H. Smith and William Kerrigan, 113–138. New Haven: Yale University Press, 1983.

Vinge, Louise. *The Narcissus Theme in Western European Literature Up to the Early 19th Century.* Translated by Robert Dewsnap et al. Lund: Gleerups, 1967.

Virūpākṣa. "The *Virūpākṣa-Pañcāśikā*." Edited by L. D. Barnett. *Le Museon* 9 (1908): 299–309.

Virūpākṣa and Vidyācakravartin. *Virūpākṣapañcāśikā Vidyācakravartikṛtavivṛtisametā*. Edited by Gopinath Kaviraj. In *Tantrasaṁgraha (Part 1)*, ed. Gopinath Kaviraj, 1–22. *Yogatantra-granthamālā*, ed. Badarinath Sukla, vol. 3. Varanasi: Sansar Press, 1970.

———. *Virupakshapanchasika*. Trivandrum Sanskrit Series, no. 9. Edited by T. Ganapati Sastri. Trivandrum: Travancore Government Press, 1910.

Visuvalingam, Sunthar. "The Transgressive Sacrality of the Dīkṣita: Sacrifice, Criminality and *Bhakti* in the Hindu Tradition." In *Criminal Gods and Demon Devotees: Essays on the Guardians of Popular Hinduism*, ed. Alf Hiltebeitel, 427–462. Albany: State University of New York Press, 1989.

Waghorn, Joanne, Norman Cutler, and Vasudha Narayanan. *Gods of Flesh, Gods of Stone: The Embodiment of Divinity in India*. New York: Columbia University Press, 1985.

Wayman, Alex. *The Buddhist Tantras: Light on Indo-Tibetan Esotericism*. New York: Samuel Weiser, 1973.

———. "The Mirror as a Pan-Buddhist Metaphor-Simile." *History of Religions* 13 (1974): 251–269.

———. *Yoga of the Guhyasamājatantra: The Arcane Lore of Forty Verses*. Delhi: Motilal Banarsidass, 1977.

Weiss, Gail. *Body Images: Embodiment as Intercorporeality*. New York: Routledge, 1999.

White, David Gordon. *The Alchemical Body: Siddha Traditions in Medieval India*. Chicago: University of Chicago Press, 1996.

———. *Kiss of the Yoginī: "Tantric Sex" in Its South Asian Contexts*. Chicago: University of Chicago Press, 2003.

———, ed. *Tantra in Practice*. Princeton: Princeton University Press, 2000.

———. "Why Gurus Are Heavy." *Numen* 31 (1984): 40–73.

Wilber, Ken, Jack Engler, and Daniel P. Brown. *Transformations of Consciousness: Conventional and Contemplative Perspectives on Development*. Boston: Shambhala, 1986.

William of St. Thierry. *Exposition on the Song of Songs*. Translated by Columba Hart. Kalamazoo, MI: Cistercian Publications, 1968

Winnicott, D. W. *Playing and Reality*. New York: Tavistock, 1982.

Wolf, Ernest. "The Search for Confirmation: Technical Aspects of Mirroring." In "The Mirror: Psychoanalytic Perspectives." Edited by Melvin Bornstein, Donald Silver, and Warren Poland. *Psychaonalytic Inquiry: A Topical Journal for Mental Health Professionals* 5, 2 (1985): 271–282.

Woodroffe, Sir John. *Principles of Tantra*. 2 vols. Madras: Ganesh & Company, 1986.

———, trans. *The Serpent Power: The Secrets of Tantric and Shaktic Yoga*. New York: Dover, 1974.

———. *The World as Power.* Madras: Ganesh & Company, 1981.

Zaehner, R. C., ed. and trans. *The Bhagavad Gītā: With a Commentary Based on the Original Sources.* Oxford: Oxford University Press, 1973.

———. *Mysticism, Sacred and Profane: An Inquiry into Some Varieties of Praeternatural Experience.* Oxford: Oxford University Press, 1975.

Zimmer, Heinrich. *Myths and Symbols in Indian Art and Civilization.* Edited by Joseph Campbell. Princeton: Princeton University Press, 1974.

Žižek, Slavoj. *The Indivisible Remainder: An Essay on Schelling and Related Matters.* London: Verso, 1996.

———. *Tarrying with the Negative: Kant, Hegel, and the Critique of Ideology.* Durham, North Carolina: Duke University Press, 1993.

———. *The Ticklish Subject: The Absent Centre of Political Ontology.* London: Verso, 1999.

Žižek, Slavoj, and F. W. J. von Schelling. *The Abyss of Freedom/Ages of the World: An Essay by Slavoj Žižek with the text of Schelling's* Die Weltalter (Second Draft, 1813) *in English translation by Judith Norman.* Ann Arbor: University of Michigan Press, 1997.

Zweig, Paul. *The Heresy of Self-Love: A Study of Subversive Individualism.* Princeton: Princeton University Press, 1980.

Index

Note: Parentheses after English entries provide only the most common, and not necessarily the only corresponding Sanskrit terms.